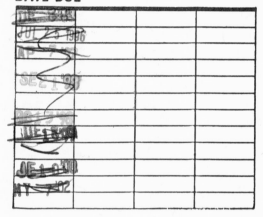

CHELSEA HOUSE PUBLISHERS
Modern Critical Views

HENRY ADAMS
EDWARD ALBEE
A. R. AMMONS
MATTHEW ARNOLD
JOHN ASHBERY
W. H. AUDEN
JANE AUSTEN
JAMES BALDWIN
CHARLES BAUDELAIRE
SAMUEL BECKETT
SAUL BELLOW
THE BIBLE
ELIZABETH BISHOP
WILLIAM BLAKE
JORGE LUIS BORGES
ELIZABETH BOWEN
BERTOLT BRECHT
THE BRONTËS
ROBERT BROWNING
ANTHONY BURGESS
GEORGE GORDON, LORD BYRON
THOMAS CARLYLE
LEWIS CARROLL
WILLA CATHER
CERVANTES
GEOFFREY CHAUCER
KATE CHOPIN
SAMUEL TAYLOR COLERIDGE
JOSEPH CONRAD
CONTEMPORARY POETS
HART CRANE
STEPHEN CRANE
DANTE
CHARLES DICKENS
EMILY DICKINSON
JOHN DONNE & THE
    17th-CENTURY POETS
ELIZABETHAN DRAMATISTS
THEODORE DREISER
JOHN DRYDEN
GEORGE ELIOT
T. S. ELIOT
RALPH ELLISON
RALPH WALDO EMERSON
WILLIAM FAULKNER
HENRY FIELDING
F. SCOTT FITZGERALD
GUSTAVE FLAUBERT
E. M. FORSTER
SIGMUND FREUD
ROBERT FROST

ROBERT GRAVES
GRAHAM GREENE
THOMAS HARDY
NATHANIEL HAWTHORNE
WILLIAM HAZLITT
SEAMUS HEANEY
ERNEST HEMINGWAY
GEOFFREY HILL
FRIEDRICH HÖLDERLIN
HOMER
GERARD MANLEY HOPKINS
WILLIAM DEAN HOWELLS
ZORA NEALE HURSTON
HENRY JAMES
SAMUEL JOHNSON
BEN JONSON
JAMES JOYCE
FRANZ KAFKA
JOHN KEATS
RUDYARD KIPLING
D. H. LAWRENCE
JOHN LE CARRÉ
URSULA K. LE GUIN
DORIS LESSING
SINCLAIR LEWIS
ROBERT LOWELL
NORMAN MAILER
BERNARD MALAMUD
THOMAS MANN
CHRISTOPHER MARLOWE
CARSON MCCULLERS
HERMAN MELVILLE
JAMES MERRILL
ARTHUR MILLER
JOHN MILTON
EUGENIO MONTALE
MARIANNE MOORE
IRIS MURDOCH
VLADIMIR NABOKOV
JOYCE CAROL OATES
SEAN O'CASEY
FLANNERY O'CONNOR
EUGENE O'NEILL
GEORGE ORWELL
CYNTHIA OZICK
WALTER PATER
WALKER PERCY
HAROLD PINTER
PLATO
EDGAR ALLAN POE

POETS OF SENSIBILITY &
    THE SUBLIME
ALEXANDER POPE
KATHERINE ANNE PORTER
EZRA POUND
PRE-RAPHAELITE POETS
MARCEL PROUST
THOMAS PYNCHON
ARTHUR RIMBAUD
THEODORE ROETHKE
PHILIP ROTH
JOHN RUSKIN
J. D. SALINGER
GERSHOM SCHOLEM
WILLIAM SHAKESPEARE (3 vols.)
    HISTORIES & POEMS
    COMEDIES
    TRAGEDIES
GEORGE BERNARD SHAW
MARY WOLLSTONECRAFT SHELLEY
PERCY BYSSHE SHELLEY
EDMUND SPENSER
GERTRUDE STEIN
JOHN STEINBECK
LAURENCE STERNE
WALLACE STEVENS
TOM STOPPARD
JONATHAN SWIFT
ALFRED LORD TENNYSON
WILLIAM MAKEPEACE THACKERAY
HENRY DAVID THOREAU
LEO TOLSTOI
ANTHONY TROLLOPE
MARK TWAIN
JOHN UPDIKE
GORE VIDAL
VIRGIL
ROBERT PENN WARREN
EVELYN WAUGH
EUDORA WELTY
NATHANAEL WEST
EDITH WHARTON
WALT WHITMAN
OSCAR WILDE
TENNESSEE WILLIAMS
WILLIAM CARLOS WILLIAMS
THOMAS WOLFE
VIRGINIA WOOLF
WILLIAM WORDSWORTH
RICHARD WRIGHT
WILLIAM BUTLER YEATS

Further titles in preparation.

Modern Critical Views

CHRISTOPHER MARLOWE

Modern Critical Views

CHRISTOPHER MARLOWE

Edited with an introduction by

Harold Bloom

Sterling Professor of the Humanities
Yale University

1986
CHELSEA HOUSE PUBLISHERS
New York
New Haven   Philadelphia

PROJECT EDITORS: Emily Bestler, James Uebbing
ASSOCIATE EDITOR: Maria Behan
EDITORIAL COORDINATOR: Karyn Gullen Browne
EDITORIAL STAFF: Perry King, Bert Yaeger
DESIGN: Susan Lusk

Cover illustration by Bill Purdom

Library of Congress Cataloging in Publication Data

Christopher Marlowe.
    (Modern critical views)
    Bibliography: p.
    Includes index.
    Summary: A collection of critical essays on Marlowe
and his works. Also includes a chronology of his life.
    1. Marlowe, Christopher, 1564–1593—Criticism and
interpretation—Addresses, essays, lectures.
[1. Marlowe, Christopher, 1564–1593—Criticism and
interpretation—Addresses, essays, lectures]
2. English literature—Criticism and interpretation—
Addresses, essays, lectures]   I. Bloom, Harold.
II. Title.   III. Series.
PR2674.C57 1986   822'.3   85–29091
ISBN 0–87754–666–5

Chelsea House Publishers
Harold Steinberg, Chairman and Publisher
Susan Lusk, Vice President
A Division of Chelsea House Educational Communications, Inc.

133 Christopher Street, New York, NY 10014

345 Whitney Avenue, New Haven, CT 06510

5014 West Chester Pike, Edgemont, PA 19028

Contents

Editor's Note

This volume brings together a representative selection of the best modern criticism devoted to the dramas and poems of Christopher Marlowe. The editor's "Introduction" centers upon *The Jew of Malta*, as the largest single instance of the survival of Marlowe's radical originality.

Harry Levin's masterly reading of *Edward II* begins the sequence of modern criticism, printed here in the chronological order of its publication. Levin is followed by David Bevington's judicious account of *The Jew of Malta*, an account deeply informed by Bevington's expert knowledge of Tudor politics.

The Australian poet A. D. Hope's exegesis of "the argument of arms" in *Tamburlaine* introduces the crucial and problematical theme of the Marlovian Sublime, at once agonistic and subversive. Hope's emphases are complemented by his fellow Australian's remarkable reading of the realism of *The Jew of Malta*, in Wilbur Sanders's learned essay, and by the study of the language of action in *Tamburlaine* by the Scottish critic David Daiches.

Two related studies of *Doctor Faustus* follow: an exacting analysis of the unity of the play by Cleanth Brooks, and a subtle reflection upon the arts of illusion by President Giamatti of Yale University. With the novelist Erich Segal's meditation upon Barabas as comic hero, we return to *The Jew of Malta* and Marlowe's fierce satire of Christian pretensions.

The volume takes a new turn with Jackson I. Cope's witty excursion into theatrical history, centering upon Marlowe's minor play, *Dido, Queen of Carthage*. William Keach's sensitive reading of the poem *Hero and Leander* is followed by Edward A. Snow's strikingly visual analysis of *Doctor Faustus*. A general overview, focusing upon Marlowe's skepticism, by Lawrence Danson provides the reader with a shrewd comprehensive judgment upon most of Marlowe's work. Kimberly Benston's brilliant account of Tamburlaine's sublime meditation upon beauty serves as coda, rounding this book off by returning to the emphasis given in my introductory comments to the agonistic stance of Marlowe, and to the rhetorical gusto of his great hero-villains.

Introduction

I

Like Shakespeare, born only a few months after him, Marlowe began as an Ovidian poet. Killed at twenty-nine, in what may have been a mere tavern brawl, or possibly a political intrigue (fitter end for a double agent), Marlowe had the unhappy poetic fate of being swallowed up by Shakespeare's unprecedented powers of dramatic representation. We read Marlowe now as Shakespeare's precursor, remembering that Shakespeare also began as a poet of Ovidian eros. Read against Shakespeare, Marlowe all but vanishes. Nor can anyone prophesy usefully how Marlowe might have developed if he had lived another quarter century. There seems little enough development between *Tamburlaine* (1587) and *Doctor Faustus* (1593), and perhaps Marlowe was incapable of that process we name by the critical trope of "poetic development," which seems to imply a kind of turning about or even a wrapping up.

There has been a fashion, in modern scholarly criticism, to baptize Marlowe's imagination, so that a writer of tragic caricatures has been converted into an orthodox moralist. The vanity of scholarship has few more curious monuments than this Christianized Marlowe. What the common reader finds in Marlowe is precisely what his contemporaries found: impiety, audacity, worship of power, ambiguous sexuality, occult aspirations, defiance of moral order, and above all else a sheer exaltation of the possibilities of rhetoric, of the persuasive force of heroic poetry. The subtlest statement of the scholar's case is made by Frank Kermode:

> Thus Marlowe displays his heroes reacting to most of the temptations that Satan can contrive; and the culminating temptation . . . is the scholar's temptation, forbidden knowledge . . . [Marlowe's] heroes do not resist the temptations, and he provides us, not with a negative proof of virtue and obedience to divine law, but with positive examples of what happens in their absence. Thus, whatever his intentions may have been, and however much he flouted conventions, Marlowe's themes are finally reducible to the powerful formulae of contemporary religion and morality.

"Finally reducible" is the crucial phrase here; is final reduction the aim of reading or of play-going? As for "Marlowe's themes," they count surely rather less than Marlowe's rhetoric does, and, like most themes or topics, indubitably do ensue ultimately from religion and morality. But Marlowe is not Spenser or Milton, and there is one originality he possesses that is not subsumed by Shakespeare. Call that originality by the name of Barabas, Marlowe's grandest character, who dominates what is certainly Marlowe's most vital and original play, *The Jew of Malta*. Barabas defies reduction, and his gusto represents Marlowe's severest defiance of all moral and religious convention.

II

Barabas (or Barabbas, as in the Gospels) means "son of the Father" and so "son of God," and may have begun as an alternate name for Jesus. As the anti-Jewish tenor of the Gospels intensified from Mark to John, Barabbas declined from a patriotic insurrectionist to a thief, and as either was preferred by "the Jews" to Jesus. This is a quite Marlovian irony that the scholar Hyam Maccoby puts forward, and Marlowe might have rejoiced at the notion that Jesus and Barabbas were historically the same person. One Richard Baines, a police informer, insisted that Marlowe said of Jesus: "If the Jews among whom he was born did crucify him they best knew him and whence he came." The playwright Thomas Kyd, arrested after his friend Marlowe's death, testified that the author of *The Jew of Malta* tended to "jest at the divine Scriptures, gibe at prayers, and strive in argument to frustrate and confute what hath been spoke or writ by prophets and such holy men." Are we to credit Baines and Kyd, or Kermode and a bevy of less subtle scholars?

Marlowe, who was as sublimely disreputable as Rimbaud or Hart Crane, is more of their visionary company than he is at home with T.S. Eliot or with academic moralists. *The Jew of Malta* contrasts sharply with *The Merchant of Venice*, which may have been composed so as to overgo it on the stage. It cannot be too much emphasized that Marlowe's Barabas is a savage original, while Shakespeare's Shylock, despite his supposed human-ization, is essentially the timeless anti-Semitic stock figure, devil and usurer, of Christian tradition. Stating it more plainly, Shakespeare indeed is as anti-Semitic as the Gospels or T.S. Eliot, whereas Marlowe employs his Barabas as a truer surrogate for himself than are Tamburlaine, Edward II, and Dr. Faustus. Barabas is Marlowe the satirist:

> It's no sin to deceive a Christian;
> For they themselves hold it a principle,

Faith is not to be held with heretics.
But all are heretics that are not Jews;
This follows well . . .

And so indeed it does. The art of Barabas is to better Christian
instruction, unlike Shylock, who has persistence but who lacks art. Shylock is obsessive-compulsive; Barabas delights because he is a free man, or
if you would prefer, a free fiend, at once a monstrous caricature and a
superb image of Marlowe's sly revenge upon society. What Hazlitt gave us
as a marvelous critical concept, gusto, is superbly manifested by Barabas,
but not by poor Shylock. "Gusto in art is power or passion defining any
object." Hazlitt accurately placed Shakespeare first among writers in this
quality:

> The infinite quantity of dramatic invention in Shakespeare takes from
> his gusto. The power he delights to show is not intense, but discursive.
> He never insists on anything he might, except a quibble.

But Shylock is the one great exception in Shakespeare, and sur-
prisingly lacks invention. Marlowe's superior gusto, in just this one instance, emerges as we contrast two crucial speeches. Barabas is outrageous,
a parody of the stage-Jew, and Shylock speaks with something like Shakespeare's full resources, so that the power of language is overwhelmingly
Shakespeare's, and yet Barabas becomes an original representation, while
Shylock becomes even more the nightmare bogey of Christian superstition
and hatred:

> SALERIO: Why, I am sure if he forfeit thou wilt not take his flesh. What's
> that good for?
> SHYLOCK: To bait fish withal. If it will feed nothing else, it will feed my
> revenge. He hath disgraced me, and hind'red me half a million,
> laughed at my losses, mocked at my gains, scorned my nation,
> thwarted my bargains, cooled my friends, heated mine enemies—
> and what's his reason? I am a Jew. Hath not a Jew eyes? Hath not a
> Jew hands, organs, dimensions, senses, affections, passions?—fed
> with the same food, hurt with the same weapons, subject to the
> same diseases, healed by the same means, warmed and cooled by the
> same winter and summer as a Christian is? If you prick us, do we not
> bleed? If you tickle us, do we not laugh? If you poison us, do we not
> die? And if you wrong us, shall we not revenge? If we are like you in
> the rest, we will resemble you in that. If a Jew wrong a Christian,
> what is his humility? Revenge! If a Christian wrong a Jew, what
> should his sufferance be by Christian example? Why revenge! The
> villainy you teach me I will execute, and it shall go hard but I will
> better the instruction.

"If you prick us, do we not bleed? If you tickle us, do we not laugh?" Shylock himself is not changed by listening to these, his own words, and neither are the audience's prejudices changed one jot. No one in that audience had seen a Jew, nor had Shakespeare, unless they or he had watched the execution of the unfortunate Dr. Lopez, the Queen's physician, condemned on a false charge of poisoning, or had glimpsed one of the handful of other converts resident in London. Shylock is rendered more frightening by the startling reminders that this dangerous usurer is flesh and blood, a man as well as a devil. Jews after all, Shakespeare's language forcefully teaches his audience, are not merely mythological murderers of Christ and of his beloved children, but literal seekers after the flesh of the good and gentle Antonio.

Can we imagine Barabas saying: "If you prick us, do we not bleed? If you tickle us, do we not laugh?" Or can we imagine Shylock intoning this wonderful and parodistic outburst of the exuberant Barabas?

> As for myself, I walk abroad a-nights,
> And kill sick people groaning under walls.
> Sometimes I go about and poison wells;
> And now and then, to cherish Christian thieves,
> I am content to lose some of my crowns,
> That I may, walking in my gallery,
> See 'em go pinion'd along by my door.
> Being young, I studied physic, and began
> To practise first upon the Italian;
> There I enrich'd the priests with burials,
> And always kept the sexton's arms in ure
> With digging graves and ringing dead men's knells.
> And, after that, was I an engineer,
> And in the wars 'twixt France and Germany,
> Under the pretence of helping Charles the Fifth,
> Slew friend and enemy with my stratagems:
> Then after that was I an usurer,
> And with extorting, cozening, forfeiting,
> And tricks belonging unto brokery,
> I fill'd the gaols with bankrupts in a year,
> And with young orphans planted hospitals;
> And every moon made some or other mad,
> And now and then one hang himself for grief,
> Pinning upon his breast a long great scroll
> How I with interest tormented him.
> But mark how I am blest for plaguing them:
> I have as much coin as will buy the town.
> But tell me now, how has thou spent thy time?

This would do admirably in a Gilbert and Sullivan opera, had the anti-Semitic Gilbert (see *The Bab Ballads*) been willing to mock his own prejudices. We do not know how the more sophisticated among Marlowe's audience received this, but properly delivered it has the tang and bite of great satire. A more fascinating surmise is: How did Shakespeare receive this? And how did he react to Barabas in what we can call the mode of Hemingway, sparring with his holy friars?

> FRIAR BARNARDINE: Barabas, thou has—
> FRIAR JACOMO: Ay, not what thou hast—
> BARABAS: True, I have money; what though I have?
> FRIAR BARNARDINE: Thou art a—
> FRIAR JACOMO: Ay, that thou art, a—
> BARABAS: What needs all this? I know I am a Jew.
> FRIAR BARNARDINE: Thy daughter—
> FRAIR JACOMO: Ay, thy daughter—
> BARABAS: O, speak not of her! Then I die with grief.
> FRIAR BERNARDINE: Remember that—
> FRIAR JACOMO: Ay, remember that—
> BARABAS: I must needs say that I have been a great usurer.
> FRIAR BERNARDINE: Thou hast committed—
> BARABAS: Fornication: but that was in another country,
> And besides the wench is dead.

We can say that Shakespeare refused the hint. Shylock's grim repetitions ("I will have my bond") come out of a different universe, the crimes of Christendom that Shakespeare had no thought of rejecting. This is hardly to say that Marlowe was in any sense humane. *The Jew of Malta* is bloody farce, more than worthy of Jarry or Artaud. Barabas emerges from the world of Thomas Nashe and Thomas Kyd, Marlowe's half-world of espionage and betrayal, of extravagant wit and antithetical lusts, which was the experiential scene that must have taught Shakespeare to go and live otherwise, and write otherwise as well.

II

The Australian poet Alec Hope, in a remarkable essay upon Marlowe, reprinted in this volume, ascribes to *Tamburlaine* "a thorough-going morality of power, aesthetics of power and logic of power." Hope is clearly right about *Tamburlaine*. I would go further and suggest that there is no other morality, aesthetics or logic anywhere in Marlowe's writings.

Where Hope usefully quotes Hazlitt on the congruence between the language of power and the language of poetry, I would cite also the great American theoretician of power and poetry, the Emerson of *The Conduct of Life*:

> A belief in causality, or strict connection between every trifle and the principle of being, and, in consequence, belief in compensation, or, that nothing is got for nothing,—characterizes all valuable minds, and must control every effort that is made by an industrious one. The most valiant men are the best believers in the tension of the laws . . .
>
> All power is of one kind, a sharing of the nature of the world. The mind that is parallel with the laws of nature will be in the current of events, and strong with their strength.

Like Marlowe, Hazlitt and Emerson are agonists who understand that there are no accidents. In Marlowe, the implicit metaphysics of this understanding are Epicurean-Lucretian. Barabas and Tamburlaine seek their own freedom, and ultimately fail, but only because they touch the ultimate limits at the flaming ramparts of the world. Edward II and Dr. Faustus fail, but they are weak, and their fate does not grieve Marlowe. Indeed, the aesthetic satisfaction Marlowe hints at is not free from a sadistic pleasure the poet and his audience share at observing the dreadful ends of Edward and Faustus. Marlowe's heroes, Tamburlaine and Barabas, die defiantly, with Tamburlaine still naming himself "the scourge of God," and Barabas, boiling in a cauldron, nevertheless cursing his enemies with his customary vehemence:

> And, villains, know you cannot help me now.
> Then, Barabas, breathe forth thy latest fate,
> And in the fury of thy torments strive
> To end thy life with resolution.
> Know, Governor, 'twas I that slew thy son,
> I fram'd the challenge that did make them meet.
> Know, Calymath, I aim'd thy overthrow:
> And, had I escap'd this stratagem,
> I would have brought confusion on you all,
> Damn'd Christians, dogs, and Turkish infidels!
> But now begins the extremity of heat
> To pinch me with intolerable pangs.
> Die, life! fly, soul! tongue, curse thy fill, and die!

Shylock, alas, ends wholly broken, "content" to become a Christian, a resolution that is surely the most unsatisfactory in all of Shakespeare. I cannot envision the late Groucho Marx playing Shylock, but I sometimes read through *The Jew of Malta*, mentally casting Groucho as Barabas. T.S. Eliot, whose admiration for *The Jew of Malta* was strong, was also a fan of the sublime Groucho. I rejoice, for once, to share two of Eliot's enthusiasms, and enjoy the thought that he too might have wished to see Groucho play Barabas.

HARRY LEVIN

"*Edward II*": State Overturned

The tragic view is never a simple one. It is not a spontaneous reaction to a given situation, but a gradual recognition of the sternest facts that govern the whole of life. It came as the hard-won guerdon of maturity to Sophocles and Shakespeare; and even Marlowe, for all his precocity, had to ripen into it. *The Jew of Malta* provokes less pity than terror; most of its terrors, indeed, are merely horrors; and in so far as it subordinates everything else to contrivance, it deserves to be classed as a farce—or, at any rate, a melodrama. That little room, that self-contained island are quite incommensurable with the geopolitical expanses of *Tamburlaine*; but their angularity and narrowness frame a more realistic picture of society, as scaled down by the law of diminishing returns. The tragedy that overtakes Tamburlaine is almost an afterthought, although his centrifugal route is strewn with lesser tragedies. Similarly, *The Tragedy of Dido* is incidental to the epic adventures of Æneas. In those plays which we have thus far considered, Marlowe seems to stand like his Leander, poised upon the very brink of tragedy. He has provided a *sine qua non* by creating extraordinarily powerful protagonists; had he stopped there, his genre would have been monodrama; and though effective drama has been built around single figures—Eugene O'Neill's *Emperor Jones*, Büchner's *Dantons Tod*, to some extent *Macbeth*—the overbalance is too precarious to be long sustained. Marlowe has taken another step, and introduced a framework of ethical reference, by stigma-

From *The Overreacher: A Study of Christopher Marlowe.* Copyright © 1952 by the President and Fellows of Harvard College. Harvard University Press.

tizing his hero as a villain. If he does nothing else in *The Massacre at Paris*, he exorcises this devil that he has raised. And in *Edward II* he sets forth his discovery that tragic life needs no villains; that plots are spun by passions; that men betray themselves.

Meanwhile, his imagination has been traveling closer to home, sweeping from Asia and Africa through the Levant, and thence to western Europe. In the prologue of *The Jew of Malta*, Machiavel announces that he has crossed the Alps from Italy toward England, and that he has crossed over from France after the assassination of his most enterprising disciple, the Duke of Guise. That event, which happened late in 1588, furnishes the climactic episode in *The Massacre at Paris*, which was produced as a new play four years later. Marlowe gathered his material out of the flux of current history, much as he had done in *The Jew of Malta*; and on his brief excursion into the troubled realm of French politics, he discovered a vein which would afterward be exploited by the tragedies of George Chapman. The massacre of Marlowe's title was the notorious holocaust of Saint Bartholomew's day, 1572, sometimes called Machiavelli's holiday by Protestants—who, hating Catherine de Medici as the chief disseminator of Italian influence beyond the Alps, called *The Prince* the Queen-Mother's Bible. For the subjects of Queen Elizabeth, who is thrice saluted as the leading defender of the Protestant faith, the play is by implication a tale of two cities, Paris and London. Huguenots are referred to as Puritans, and suspicion is directed toward the English Catholic exiles at Douai and Reims. It is not surprising that the French government objected to its performance on one occasion. If Marlowe had lived a few months longer, he would doubtless have been surprised to learn that Henry of Navarre, the spokesman for his anticlericalism, had joined the Catholic church. Marlowe's own attitude toward the Pope is intensified in two lines assigned to the previous king, Henry III:

> Ile fire his crased buildings and inforse
> The papall towers to kisse the holy earth.
> (1214–15)

The same lines occur in *Edward II*, with "lowlie ground" instead of "holy earth" (397)—a difference which suggests that an actor's fallible memory is responsible for our text of *The Massacre at Paris*. Notwithstanding, the speech is more appropriate to the latter play than it is from the mouth of the ineffectual Edward. His expulsion of the Templars is not mentioned in Marlowe's account, which concentrates its antireligious sniping on Edward's humiliation of the Bishop of Coventry. At a time when hatred of the papacy ran so high in England that King John could be something of a hero upon the popular stage, Marlowe could enjoy immunity in expressing Barabas' impulse to burn churches. The recurrence is peculiarly Marlovian in its juxtaposition of prideful towers and purging fires.

Heretofore the protagonist has been an infidel: an Atheist or a pagan, a Mohammedan or a Jew. To this rule the Guise is no exception, since his religious fanaticism is a thin disguise for political opportunism. His "aspiring thoughts" (930) reflect the anti-Machiavellian presumption that Catholics were really Atheists who professed to believe in Christ for reasons of policy—what John Donne would call "perfidiousenesse or dissembling of Religion." Where Barabas believed in Jehovah and emulated the Christians in failing to practice what he preached, the Guise is a complete unbeliever at heart. "Religion: *O Diabole*," he snarls in the candor of soliloquy (123), even as his master, Machiavel, counts religion but a childish toy. Nevertheless, through lip-service he commands the infiltrating ranks of the priesthood, and draws upon the sinister gold that his Catholic majesty, Philip of Spain, is currently extracting from the Americas. The Guise is a born gambler, ever ready to stake his all for the prize of the hour, to pose the absolute alternative: *Aut Cæsar aut nullus*. With all his cards in his hand "to shuffle or cut" (147), he coolly reckons on dealing himself a king. Yet the crown itself seems less desirable to him than the ceaseless conspiracy wherewith he strives for it. It is not so much *libido dominandi* as sheer appetency, *libido* unsated and insatiable, that drives him on. "For this," he reiterates, he has contrived his stratagems: not for the end but for the means, not for the fruit but for the experience. For this he builds upon his "quenchles thirst" (107), utilizing a curious metaphor which intermixes the acts of construction and consumption, as with the pyramid that he soon is promising either to climb or destroy. Truly, as he has stated at the outset, his thoughts are bursting into flames which can only be quenched with blood. Not only Marlowe's *Doctor Faustus* but even Goethe's *Faust* is foreshadowed by the Guise's doctrine

That perill is the cheefest way to happines.
(95)

Except for this soliloquy, Marlowe's longest, and a few other speeches by or about the Guise, *The Massacre at Paris* is a singularly crude and unpoetic potboiler—at least in the abridged and garbled redaction that has survived. The upshot is a stronger emphasis than ever upon the force of a single personality, a heroic torso prone on a crumbling pedestal. In the original version, which must have been twice as long, this may have been counterweighted with the other parts; but the play, like all of Marlowe's, was known by its title role and listed as *The Guise* on the

books of his theatrical manager, Philip Henslowe. In *Tamburlaine* character is destiny; in *The Jew of Malta* destiny is character; perhaps there is not
enough plot in the one and too much in the other. In *The Massacre at
Paris* there seems to be a schism between character and plot. The restless
egoism of the Guise cuts through the tangled motives of the others; three
successive kings are dwarfed by his failure to attain the throne; the one
who sits upon it through most of the play, Henry III, closely resembles
Edward with his minions and his "pleasure vncontrolde" (127). But the
Guise too has his soft spot; his isolation from everyone else is confirmed
when his wife betrays him; he gains a pair of horns, if not a crown; and
that brutal irony is the theme of the one comic scene—a scene which, as
chance or forgery will have it, survives in extended detail from an early
transcript. The Guise regains his dignity at his death, after the classical
moment of exultation:

> As ancient Romanes ouer their Captiue Lords,
> So will I triumph ouer this wanton King,
> And he shall follow my proud Chariots wheeles.
> (989–91)

But there is to be no triumphal procession for him. It is not in a little
room, but in an apartment of the palace, that he is finally trapped. He
responds to the royal challenge and strides through the claustral seclusion:
"Yet Cæsar shall goe forth" (1005). Cæsar has been his epithet for
himself, and it is no less apt for his fate than for his ambition. Whether
Julius Cæsar echoed this line, or whether the Shakespearean line was
interpolated into Marlowe's script, is one of the many uncertainties that
hedge *The Massacre at Paris*. The Guise, drawing back in aristocratic
aloofness from his assassins, dies with a Senecan declaration of identity in
the midst of adversity:

> But they are pesants, *I* am Duke of *Guise*.
> (1007)

What he likes best, he has boasted, is what flies beyond his reach. Now we
behold, the King points out, "traiterous guile outreacht" (969). And,
since no one is more abject than the opportunist who has missed his
opportunity, the overreaching Guise now devolves to the very nadir of
fortune. It is left for Shakespeare to formulate an epitaph in *Antony and
Cleopatra*:

> Tis paltry to be *Cæsar*:
> Not being Fortune, hee's but Fortunes knaue.
> (V, ii, 2–3)

With this final spin of Fortune's wheel, Cæsarism exhausts its possibilities. Marlowe already had gone on to investigate the problem of kingship from the other side, the side of the legitimate monarch who forfeits his crown, the unheroic hero at whose expense the interloper achieves his self-made greatness, the weak and unambitious inheritor of high place caught in the conflict of strong and ambitious men. Marlowe's cult of strength, from the beginning, carried along its explicit corollary, the scorn of weakness. *Tamburlaine* begins with a sketch of the weakling Mycetes, lacking in wit but interested in poetry, esthetically preoccupied with the sight of blood on the battlefield, wistfully clinging to the smooth-spoken courtier whom he terms his "Damon" (58). Though Tamburlaine is all that Mycetes is not, the strain of effeteness turns up again in Calyphas, the Phaëthon-like son who proves incapable of taking over his father's reins. Tamburlaine's virtue is capable of both conceiving and subduing, as he asserts in one of his rare moments of introspection; but his behavior is so externalized that we scarcely see him when he is not subduing. The conceiving is actually done by Marlowe, who accompanies his conqueror—as poets do—"in conceit" (260). As his dramaturgy matured, he would concentrate more upon passion and less upon action, less upon externals and more upon feeling. *The Jew of Malta* glanced behind obvious surfaces and purchased with grief its glimpse of experience. But with Barabas, as with Tamburlaine and the Guise, the impact is registered on us—as on their victims—from the outside; whereas with Edward, because he is the victim, we feel the effect of people and circumstances on him. Because he is passive rather than active, he cuts much less of a figure; but he is more deeply grounded within the psychological range of his creator; and his sensations are relayed to us more fully and faithfully.

Above all, he is a man who lives by his senses, an exponent of *libido sentiendi*. Being a king, he has no need to seek power; it is thrust upon him; and, being a hedonist, he wants to enjoy it. He is kept from doing so by the agitations of those careerists who surround and harass him. In his vacillations with them, his yearning for affection, and his continual yielding, he utterly reverses the pattern of *Tamburlaine*. Tucker Brooke stresses the fact that *Edward II*, unlike Marlowe's more characteristic plays, was not performed by Henslowe's companies; and draws the interesting inference that Marlowe, unable for once to count upon Edward Alleyn for a dominating role, was attempting to distribute the equilibrium more evenly among the dramatis personæ. This is the kind of functional sidelight that is seldom irrelevant to our understanding of Elizabethan drama; it illuminates both the technique of the one-man play and the emergence of an ampler and more varied characterization. But it should

not deflect our attention from Marlowe's increasing flexibility, his matur-
ing sympathies, and his unexpected insight into human frailties. Nor
should it, within the precincts of the theater, persuade us that Edward's
part is somehow negligible. Rather, what is envisaged may be a new style
of acting, more rounded and subtle than Alleyn's elocution, ultimately to
be associated with Richard Burbage and the major Shakespearean roles.
We are reminded, as we enter the 1590's, that Shakespeare will soon be
catching up with Marlowe. He will be imitating his contemporary, out-
Marlowing the Marlovian idiom, in *Richard III*. But Shakespeare may have
meanwhile established, with *Henry VI*, a dramatic balance and a lyrical
modulation which Marlowe may well be emulating in *Edward II*.

During the patriotic decade between the rout of the Spanish
Armada and the downfall of the Earl of Essex, between *Tamburlaine* and
Shakespeare's *Henry V*, the dramatic repertory was dominated by the
vogue of the chronicle history. In trying his hand at it, Marlowe addressed
his iconoclastic talent to a highly traditional form, which was fast becoming a quasi-official vehicle for keeping tradition alive. Tragedy, which was
also founded on some historical matter, differed from the history play by
being set in some other country than England. Hence, while the tragic
playwright could take many liberties in the interest of his artistic conception, the historical playwright was obliged to respect the common precon-
ception of his material as crystallized by legend, if not by history more
rigorously construed. Much of this material, in fact, was taken from the
Elizabethan historians, notably from the second edition of Raphael Holinshed's
Chronicles, published in 1587. These chronicles are essentially annals,
recording events as they happened, year by year and reign by reign. The
result, transferred to the stage, was bound to be clumsily episodic in
structure, and to derive such unity as it possessed from the personality of
the reigning monarch. Much could be done if he was a popular hero, like
Henry V. When he was a villainous usurper, like Richard III, Shakespeare
could blend in him the qualities of Tamburlaine and Barabas, and moti-
vate the plot by the interplay of ambition and revenge. But those were the
great exceptions, and they remain among the few English kings who have
continued to live in the theater. The long-drawn-out and unhappy reign
of Henry VI was more difficult to resolve dramatically. Marlowe might
have been attracted by that ill-fated ruler, who would so much rather have
been a shepherd; but Shakespeare relegates him to the background, where he
does all too little to unify the three plays treating York and Lancaster, Joan
of Arc and Jack Cade, and a miscellany of problems, foreign and domestic.

The grand design of Shakespeare's histories is delineated through a
series of lessons in ethics and politics. In general, the king can do no

wrong; sometimes, alas, he is led astray by evil counselors and false favorites; yet nothing ever justifies the dethronement of God's anointed. On the other hand, the commons are usually right, except when they are misled by demagogues. The sovereign and the people working happily together, in a popular monarchy where the feudal barons are kept well under control, fulfill the Tudor ideal of commonwealth. The primary function of the dramatic chronicler is to reinforce such precepts as these by examples—as crudely and naïvely, more often than not, as Peele in his jingoistic *Edward I*. No one would or could have questioned this ethos, but Marlowe shows no special concern to apply it; he is not concerned with the state but, as always, with the individual; and, in this case, it is a poignant irony that the individual happens to be the head of a state. Where Shakespeare's rulers prefigure Queen Elizabeth in various ways, the court of Edward almost seems to anticipate the absolutism and favoritism of the Stuarts. Thomas Heywood claims, in his *Apology for Actors*, that the whole of English history has been dramatized, from the landing of the legendary Brut up to the day of writing in 1612. Out of that continuous procession, Marlowe's single choice is significant. Other University Wits, if they preceded him in taking up the chronicle history, brought to it techniques he had used in his tragedies: the blank verse, the pageantry, the handling of conquests and conspiracies. His unique contribution was to bring the chronicle within the perspective of tragedy, to adapt the most public of forms to the most private of emotions.

The prologue to *Doctor Faustus*, apologizing for the private nature of the story, casts a backward glance at certain other plays. One is about Carthaginians, though it can hardly be *Dido*; another might well be *Tamburlaine*, aptly summed up in "the pompe of prowd audacious deedes" (5). Still another may be *Edward II*, whose issue is sharply presented when the Chorus speaks of:

> sporting in the dalliance of loue,
> In courts of Kings where state is ouerturnd.
> (3–4)

Love is an unseasonable motive, in the face of political responsibility, as Æneas demonstrated when he abandoned Dido. "*Quam male conueniunt*" —the fragment cited from Ovid in *Edward II* (308) is completed and translated when the effeminate Henry III in *The Massacre at Paris* speaks of "loue and Maiestie" (609). *Amor et maiestas*—how badly they suit each other! The complaint has been softened from Machiavelli's hard-boiled remarks on whether princes ought to be loved or feared. The pride of the Guise is conveyed, in an image of overeating, as a "surfet of ambitious thoughts" (960). The tragic flaw of *Edward II*, as Gaveston conveys it in his opening soliloquy, is to "surfet with delight" (3). Where the Guise exultantly contemplated the prospect of a Roman triumph over Henry III, Gaveston evokes it metaphorically as the measure of his relationship with Edward:

> It shall suffice me to enioy your loue,
> Which whiles I haue, I thinke my selfe as great,
> As *Cæsar* riding in the Romaine streete,
> With captiue kings at his triumph Carre,
> (171–4)

This was an actuality for Tamburlaine, and these last two lines appear to be echoes from both *Edward I* and *Henry VI*. There the procession is taken quite literally, whereas in *Edward II* amorous fulfillment is preferred to military victory. When the future Richard III panegyrizes the sweetness of a crown, in the third part of *Henry VI*, he outdoes Tamburlaine by exclaiming:

> How sweet a thing it is to weare a Crowne,
> Within whose Circuit is *Elizium*,
> And all that Poets faine of Blisse and Ioy.
> (I, ii, 29–31)

Tamburlaine made the identical value-judgment, in equating the diadem with bliss and felicity, that Barabas did in evaluating his gold. Somewhat differently, the returning Gaveston salutes London as his Elysium and finds no greater bliss than to bask in the sunshine of royalty, to "liue and be the fauorit of a king" (5). Nemesis manages, when he is executed, to repeat the key-word in his final speech:

> O must this day be period of my life!
> Center of all my blisse!
> (1290–1)

His affinity with the King is reaffirmed, across an eventful interval, when Edward meets his fate:

> O day! the last of all my blisse on earth,
> Center of all misfortune.
> (1928–9)

Edward's admission of defeat is a reversal for all that Marlowe's heroes have represented:

> To wretched men death is felicitie.
> (2114)

While other playwrights were following Marlowe's lead and drama-tizing kingly success, he chose to occupy himself with conspicuous failure. There are no unhappier pages in English history than those which record "the pitifull tragedie of this kings time"—for even Holinshed so described the regime of Edward II. Holinshed sympathized with the baronial party in its internal struggle against the King, and deplored the loss of national prestige that England suffered in its wars with Ireland, Scotland, and France. Marlowe touches upon these very lightly, treats the King much more sympathetically, and centers his dramatization on Edward's relations with his antagonist, Mortimer, and his favorite, Gaveston. Since the latter has to be executed midway through the drama, Marlowe fills in the gap and preserves the dramatic continuity by introducing the two Spen-cers, as Gaveston's protégés, ten years before their historical models emerged as Edward's favorites. The chronological sequence, whch extends from Edward's accession in 1307 to Mortimer's execution in 1330, is concentrated into a time scheme which seems fairly short and consecu-tive, albeit Edward progresses from youth to old age. Early editions, which yield a more satisfactory text than we have for any of Marlowe's other plays, indicate his emphasis on the title page: *The troublesome raigne and lamentable death of Edward the second, King of England: with the tragicall fall of proud Mortimer*. Edward's reign was a time of troubles, yet his death is to be lamented. His brother, Edmund of Kent, blames "the ruine of the realme" first on Gaveston and later on Edward (1011, 1832). But when Edward is deposed, "the murmuring commons," as Mortimer recognizes, "begin to pitie him" (962, 2334). Mortimer is emphasized, as a more distinctively Marlovian figure, in the octavo of 1594; but the quartos of 1598 and thereafter add another flourish to the subtitle: *And also the life and death of Peirs Gaueston, the great Earle of Cornewall and mighty fauorite of King Edward the second.*

With Gaveston, Marlowe goes beyond Tamburlaine and Barabas in charting a new and dangerous way to rise in the world, to out-Herod monarchs. To charm their affections is to be exposed to the hatred of all their other courtiers, as was the actual Piers Gaveston, the leader of the French party at the court of the Plantagenets. Mortimer voices the attitude of the barons when he scorns "that slie inueigling Frenchman" (264), and what is said about Gaveston's aspirations and extravagances seems to be historically warranted. But Marlowe goes out of his way to make Gaveston a baseborn social climber, a "night growne mushrump" (581), just as he makes parvenus out of the respectable Spencers, in order to humble the pride of their courtly rivals. Gaveston inaugurates the drama by reading aloud the "amorous lines," the welcoming letter of Edward,

> The king, vpon whose bosome let me die,
> And with the world be still at enmitie.
>
> (14–5)

Gaveston's insouciant hostility toward the peers is matched by his cynical contempt for the multitude, which he exhibits next in his encounter with the three poor men. This is not the right chorus for his mounting fortunes, he soliloquizes, as soon as he has dismissed them:

> I must haue wanton Poets, pleasant wits,
> Musitians, that with touching of a string
> May draw the pliant king which way I please:
> Musicke and poetrie is his delight,
> Therefore ile haue Italian maskes by night,
> Sweete speeches, comedies, and pleasing showes,
> And in the day when he shall walke abroad,
> Like *Syluan* Nimphes my pages shall be clad.
>
> (51–8)

Marlowe is here refining on Holinshed's description of Edward "passing his time in voluptuous pleasure, and riotous excesse," corrupted by Gaveston, who "furnished his court with companies of iesters, ruffians, flattering parasites, musicians, and other vile and naughtie ribalds, that the king might spend both daies and nights in iesting, plaieng, blanketing [*sic*], and in such other filthie and dishonorable exercises." Between that medieval brawl and Marlowe's Renaissance pageant, the contrast is brilliantly illuminating. Marlowe's anachronistic Gaveston, in anticipation of such entertainments as the Earl of Leicester gave for Queen Elizabeth at Kenilworth, becomes a lord of misrule, a master of the revels, as well as a stage manager of palace intrigue. The Machiavellian becomes an Epicurean, maintaining his sway through the elusive and disturbing power of the arts. The Marlovian flattery, the speech of esthetic persuasion, is embellished with scenery and choreography; sound and spectacle are bracketed together by the casual couplet that rhymes "night" with "delight." And Gaveston proceeds to imagine a masque which can be taken as a portent, since its hero, Actæon, was hunted down for having gazed on a sight forbidden to men.

Its heroine is sexually ambiguous, a "louelie boye in *Dians* shape" (61), like the epicene pages or—for that matter—the boys who took feminine parts in the Elizabethan theater. The heroine of the play, the Queen neglected by Edward, wishes that her own shape had been changed by Circe (469), while Gaveston himself is compared to "*Proteus* god of shapes" (708). Examples of metamorphosis are frequently adduced, along with such standard mythological prototypes as Phaëthon; and the elder Mortimer evokes a long series of classical precedents to show that heroes and wise men "haue had their minions" (688)—Achilles and Patroclus, Socrates and Alcibiades, and other names still cited by apologists. Comparisons of Gaveston to Ganymede, and to Leander as well, link *Edward II* with *Dido* on the one hand and with *Hero and Leander* on the other. But the most suggestive comparison looks back to Tamburlaine's lament for Zenocrate and ahead to Faustus' vision of Helen of Troy, when Lancaster addresses Gaveston as

> Monster of men,
> That like the Greekish strumpet traind to armes
> And bloudie warres, so many valiant knights.
> (1182–4)

The epithet most commonly applied to Gaveston, "minion," is etymologically the French term of endearment, *mignon*, which now begins to acquire pejorative overtones. Though it is sounded only nine times, it charges the atmosphere, just as "policy" does in *The Jew of Malta*. The King, says Mortimer, "is loue-sick for his minion" (382). As the Queen says, "his minde runs on his minion" (806). And again, and always:

> Harke how he harpes vpon his minion.
> (608)

His obsession is carefully underlined by the repetition of the proper name. "Gaveston." The very word is like a charm, like "Tamburlaine" and "Barabas" in their different ways; and all three are alike in being amphimacers, which fit so effectively into Marlovian verse: "Bajazeth," "Abigall," "Mortimer." Beginning with the first line, and largely confined to the first half of the play, "Gaveston" is sounded 110 times, fifty-six times at the end of a line. Thus Edward, posing the absolute alternative, will "eyther die, or liue with *Gaueston*" (138). He is perfectly willing to divide his kingdom among his nobles,

> So I may haue some nooke or corner left,
> To frolike with my deerest Gaueston.
> (367–8)

It is the old story, so often renewed by life and repeated by drama, of neglecting one's duty to realize one's individuality: *All for Love, or the World Well Lost*. By dwelling upon the emotional conflict between majesty and love, Marlowe resolves the technical conflict between the claims of history and of tragedy. Edward's infatuation, though it impels him in the opposite direction, is just as extreme as Tamburlaine's domination or Barabas' cunning. His irresponsibility is rendered peculiarly flagrant by the unsanctioned nature of his indulgences. It cannot pass without comment that this, the most wholehearted treatment of love in any of Marlowe's plays, involves the erotic attachment of man to man. Friendship, as classically illustrated by Richard Edwardes' tragicomedy of *Damon and Pythias*, was a major Elizabethan theme; but to glance no farther than Shakespeare's sonnets, the ardor with which both sexes are celebrated is such as to elude academic distinctions between the sensual and the Platonic. Gaveston is more and less than a friend to Edward, who devotes to him an overt warmth which Marlowe never displays toward the female sex. The invitation to love, "Come live with me," the mode of enticement so richly elaborated in Gaveston's monologue on music and poetry, soon found its echo in Richard Barnfield's amorous appeal of a swain to a youth, *The Affectionate Shepherd*, thereby joining a literary tradition of homoeroticism which can be traced through Vergil's second Eclogue to the Greek bucolic poets. To ignore the presence or to minimize the impact of such motivation in *Edward II*, as most of its critics discreetly tend to do, is to distort the meaning of the play. According to the testimony of Kyd, Marlowe dared to suspect "an extraordinary loue" between Saint John and Jesus—even comparing them, according to Baines, with "the sinners of Sodoma." It seems unlikely, when the chronicles hinted at such a scandal as he had read into the Gospels, that Marlowe should have looked the other way.

In Michael Drayton's *Legend of Piers Gaveston*, the monologuist adapts a familiar Marlovian symbol to characterize his relationship with the King:

> I waxt his winges, and taught him art to flye,
> Who on his back might beare me through the skye.
> (281–2)

When the "mounting thoughts" (879) of Marlowe's Gaveston are blocked by the opposition, there is a residue of genuine pathos in his response to Edward's commiseration:

> Tis something to be pitied of a king.
> (426)

Their dalliance, which could be profitable to Gaveston, can only be harmful to Edward, who is the lone disinterested character; or rather, as a lover, he projects his innate egoism into a second self which transcends the rest of the world. Pliant to the caprices of his flattering favorite, "the brainsick king" (125) is petulant with his "head-strong Barons" (1065), vainly commanding and pleading by turns, a spoiled child now cajoling and now capitulating. "Ile haue my will" (78), he declares on his first entrance, and a moment later: "I will haue *Gaueston*" (96). But Mortimer and the other nobles, taking their stand upon an absolute alternative, decide to be resolute,

> And either haue our wils, or lose our liues.
> (341)

In the ensuing battle of wills, Edward is predestined to be "ouerrulde" by his "ouerdaring peeres" (333, 342):

> The Barons ouerbeare me with their pride.
> (1315)

Every other speech of the King's is an order, which is generally flouted and countermanded, while the Mortimers issue orders of their own. When Edward decrees of the younger,

> Lay hands on that traitor *Mortimer*,
> (315)

the elder Mortimer treasonably retorts,

> Lay hands on that traitor *Gaueston*.
> (316)

Edward has the regal habit of likening himself, or being likened, to the king of beasts; he is a lion, not to be intimidated by the crowing of "these cockerels" (1005). Yet, after he has fallen, he is a wren, striving against "the Lions strength" of Mortimer (2299)—or, more appropriately, "a lambe, encompassed by Woolues" (2027). It is perversely characteristic of him that he reads his destiny in the emblems of eagles and flying fish, the heraldic devices of temporary reconciliation that Mortimer and Lancaster bear to his "generall tilt and turnament" (673).

Edward is good at such charades, his enemies concede, at "idle triumphes, maskes, lasciuious showes" (959). Mortimer understands him as well as Gaveston does, and Mortimer's reproach is as pertinent as Gaveston's artistic plan of campaign:

> When wert thou in the field with banner spred?
> But once, and then thy souldiers marcht like players,
> With garish robes, not armor.
> (984–6)

For Edward is not a soldier or a commander, he is an esthete and a voluptuary. Glorified by masques or defamed by ballads, he is a king with the soul of an actor, where Tamburlaine was more like an actor in the role of a king. Rhetoric and pageantry existed on the surface in *Tamburlaine*, objective and unreal; but in *Edward II* they are of the essence, subjective and real. Here the theatricality is not conventional but psychological, conceived as a trait of Edward's character. No longer is it taken for granted that words and deeds must coincide; on the contrary, his chronic fault is his inability to substantiate his vaunts. He is steeled by the news of Gaveston's death to make the one vow that he is able to execute. Then, when the parasite is avenged at Boroughbridge, Edward must stage a triumphal ceremony in his memory and in honor of newer favorites:

> Thus after many threats of wrathfull warre,
> Triumpheth Englands *Edward* with his friends,
> And triumph *Edward* with his friends vncontrould.
> (1695–7)

But his triumph, like the Guise's, is short-lived, and shortly he has reason to complain that he is "contrould" by the Queen and Mortimer (2015). When his infelicitous crown is demanded, he prays that it be transmuted into "a blaze of quenchelesse fier" (2030). Then, in accordance with the stage direction, "*The king rageth.*" In his eagerness before the battle, he invoked the sun, with an invocation that Juliet would use at a happier juncture: "Gallop a pace" (1738). His vain command, on the point of abdication, is for the elements to stand still. Now he feels, as Gaveston did when banished, "a hell of greefe" (412, 2538). But, just as Gaveston nonchalantly surrendered with the maxim that "death is all" (1199), so Edward asserts in yielding that "death ends all" (2140). That is a pagan sentiment which sorts, at all events, with his prayer to "immortal *Ioue*." In the dark and muddy dungeon where he encounters his end, he pays the most ironic penalties for the frolicking prodigality of his kingship. Tortured physically and mentally, humiliated by the loss of his beard, shaved and washed in puddle water, he rises to a sense of his tragic role with his remembrance of a forgotten victory:

> Tell *Isabell* the Queene, I lookt not thus,
> When for her sake I ran at tilt in Fraunce,
> And there vnhorste the duke of *Cleremont*.
> (2516–8)

It is a far cry of triumph, more theatrical than chivalric; but Shakespeare must have borne it in mind when Othello, on the verge of suicide, remembered his victory over the Turk at Aleppo. The striking feature of Edward's catastrophe is the total absence of anything spectacular. After all the talk about pageants, the tourneys and processions, they seem to have completely melted away. We are left with a bare stage which pretends to be nothing more, and with a hero stripped of any claim to distinction except his suffering.

> Hence fained weeds, vnfained are my woes.
> (1964)

Edward, on his imaginative flights, is the heir of Marlowe's earlier and more exotic heroes.

> Ere my sweete *Gaueston* shall part from me,
> This Ile shall fleete vpon the Ocean,
> And wander to the vnfrequented Inde.
> (343–5)

Such is his vaunt, at least, but harsh reality tests and deflates the gorgeous hyperbole. The state rests secure, the island remains terra firma, while Gaveston is whirled away by the currents of lawless dalliance. And Edward's recognition of his own powerlessness, hyperbolic though it sounds, is quite literal:

> Ah *Spencer*, not the riches of my realme
> Can ransome him, ah he is markt to die.
> (1309–10)

The style of the play, toned down to accord with its subject matter, has its pedestrian stretches as well as its minor harmonies. Numerous commas indicate varying pauses, as well as improvement upon the other texts in punctuation, and lines run over more limpidly than before. The dialogue makes flexible use of short speeches, sharp interchanges, and subdivided lines; yet, in the later scenes particularly, it crystallizes again into monologues, soliloquies, and set pieces. Marlovian allusion sounds out of place when—to cite an anticlimactic example—the Queen, setting out for Hainault in near-by Belgium, avows her willingness to travel as far as the Don,

> euen to the vtmost verge
> Of *Europe*, or the shore of *Tanaise*.
> (1640–1)

The blare of Marlowe's nomenclature is subdued when his characters' names are domesticated, and the verse halts when the Earl of Lancaster boasts of his four other earldoms,

> Darbie, Salsburie, Lincolne, Leicester.
> (103)

Gaveston mocks at those titles in a subsequent scene which comprises a single speech, five lines of ironic exposition while he is crossing the stage with the Earl of Kent. Such is Marlowe's technical self-consciousness that, when the Queen breaks down in the midst of a formal utterance, she is interrupted by Mortimer:

> Nay madam, if you be a warrier
> Ye must not grow so passionate in speeches.
> (1762–3)

The Queen's rhetorical abilities are put to an even severer test when Edward forces her to plead for the repeal of her rival's banishment. The usual plea is reversed, and persuasion gives way to dissuasion, when she dissuades Mortimer and he dissuades the barons from standing by their resolve. He complies out of love for her, while she has complied out of love for her husband; and Gaveston, the object of her husband's love, completes the unnatural quadrangle of compliance by virtually driving her into Mortimer's arms. Meanwhile Edward, reconciled with her, ironically accepts the situation as "a second marriage" (632).

Isabell, his queen, is a split personality. Though she does not live up to the accusation of being "subtill" (1581), it would be unfair to assume that characterization of women had as yet been developed to any degree of subtlety. She is more alive, at any rate, than the corpse of Zenocrate or the wraith of Helen. The theater was still a man's world; its heroines, as played by boys, were not unnaturally somewhat androgynous; they could behave without effort like shrews or viragoes or the proverbial Hyrcanian tigresses. Somewhat more feminine, though awkwardly depicted, was the saintly, long-suffering type of the patient Griselda, like the women so consistently neglected by the men in the plays of Robert Greene. Isabell enacts both types with manic-depressive inconsistency. She is pathetically devoted to Edward when, prompted by Gaveston, he repels her as a "French strumpet" (441). Subsequently, it is he who talks of "outragious passions" and denounces her as "vnnaturall" (2003). But the interim, and the downfall of her rival, have changed the forlorn wife into the scheming adulteress; and the transition is abruptly made in two brief soliloquies, which stand no more than a page or a scene apart. Despite the modifications that have been effected in order to give the drama a semblance of unity, the elaborate construction that differentiates it from all the others, there is still a break in the middle of *Edward II*, a watershed which divides our sympathies. Up to that point, Edward's follies alienate us, and afterward his trials win us back; while Isabell, who starts by being ungallantly abused, ends by justifying his antipathy. Amid these bewildering shifts of the moral winds, Kent is a sort of weathervane whose turnings veer with the rectitude of the situation, not unlike his namesake in *King Lear*—or possibly a Shakespearean *raisonneur* like John of Gaunt or Humphrey, the good Duke of Gloucester.

Our impression of Mortimer, too, is jeopardized by the same discontinuity that splits the characters of Edward and Isabell. Originally, when the King is so unreasonable, Mortimer seems not merely reasonable but exceptionally downright and hearty, the very antithesis of the intriguing courtier. One of the play's most observant commentators, W. D. Briggs, has even observed in him a model for Hotspur. In that respect he is the natural spokesman for Gaveston's enemies, ultimately becoming a foil for Edward himself, and maintaining a hold upon Isabell that parallels Gaveston's ascendancy over the King. But, as the play moves from open hostilities to more devious conspiracies, Mortimer becomes increasingly Machiavellian and thus more characteristically Marlovian. Whereas Edward and Gaveston cling to each other, he stands—and falls—by himself. When Edward, "Englands scourge" (1567), defeats the barons, and Mortimer is taken prisoner, the latter asks himself:

> What *Mortimer*? can ragged stonie walles
> Immure thy vertue that aspires to heauen?
> (1565–6)

Soon enough he "surmounts his fortune" and makes his escape from the Tower of London; before long he has dethroned the King and become the Lord Protector. In his quickly accumulating *hubris*, quoting a verse from Ovid, he declares that greatness has placed him beyond the reach of fortune; in Senecan terms, he is the Olympian oak, to whom all others are but humble shrubs: yet the shrub is safer than the lofty tree from the whirlwind. He exults, as Tamburlaine did, that he can make "Fortunes wheele turne as he please" (2197). But his own death, compressing three years of history into a crowded final scene, is the immediate consequence of Edward's. Young Edward, having succeeded his late father as King, at once denounces Mortimer as "Villaine" (2593). Mortimer's acceptance of the fatal decree is a belated recognition that his strivings do not exempt him from the common lot:

> Base fortune, now I see, that in thy wheele
> There is a point, to which when men aspire,
> They tumble hedlong downe: that point I touchte,
> And seeing there was no place to mount vp higher,
> Why should I greeue at my declining fall?
> (2627–31)

Mortimer has viewed himself, in his heyday, rather as Fortune's successful foe than as her erstwhile favorite. With her triumph and his decline, he still may depend on his virtue; but virtue, at this point, devolves from Machiavelli's conception back to Seneca's. The individual, in a narrowing world, has less room to act and more occasion to suffer. The ethical criterion is the stoical resignation with which he meets inevitable and overwhelming odds. Where Barabas died cursing, Mortimer's last lines are profoundly meditative. In the seriocomic realm of *The Jew of Malta*, sin could be temporarily dismissed as something that happened in another country. Tragedy, however, must face consequences. Mortimer faces them with curiosity as well as fortitude, readily dismissing the limited sphere of his worldly activities and welcoming death as a further adventure, an Elizabethan voyage of exploration:

> Farewell faire Queene, weepe not for *Mortimer*,
> That scornes the world, and as a traueller,
> Goes to discouer countries yet vnknowne.
> (2632–4)

Not Hotspur but Hamlet is adumbrated by Mortimer, when he sets out toward that undiscovered country from whose bourne no traveler returns. His augmented stature, outshadowing the other characters, largely determines the after-effect of the play. Ben Jonson apparently thought of expanding Marlowe's denouement into a neoclassical tragedy, *The Fall of Mortimer*; and though he left no more than a page or two, it constitutes another link between his work and Marlowe's, and projects a course for the hero-villains of Jonson's two completed tragedies. Michael Drayton was so impressed by Mortimer, "that some-what more than Man" (147), that he cast him as hero in his epic of Edward's reign, *The Barons' Wars*, which in its early version was entitled *Mortimeriados*. In addition to chanting—as Lucan had done—"a farre worse, then Civill Warre" (8), Drayton poetized the romance between Isabell and Mortimer with a pair of his Ovidian *Epistles*. It is noteworthy that Bertolt Brecht, in adapting *Edward II* to the modern German stage, vulgarizes Gaveston, whose music and poetry are reduced to drinking ale and playing whist, while refining and rationalizing Mortimer into a classical scholar turned politician. Marlowe may offer a cue for that interpretation in the soliloquy where Mortimer cites Ovid, and looks upon the Prince with the furrowed brow of a pedantic schoolmaster. Somewhere, conceivably during his short imprisonment in the Tower, Mortimer has picked up his sudden flair for disguises, equivocating letters, and the other ruses of Machiavellianism: his sentence of death for Edward has its counterpart in Ferdinand's condemnation of Antonio in *The Duchess of Malfi.* Edward, hesitating to commit Mortimer, acknowledged that "the people loue him well" (1036). Mortimer, in his Machiavellian phase, acknowledges: "Feard am I more than lou'd" (2383). The sinister aspect of his character is shadowed in the accomplice he chooses for Edward's assassination. The assassin, Lightborne, naïvely and proudly boasting of his Italianate poisons and more ingenious professional tricks, is to Mortimer what the slave Ithamore was to Barabas. And Lightborne's name reveals the cloven hoof; for it had also belonged to one of the devils in the Chester cycle, and is neither more nor less than an Anglicization of "Lucifer."

In his grimly diabolical banter with Mortimer, Lightborne undertakes to murder the King by "a brauer way" than any of the tortures he has enumerated (2369). The horrendous details are decently obscured, both in the dialogue and in the business; but legend was painfully explicit in specifying how a red-hot spit had been plunged into Edward's intestines. The sight of the instrument would have been enough to raise an excruciating shudder in the audience; and subtler minds may have perceived, as does William Empson, an ironic parody of Edward's vice. It is when he beholds the frown of Lightborne that Edward knows the worst:

> I see my tragedie written in thy browes.
> (2522)

So, in the next scene, Isabell tells Mortimer: "Now . . . begins our tragedie" (2591). Edward's tragical history, like Tamburlaine's, is compounded of many tragedies. That of the Mortimers stood out among the stock narratives of unlucky statesmanship in the *Mirror for Magistrates.* Marlowe's Edward self-consciously catches the exemplary tone of that compilation:

> Stately and proud, in riches and in traine,
> Whilom I was powerfull and full of pompe,
> But what is he, whome rule and emperie
> Haue not in life or death made miserable?
> (1879–82)

The Earl of Leicester, in arresting him, garbs the humiliation in borrowed garments of Roman sententiousness:

> *Quem dies vidit veniens superbum,*
> *Hunc dies vidit fugiens iacentem.*
> (1920–1)

This was Seneca's formula for Thyestes, yet it applies to all tragic vicissitudes. Thus Jonson translates it, at the conclusion of *Sejanus*:

> For, whom the morning saw so great, and high,
> Thus low, and little, 'fore the 'euen doth lie.
> (V, 902–3)

Classical or medieval, the peripety is the same, the overturn from grandeur to misery. Edward, the slave of passion, diverges from the man of action, Tamburlaine, by suddenly moving away from the grandeurs of morning and lingering over the miseries of night. Should we conclude that Marlowe was moving back toward a more traditional concept of tragedy? "All liue to die," as Edward tells Spencer, "and rise to fall" (1979). All are corrupted by life, except for his son—who survives to exhibit, in Heywood's *Edward III*, the manly qualities his father has lacked. Marlowe's boyish Edward III, with the innocent wisdom of the stage-child, proclaims in three last words his "greefe and innocencie" (2670). Yet the process of corruption, as Marlowe implied in *The Jew of Malta*, has been a kind of experience purchased with grief and repaid by an awareness of the difference of things. The relative maturity of *Edward II* seems to mark some progression from innocence into experience. Lightborne's spit is an unspeakable counterpart for the scourge of the Scythian conqueror; and the moral advantage of masochism over sadism is, to say the least, a delicate question. But it marks a psychological advance, from terror to pity, when the protagonist experiences genuine agony; while, in philosophical terms, it replaces the values of Epicureanism with those of Stoicism.

Resignation is not the attitude that we intrinsically associate with Marlowe. The frailty of the body, the fallibility of the mind, and the transience of human glory come as highly reluctant admissions in his other tragedies. *Edward II* would prove, if it proved no more, Marlowe's ability to challenge his own assumptions. To see him reverse himself, to see his idiosyncrasies stamped upon a conventional formula, to see for once the would-be tyrant tyrannized over, is more than we might have expected.

> But what are kings, when regiment is gone,
> But perfect shadowes in a sun-shine day?
> (2012–3)

Shakespeare could hardly push that line of inquiry much farther. "The reluctant pangs of abdicating Royalty," Charles Lamb would argue, are often as poignantly rendered in *Edward II* as in *Richard II*; and Edward's death scene was as moving, to Lamb, as anything in ancient or modern drama. Shakespeare could balance his tragedy by handling the counter-claims of the opponents more sympathetically, envisioning the whole as a problem in statecraft, where Marlowe saw little save individual rivalries. Richard's mistakes are due to lack of judgment, where Edward's are attributable to will; and in his willfulness he knows his mind, as Richard in his vacillation does not. The inconsistencies of the latter, his frivolity and his dignity, are more consistently portrayed; yet it is the former whose maladjustment seems more fundamental and whose suffering seems more intense. Richard's death, unlike his life, is an imitation of Christ, a passion play in which an earthly crown is superseded by a crown of thorns. Yet Shakespeare seems to be universalizing the plight that Marlowe had discerned and isolated; and Shakespeare's king is illuminated, like a gilded page from a medieval manuscript, by such lyrical trappings and masquerading embellishments as Marlowe had devised. Richard, descending symbolically into the base court, visualizes himself as Phaëthon. He plays his climactic scene, the deposition, even more histrionically than his predecessor. When he dashes the looking-glass to the floor, his gesture is a farewell to the *Mirror for Magistrates*. The reflection that has been conveyed to him is a reverberation, not from *Edward II*, but from *Doctor Faustus*:

> Was this Face, the Face,
> That euery day, vnder his House-hold Roofe,
> Did keepe ten thousand men?
>
> (IV, i, 281–3)

When Marlowe's Edward finds brief sanctuary in the Abbey of Neath, for a fleeting moment of serenity he feels that he may have missed his real vocation, that he might better have lived in philosophical retreat, and that "this life contemplatiue is heauen" (1887). He exhorts his companions, and especially Baldock, to console themselves with Plato and Aristotle, counselors whom they have all too cynically laid aside for careers of action. The minor character Baldock, "that smoothe toongd scholler" (1845) who has urged the King not to behave like a schoolboy, is the representative of *libido sciendi* in this play, in so far as Edward and Mortimer represent *libido sentiendi* and *libido dominandi*. Baldock's gentry, as he puts it, derives "from Oxford, not from Heraldrie" (1046). Thence he has brought a "speciall gift to forme a verbe" (775)—the talent for putting words together, in Quintilian's phrase—and now he would like "to court it like a Gentleman" (752). Having graduated into the world as the tutor of Gaveston's future countess, he is prepared, when we meet him, to join the Spencers in their campaign for Edward's patronage. The elder Spencer, advising him to "cast the scholler off" along with his curate-like attire, reads him a Machiavellian lecture on worldly wisdom:

> You must be proud, bold, pleasant, resolute,
> And now and then, stab as occasion serues.
>
> (762–3)

Interesting advice which a young Cambridge scholar, smooth-tongued and gifted at forming verbs, would take at his everlasting peril. Though prophecy doubtless went beyond Marlowe's intention, he may have deliberately added one or two strokes of self-caricature to this University Wit who comes to grief among the intrigues and politics of court. Since the historical Sir Robert Baldock had been Edward's Lord Chancellor, a man of affairs whose origin was by no means obscure and whose background was not specially academic, Marlowe must have gone out of his way to manifest the wry preoccupation he shared with Nashe and Greene and the other masters of arts who had rashly decided to practice the dubious trade of literature in the wicked city of London.

It is as if a painter, half in earnest and half in jest, had painted himself in the corner of some panoramic canvas. When we turn from *Edward II* to *The Massacre at Paris*, we note that Marlowe again has appended a signature in the secondary figure of Ramus. A recent discussion of that confused and confusing play, by P. H. Kocher, pertinently notices how Marlowe seems to delight in shedding the blood of preachers and scholars. Petrus Ramus, whose murder was for Protestants a martyrdom, could be considered the scholar's patron saint. His works, which so drastically simplified the relations between logic and rhetoric, and which attempted to devise a more pragmatic approach to both, had set off an intellectual revolution in the Cambridge of Marlowe's day. Although his endless dichotomies turned out to be as rigid as those scholastic predicaments which he strove to abolish, Ramus was the Reformation's strongest champion in questioning Aristotle and the Schoolmen. Marlowe's depiction shows him "*in his studie*" with his "bedfellow," Taleus, (376) who escapes. Since Ramus has dedicated his existence to learning, he has no gold and cannot ransom himself—a special twist of the frequent Marlovian plaint. The humbleness of his birth is contrasted with the pride of his reason, in his dialectical interchange with the Guise. The Guise resorts to the argument of force, and Ramus dies reasoning to the very last. Although the portrait is stiff and fragmentary, it should stay in our minds as an affirmation of that scholarly ideal from which Dr. Faustus so egregiously deviates. If Edward II fails to justify his own lofty calling, that may be in part because Marlowe owes his allegiance to an even loftier one. Consciously, he may be allegorizing his autobiography, as Keats maintained that Shakespeare did; he may be miscasting the artist as a king, like Thomas Mann in his twentieth-century novel of kingship, *Königliche Hoheit*. Art, which is notoriously protean, can assume innumerable shapes; yet, as we grapple with it, we come to apprehend the intelligence behind it; and where, if not in *Doctor Faustus*, are we able to overtake the artist within his elusive sphere, the intellect?

DAVID BEVINGTON

"The Jew of Malta"

Much of the difficulty in interpreting *The Jew of Malta* stems from the same uneasy juxtaposition of moral structure and secular content already found in *Tamburlaine*. The protagonist, Barabas, is in part a lifelike Jewish merchant caught in a political feud on Malta, and in part an embodiment both of the morality Vice and of the unrepenting protagonist in homiletic "tragedy." In some early scenes of the play he is psychologically complex and briefly pitiable; and yet T. S. Eliot astutely interprets *The Jew* as a savage farce. Spivack traces the farcical nature of Barabas to the stage tradition of the Vice: the way in which Barabas puts himself on show to the audience, the treachery to friend and foe alike, the theatrical laughing and weeping, the expert intrigue for its own sake. The attempt to reconcile these strange opposites of plausibility and farce in Barabas' character leads to a series of moral uncertainties. H. S. Bennett calls *The Jew* "a challenge to our powers of assimilation," and most of its critics have pointed to the play's unevenness of tone and incongruity of effect.

Some critics and editors have attributed the lack of consistency in *The Jew* to a supposedly unreliable text, containing substantial revisions penned during the long years between the original production of 1589–1591 and the earliest printed version of 1633. Tucker Brooke, for example, believes it "probable that the extant text incorporates the results of at least two separate revisions; the first carried out before the revival of 1601, to which Henslowe alludes, the second that which must have been

From *Mankind to Marlowe: Growth of Structure in the Popular Drama of Tudor England.* Copyright © 1962 by the President and Fellows of Harvard College. Harvard University Press.

necessary before so old a work could be presented at Court and at the Cock-pit." These two assumptions are based only on a priori reasoning; Henslowe alludes merely to a performance in 1601, not to a revision. Nevertheless the argument has received widespread support, seemingly because scholars in search of classically "pure" tragedy have not wished to ascribe to Marlowe both the early scenes of tragic conflict and the later scenes of vicious and farcical degeneracy.

Recent studies have suggested, however, that the text of The Jew is not unreliable, and that the discrepancies between the 1633 quarto and the original performance are probably not fundamental. Margarete Thimme asserts with conviction that the text is all Marlowe's work. H. S. Bennett, although believing that some drastic changes may have occurred, notes that there was "j cauderm [cauldron] for the Jewe" in the Admiral's inventory of 1598, and concludes that the final scene has not been vitally tampered with in any revision. J. C. Maxwell finds by bibliographical analysis that the deficiencies in the 1633 text are far less the result of changes in manuscript than of an admittedly bad printing. The length of time between composition and publication, he argues, is not so serious as is commonly imagined, since the doctrine of "continuous copy" is an editorial fiction, and since "manuscripts, unlike apples, do not become corrupt simply by lying in a drawer." To class The Jew as a text with The Massacre at Paris, he concludes, "is to blur the clear distinction between memorial transmission (and, in this case, very poor memorial transmission) and careless printing from a manuscript that may have suffered some minor damage in revision and transcription."

It is not far fetched to suppose that vice comedy may have formed a part of the earliest text of The Jew, since Greg has shown vice comedy to have been a part of the basic design of Faustus. An examination of structure in The Jew confirms the likelihood of basic similarity between the 1633 text and the first performance. The vicious and degenerate comedy in the later scenes is integral to the conception of the whole work as homiletic intrigue. In its original form the play probably contained a sequence of episodic plots corresponding in structure to the plotting phases of such homiletic tragedies as The Longer Thou Livest and Enough Is as Good as a Feast.

Symmetrical suppression and alternation, although not so sharply demarcated as in Tamburlaine, are the essential methods by which The Jew is put together. Barabas' partners and victims parade before us in linear sequence, usually in pairs. The two merchants appear only in the first scene, and like homiletic figures serve the limited function of highlighting a characteristic in the protagonist, colossal wealth and mercenary ingenuity. Similarly, the three Jews function only in the first two scenes. Possibly they were originally two in number, for Barabas pointedly bids farewell to only two of them by name ("Farewell, Zaareth; farewell, Temainte"), and the third Jew speaks only one inconsequential line ("And very wisely said; it may be so") in his two appearances on stage. Once the Jews have served the purpose of evoking pity for Barabas, they are permanently suppressed. The Abbess and Nun in scene two are employed only once, as the dupes for Barabas' scheme to remove his hidden treasure from his confiscated house. Mathias and Lodowick, the first pair of victims to be slaughtered by Barabas, are introduced late in Act I and disappear in III, ii. They are superseded by the two Friars, who appear chiefly in the scenes following the murder of Mathias and Lodowick (III, iii–IV, iii), and then by the courtesan Bellamira and her accomplice Pilia-Borsa, who connive with Ithamore to blackmail Barabas after the suppression of the Friars (IV, iv–V, i). Marlowe's tendency to symmetrical pairing appears further in the combinations of Barabas and Ithamore, and of the foreign potentates Calymath and del Bosco. Thus the episodic nature of the plot is reflected in the series of groupings surrounding Barabas, as his villainous career moves forward by intrigue and duplicity.

The episodic succession must end in retribution, according to the moral formula, and in the final scenes of *The Jew* the action is dominated by political figures who engineer the retribution: the Turk Calymath, the Spaniard del Bosco, and Malta's governor Ferneze. They occupy the structural position of the judges in the homiletic drama such as Despair, God's Judgment, Correction, and Perseverance. Throughout the play, moreover, they have occupied the alternating and separate scenes of moral commentary, previously peopled by homiletic figures of moral purity whose virtuous conduct contrasted with the depravity of the vicious comedians. The political world of Malta provides this structural contrast in the second scene, after Barabas' first solo appearance, and in the fourth scene (II, ii), after Barabas' success in removing his treasures from his house. The appearance of del Bosco (III, v) punctuates the interval between the slaughter of Mathias and Lodowick and the slaughter of the two Friars. The final grouping of the governors and princes in Act V corresponds structurally not only to the avengers in morality drama but to the procession of "reward" personalities whose triumphs offset the defeat and punishment of the protagonist. Of course there is something bizarre in considering Ferneze as a judge or "reward" figure, and it is the contrast between moral justification implicit in the homiletic structure of the play and Marlowe's accurate portrayal of *Realpolitik* that we shall consider in evaluating the play's ambiguity. It is important at present to emphasize the pervasiveness of the homiletic structure in the sequential progression of Barabas' victims and in the alternating and contrasting appearance of his enemies or judges.

A feasible casting for the speaking parts of *The Jew* requires at least seven experienced actors and three boys, and demonstrates the technical advantage of suppression and alternation in pairs: (1) Barabas (2) Machiavel, Ithamore (3) Ferneze (4) Calymath, first Friar (5) first Merchant, first Jew, Lodowick, second Friar (6) second Merchant, second Jew, Mathias, del Bosco (7) Pilia-Borsa, Messenger, Guard, Basso, Slave. The ranks of the boys would have to include two seasoned performers together with one or two beginners: (1) Abigail and Bellamira (2) Abbess and Katherine (3) Nun. It is quite possible that a few more adult actors were available, and that the doubling assignments need not have been this heavy. Even if the actors themselves did little alternating of roles, however, the structural heritage of alternation survives strongly.

No nondramatic source has been discovered for the plot and order of events in *The Jew*, and Bakeless conjectures that "probably none exists." Ethel Seaton has shown that Philip Lonicerus' *Chronicorum Turcicorum tomi duo*, used by Marlowe in assembling materials for *Tamburlaine*, Part II, contains a reference to one Juan Miques or Michesius, a well-known Jewish man of affairs who may have served as a model for Barabas' character. Miques also appears in Belleforest's *Cosmographie Universelle*, and other Jews named David Passi and Alvaro Mendez may similarly have contributed to Marlowe's conception of his hero. With only these few general sources for *The Jew*, scholars have generally agreed that Marlowe (and possibly collaborators) must have improvised a great deal. "Out of a haze of surmise and unreliable report he saw clearly enough the main lines of his character. His reading and general knowledge of recent and current history gave him the rest." As in the case of *Tamburlaine*, Part II, therefore, the structural ordering of events appears to have been the creation of the dramatist and his popular company. It is probably this fact which accounts for the linear arrangement of episodes, and the prominence of homiletic intrigue, in the sequence of the action.

Even if the structure of vice "tragedy" is clearly present in *The Jew*, this element can scarcely account for the play's greatness. As in *Tamburlaine*, Marlowe's genius cannot here be forced into the restrictive mold of the homiletic drama. Marlowe sees in Barabas far more than a maliciously evil Worldly Man. He reaches beyond the type to a particular person, and is seemingly less interested in moral example than in the intricate causality of human behavior. And yet however imperfectly Marlowe may fit into the homiletic formula, that formula does exist in his drama, and it exerts a

profound if ambivalent effect. Paradoxically it is Marlowe's search for new
themes that places such emphasis upon the older format, by exaggerating
its incongruity in a drama of increasingly secular values. This incongruity
can best be measured in a scene-by-scene analysis, describing on the one
hand the elements of homiletic farce progressing to a "tragic" end for the
unrepentant protagonist, and, on the other, the elements of a psychological
treatise depicting a persecuted Maltese Jew. The study will necessarily
focus upon the protagonist, and will have to examine the delineation of
character insofar as Barabas appears to be a person of complex human
emotions as well as a purely vicious type. Nevertheless the ultimate
interest here lies in the conflict between the intricacy of character portrayal and inherited moral structure.

The prologue, spoken by Machiavel, is a conventional morality
device heralding the appearance of the unregenerate protagonist. Machiavel
himself poses as the personification of evil. This popular misconception of
the Italian writer is in fact only a veneer, a topical label for the Father of
Lies. Marlowe prefers to clothe his personifications in historical garb, but
the disguise does not conceal the fact that Machiavel's function, like that
of Satan in *Conflict of Conscience*, is to serve as the progenitor of evil for
his emissary in the world of men. Just as Satan promises to call forth his
lieutenants Hypocrisy, Avarice, and Tyranny, Machiavel (who is significantly no longer a living person but a "soul" or spirit of malevolence) bids
us prepare for his viceroy, the Jew:

> And let him not be entertain'd the worse
> Because he favours me.

Machiavel personifies in abstract and absolute form the vices that are to be
found in Barabas: utter lack of conscience ("there is no sin but ignorance") and inordinate greed:

> [He] smiles to see how full his bags are cramm'd,
> Which money was not got without my means.

The tone of Machiavel's speech is one of diabolical amusement at his own
villainy. We are to be entertained by a display of extraordinary cunning
motivated solely by the love of evil for its own sake.

The first dramatic vision of Barabas confirms the image of evil. He
is clever, miserly, devoid of conscience. His love for his daughter Abigail
proves to be merely an extension of his self-absorbed greed. His narrow
charity excludes even the three brethren of his race with whom he
discusses the expected arrival of the Turkish fleet:

> Why, let 'em come, so they come not to war;
> Or let 'em war, so we be conquerors.—
> *Nay, let 'em combat, conquer, and kill all.*
> *So they spare me, my daughter, and my wealth.*   [*Aside.*
>
> (I, i, 148–151)

In fact he deliberately dupes the three Jews in his explanation of the Turkish visit, and quiets their fears only to ponder after their departure, "These silly men mistake the matter clean." It would be an error, then, to sympathize with Barabas as the representative victim of a downtrodden race, since his ill-will applies equally to Christian, Turk, and Jew. We can no more expect him to abjure his native evil than Worldly Man in *Enough Is as Good as a Feast*, who is guaranteed by his prolocutor to be stout in villainy and "in any wise wil not bow."

After this traditional exposition of the unredeemable worldling, the moral formula introduces a confrontation in the second scene between Barabas and his dramatic counterparts. At this point the ambiguity commences, for according to the moral pattern Barabas' enemies and future victims should represent the cause of virtue. Instead, because Marlowe's interest in his protagonist is too deep for simple denunciation, we are suddenly faced with the irony of finding Barabas the sympathetic victim of Christian treachery. Ferneze's method of taxation is patently despotic, and his refusal to allow Barabas to pay the tax after momentary reconsideration, in lieu of total forfeiture, is arbitrary. Barabas' defense becomes, by a curious inversion, the pleading of a wronged, sensitive, and helpless person:

> The man that dealeth righteously shall live:
> And which of you can charge me otherwise? . . .
> Ay, let me sorrow for this sudden chance;
> 'Tis is the trouble of my spirit I speak:
> Great injuries are not so soon forgot.
>
> (I, ii, 117–118, 207–209)

The second Jew, as he and his fellows depart, expresses a choric reaction to the preceding scene:

> On, then: but, trust me, 'tis a misery
> To see a man in such affliction.
>
> (I, ii, 212–213)

An Elizabethan audience, whatever its attitudes toward Jews in general, would have reacted with some indignation to Barabas' broadly human plight. The dramatist intended his audience to view his "villain," for the moment at least, with genuine sympathy.

When Barabas is left alone on stage, however, he reveals that his noble passion was in fact contrived as a means of deceiving others and winning sympathy from them. He laughs exultingly at his cleverness in duping them, and at the pity he has evoked:

> See the simplicity of these base slaves.
> Who, for the villains have no wit themselves,
> Think me to be a senseless lump of clay,
> That will with every water wash to dirt!
> No, Barabas is born to better chance,
> And fram'd of finer mould than common men, . . .
> For evils are apt to happen every day.
>   (I, ii, 215–224)

He informs Abigail that she need not moan "for a little loss," since he has stored away more than has been confiscated. Even the news that he cannot gain access to his house to remove the treasure deters him for only a moment. He has a plan for every emergency.

Clearly Barabas' passionate reaction to the tax was all a pretense, intended to trick the audience as well as the three Jews. The revelation in soliloquy of this hypocrisy is an ironic undercutting of the apparent tragedy for a comic purpose. It shows Barabas as the "Vice," who mockingly and boastfully reveals his strategy to his audience after having cheated them into misplaced sympathy. His hate is not provoked by Ferneze's persecution; Barabas hated the world before, as a matter of policy.

At the same time, the injustice of Ferneze's decree remains a fact, and Barabas has been treated ignominiously. A second purpose of this second scene, then, is to provide an understandable motivation for the Jew's hate and his subsequent deeds of revenge. He is put in a position of having to fight back, so that his misanthropic behavior is made plausible:

> Daughter, I have it: thou perceiv'st the plight
> Wherein these Christians have oppressed me:
> Be rul'd by me, for in extremity
> We ought to make bar of no policy.
>   (I, ii, 270–273)

The Vice has been secularized in the person of Barabas, a man with dangerous enemies. This aspect of Barabas shows something far more subtle and lifelike than the type of unrepentant Worldly Man. Even Abigail, a sympathetic character, perceives at first the justice of her father's retaliatory tactics. She reluctantly agrees to help in deceiving the nuns, so that Barabas may retrieve the money from his house. The Jew's plan to win back his own property from the Christians, even if by slightly devious means, is only to demand an eye for an eye. In one sense all of

Barabas' later acts are acts of vengeance or self-defense, and stem from Ferneze's first pitiless deed. Hence the first two scenes are crucial in justifying Barabas' subsequent treachery. Nevertheless, the need for providing motivation should not obscure the purely Vice-like conception of Barabas' original character.

Critics have often contrasted the degeneracy of Barabas into pure villain in the last three acts of *The Jew* with his moral complexity as a person in the earlier scenes—a contrast usually accounted for by the theory of multiple authorship. As we have seen, however, the Jew was actually a villain when he appeared in the first scene. His later career of viciousness is simply a return to his original nature rather than a new and puzzling development in character. Once Marlowe has established Barabas' motivation for revenge, he turns again to the pattern of vicious and comic intrigue. The structure becomes that of plotting and degeneracy in the homiletic drama, such as Worldly Man's succession of unfair triumphs over his innocent victims Tenant, Servant, and Hireling in *Enough Is as Good as a Feast*.

The shift to a structure of vice intrigue commences in Act II, iii, with the alliance of Barabas and Ithamore, the slave who is to assist in the Jew's acts of "revenge." Ithamore, too, is given a motivation for anti-Christian hatred. Barabas welcomes him as a comrade in hate:

> Why, this is something: make account of me
> As of thy fellow; we are villains both:
> Both circumcised; we hate Christians both.
> (II, iii, 214–216)

Yet their alliance for the purpose of revenging themselves upon Christian persecutors is patently a pretext. They not only "hate Christians both" but "are villains both"; the former is the ostensible motivation, the latter the basically vicious fact. Barabas' victims of the past have not all been Christians. He has turned his hatred upon invalids, orphans, and helpless persons without distinction of sect or nationality:

> As for myself, I walk abroad a nights
> And kill sick people groaning under walls:
> Sometimes I go about and poison wells.
> (II, iii, 175–177)

In battle he has delighted in playing the villain with both sides:

> And in the wars 'twixt France and Germany,
> Under pretense of helping Charles the Fifth,
> Slew friends and enemy with my stratagems.
> (II, iii, 188–190)

The description here does not correspond realistically with what we know of Barabas' life. He has been a merchant, not a warrior. In earlier speeches he has deliberately relinquished temporal power to Christian kings, asking only for peace that he may gain more wealth (I, i, 127–133). The present recital of vicious accomplishments is the record of a universalized genius of evil, not of the specific man. At the same time, Barabas does have particular and valid reasons for hating Christians, especially Ferneze.

Recognizing this dual aspect in the play's exposition, we may follow in successive scenes the resulting divergence of aim between a series of psychologically motivated revenges and a parade of triumphs by the Worldly Man over his innocent victims. Barabas' first deed of "vengeance" is directed against Mathias and Lodowick, two rivals for the love of Abigail. Barabas does not object to their love for his daughter; but Lodowick is the son of Malta's governor, and his blood must pay the price of Ferneze's unjust taxation. Barabas' hatred of Lodowick is therefore understandable:

> As sure as heaven rain'd manna for the Jews,
> So sure shall he and Don Mathias die:
> His father was my chiefest enemy.
> (II, iii, 249–251)

The reason for Mathias' death is far less clear, however. It is merely specious logic on the part of Barabas to include Mathias' name with Lodowick's in the speech just quoted. Mathias is guilty of no offense. Moreover, Abigail is genuinely in love with him. She consents, though much against her will, to aid in the plot against Lodowick without realizing that her father plans to destroy her lover as well. Her love for Mathias is not a moral problem for Barabas but an opportunity for intrigue. After both young men have been slain, Abigail broken-heartedly questions the necessity of Mathias' death:

> Admit thou lov'dst not Lodowick for his sire,
> Yet Don Mathias ne'er offended thee.
> (III, iii, 43–44)

What delights Barabas in the episode of Lodowick and Mathias is the cleverness of his act. He needs two victims in order to play one against the other. Mathias must die to complete a scheme of ingenious crime. Like Iago, another descendant of the Vice, Barabas operates through false rumor, the jealousies of love, setting friend against friend by means of evil suggestion.

Once Barabas has entered upon his career of revenge, each suc-ceeding act is motivated in part by the need to suppress those who know too much or have revolted against him, or by the desire to further his revenge against Ferneze and the government. The structural result is a sequence of episodes involving a succession of victims, usually in pairs, who are suppressed with the forceful regularity of homiletic drama. Abigail learns the truth of Mathias' death, and turns nun in earnest. Consequently she is a potential enemy to the Jew on two counts, of disloyalty and possession of dangerous knowledge:

> For she that varies from me in belief,
> Gives great presumption that she loves me not;
> Or, loving, doth dislike of something done.
> (III, iv, 10–12)

Her death must be the result, as another "vengeance" stemming from Barabas' original hatred for Ferneze. At the same time Barabas' primary concern in dispatching Abigail is less with the motive of his deed than with its execution. The Italian tradition of revenge, introduced by Machiavel, may serve in part as a literary source for Barabas' method in handling poisons, but the emphasis on artistry in evil is also the mark of the Vice and Worldly Man. Barabas gloats over his precious secret poison which cannot be detected upon the victim's body, and chuckles at the ironic appropriateness of a deadly porridge sent as alms to the nunnery.

The slaughter of the nuns leads to yet another situation in which Barabas has to protect himself by further violence. Friar Barnardine receives Abigail's dying confession of her father's villainy, and with Friar Jacomo he confronts Barabas with threatened exposure. Like Abigail, therefore, the Friars have become dangerous enemies to Barabas and must be dispatched with haste and skill:

> Now I have such a plot for both their lives,
> As never Jew nor Christian knew the like:
> One turn'd my daughter, therefore he shall die;
> The other knows enough to have my life,
> Therefore 'tis not requisite he should live.
> (IV, i, 120–124)

This soliloquy emphasizes the two elements underlying Barabas' actions. The last three lines present the plausible motivation, although it is curious that the Jew speaks of only one Friar as possessing the knowledge of his crimes. Obviously Barabas realizes that both are partakers of the secret; "I fear they know we sent the poison'd broth," he whispers to Ithamore. The device of attributing a different motive to each of the two Friars is too rhetorical to be sincere. But it is in the two preceding lines that Barabas speaks as the Vice. This plot is to be a masterpiece, and the

Jew prepares his audience to admire the beauty of its conception. The execution of his design is everything that he promises. He plays on the rapacity of the Friars, and pits them against each other (as he had done with Mathias and Lodowick) in the manner of the Vice by appealing to their ruling passion, greed.

The next episode, in which Ithamore becomes infatuated with the courtesan Bellamira and conspires with her and Pilia-Borsa to blackmail Barabas, is a business of comic intrigue. The scenes here are more burlesque than in the incident with the Friars: the tavern life and brothel humor, the quarrel over a whore, the grotesque "humors" of Pilia-Borsa's affected manner, and Barabas' ingenious disguise as a French musician in order to spy on the blackmailers. This vice comedy acts as a ludicrous and degenerate parody of the more serious bloody deeds of Barabas and Ithamore.

Even in this late episode, however, the motivation depends plausibly upon the train of events that has preceded this action. Barabas' need to do away with Ithamore and his new companions is identical with that which had brought Abigail and the Friars to their deaths, disloyalty to Barabas combined with knowledge that could expose him to the law:

> Well, I must seek a means to rid 'em all,
> And presently; for in his villainy
> He will tell all he knows, and I shall die for't.
> (IV, v, 63–65)

At the same time, we know that Barabas had planned to rid himself of Ithamore sooner or later in any case. He deserves Ithamore's epithet of "bottle-nosed knave" (III, iii, 10) identifying him as a recognizable stage type. It is his nature to hate everyone, even his fellows in vice, and the destruction of Ithamore stems ultimately from this simple hate.

Thematic unity in these scenes of worldly ambition follows that of the mid-century popular play. No hypothesis of later textual emendation is required to explain the connection between these successive episodes. In one sense, Barabas' acts depend upon one another as he seeks to revenge his wrongs or to cover up for his crimes. On the other hand, insofar as each evil deed is the result of Barabas' purely evil nature, there is no development of motivation at all. Each variation on the theme of vice casts additional light on the nature and operation of evil. The process does not logically unfold, but elaborates and intensifies by repeated example. The play moves steadily toward comic decline. Each succeeding incident becomes more ludicrous and more wildly improbable than the one before, as the reign of pure vice becomes increasingly separated from its original motive.

The structure of the final act follows the inevitable conclusion of

all homiletic "tragedy," descending lower and lower into an insane depravity that can end only in punishment for the protagonist and restoration of order for those who remain. Barabas' frenzy in the manipulations of
state affairs destroys even the pretense that he is driven by a desire for
vengeance. When the Turks deliver Ferneze into his power, he is in a
position to complete the personal "revenge" that has supposedly motivated all his previous acts of violence. Instead of doing so, he plots the
destruction of his Turkish allies. The Vice traditionally knows no sides,
and always prefers to pit one side against the other rather than seek aid
against his supposed enemies. Barabas abandons the cause of revenge for
one of intrigue for its own sake:

> Thus, loving neither, will I live with both.
> (V, ii, 111)

He boasts to the audience of his treachery in turning against the Turks,
who would have helped him to destroy the uncircumcised Christians he
professedly hates:

> Why, is not this
> A kingly kind of trade, to purchase towns
> By treachery, and sell 'em by deceit?
> Now tell me, worldlings, underneath the sun
> If greater falsehood ever has bin done?
> (V, v, 46–50)

Even when he is dying, having been trapped by Ferneze's counterplot, the
Jew boasts of his villainy and promises that he had intended the destruction of both sides:

> And, had I but escap'd this strategem,
> I would have brought confusion on you all,
> Damn'd Christians, dogs, and Turkish infidels!
> (V, v, 84–86)

Barabas' farewell is that of the evil genius in the moral play who aims at
the annihilation of everything decent "underneath the sun."

Barabas' punishment appears to answer for his sins. The formula of
the moral play demands providential justice to end the worldly success of
vice, and we ought to be satisfied with Barabas' fate. His death is not
accidental, like that of Cambises or Tamburlaine. A boiling cauldron is
sufficient atonement even for a lifetime of atrocities. The Jew was evil,
and he answered for it; the lesson seems clear and edifying. The difficulty,
however, lies in the instrument of that justice. Ferneze lacks the personal
virtue to act as agent of God's righteous anger; and yet the moral frame-

work of the play puts him in a position of doing just this. In fact, Ferneze speaks of himself in this role:

> So, march away; and let due praise be given
> Neither to Fate nor Fortune, but to Heaven.
> (V, v, 123–124)

Almost in the same breath, Ferneze perpetrates his own last act of duplicity by refusing to free Calymath, whom the Jew's treason has delivered into his hands. The play ends where it began, without the establishment of a moral order on Malta but merely with the restoration of the expediency that has always been Ferneze's method of governing. His appeal to divine justice is a mockery.

This curious dilemma has come about through the transference of a secular story into the structure of moral drama. In order to rationalize the native viciousness of Barabas it is necessary to provide him with enemies and persecutors; and since he is a Jew on the island of Malta, the Christians must play the part of villainy in those crucial first scenes when for a short time our sympathy focuses on Barabas. These Christians on Malta are Roman Catholics, and Catholics frequently appeared on the Elizabethan stage as villains. Nevertheless, the portrayal of them as evil results in moral confusion in the ensuing scenes of the play, since they cannot justly provide a virtuous foil for Barabas' villainy. For example, the two Friars are presented as greedy and unscrupulous in their desire for gold. They are also lecherous, and have mistresses within the walls of the convent. To dupe such unworthy members of a much-feared church in Marlowe's day must have merited applause rather than condemnation. The anti-Papist jokes, often on Barabas' lips, surely evoked appreciation from his original audience:

> And yet I know the prayers of those nuns
> And holy friars, having money for their pains,
> Are wondrous;—and indeed do no man good.   [Aside.
> (II, iii, 80–82)

The same problem of moral ambiguity occurs in *Faustus* when the protagonist snubs the Prince of Rome and his superstitious Friars. In *The Jew*, the function of such anti-Catholicism is to provide motivation for Barabas' acts as a Maltese Jew; but because Barabas is also a villain, such factors work against the moral function of the plot, which suggests that all of his acts are wicked and are to be punished.

If the conflict is evident in Barabas' religious enemies and victims, it is even more apparent in his political antagonists. Quite early in the action Ferneze is singled out as the man who must bring the Jew to justice.

As Barabas grows more violent and evil, Ferneze comes inevitably to represent his moral opposite. The governor is prompted to revenge by the death of his son and Don Mathias:

> Upon which altar I will offer up
> My daily sacrifice of sighs and tears,
> And with my prayers pierce impartial heavens,
> Till they [reveal] the causers of our smarts,
> Which forc'd their hands divide united hearts.
> (III, ii, 31–35)

Ferneze repeatedly refers to himself as the executor of divine law in hunting down Barabas. When the supposedly dead body of the Jew is thrown over the walls of the city, Ferneze remarks:

> Wonder not at it, sir; the heavens are just.
> (V, i, 55)

It is in the context of moral drama that such a conclusion is to be expected. The structure of the play demands a relationship between cause and effect in Barabas' career. The difficulty is that in rationalizing Barabas' original plight, Marlowe has created villains out of those very persons who must later become the agents of retribution.

Ultimately, Marlowe's world of chronicle is morally neutral. Ferneze, Calymath, and del Bosco are no better and no worse than Barabas; Ferneze's final victory is merely a fact. The contest for Malta is a struggle for balance of power between leaders who are inspired by a lust for dominion and wealth:

> FERNEZE: What wind drives you thus into Malta road?
> BASSO: The wind that bloweth all the world besides,
> Desire of gold.
> (III, v, 2–4)

Abigail sees that the material world does not always proceed according to God's plan, and therefore makes a second and entirely devout conversion to the life of a nun:

> But I perceive there is no love on earth,
> Pity in Jews, nor piety in Turks.
> (III, iii, 50–51)

Such injustices are never denied or amended, and they fit uneasily into a dramatic plan inherited from a religious tradition. Once again, as in *Tamburlaine*, we find in the combination of secular material and moral structure a key to the play's characteristic ambiguity.

A. D. HOPE

"*Tamburlaine*":
The Argument of Arms

Towards the end of Marlowe's *Tamburlaine* there is a brutal scene in which the conqueror returns from his victory over the Turkish kings and calls for his son Calyphas. As Calyphas has refused to take part in the battle his father prepares to kill him with his own hands in front of his other sons, his generals and the captive kings. Although Techelles, Usumcasane and Theridamas, the generals who have followed Tamburlaine's fortunes from the start, must surely by now be inured to massacre, arbitrary judgment and brutal execution, they are shocked. They know well enough the ungovernable temper and the ferocious resolution of their master. Yet they fall on their knees and plead for the young man's life. Tamburlaine berates them like raw recruits:

> Stand up, ye base, unworthy soldiers!
> Know ye not yet the argument of arms?

As they plainly do not know it, he proceeds to tell them, and concludes the lesson by stabbing Calyphas to death.

The Argument of Arms is the argument of the play, and it is doubtful whether some editors and critics of the play have understood it any better than did Tamburlaine's generals, though in both cases it is not for want of telling. It is, indeed, just of that speech in which the argument is first and most clearly set out, in poetry so splendid as to compel understanding, that understanding has been most lacking. This is, of

---

course, the speech in the first part of the play where Cosroe, for whom
Tamburlaine has won, and from whom he has then taken, the Persian
throne, reproaches his conqueror, calling him 'bloody and insatiate
Tamburlaine'. Tamburlaine replies:

> The thirst of reign and sweetness of a crown
> That caused the eldest son of heavenly Ops,
> To thrust his doting father from his chair,
> And place himself in the imperial heaven,
> Mov'd me to manage arms against thy state.
> What better precedent than mighty Jove?
> Nature, that fram'd us of four elements
> Warring within our breasts for regiment,
> Doth teach us all to have aspiring minds:
> Our souls, whose faculties can comprehend
> The wondrous architecture of the world,
> And measure every wandering planet's course,
> Still climbing after knowledge infinite,
> And always moving as the restless spheres,
> Wills us to wear ourselves and never rest,
> Until we reach the ripest fruit of all,
> That perfect bliss and sole felicity,
> The sweet fruition of an earthly crown.

Scholars and critics have often pointed out that the first part of
this passage is the very poetry of Renaissance humanism, but they usually
show disappointment at the end of it. John Addington Symonds called it
'Scythean bathos'; Una Ellis-Fermor, after calling the passage on the Soul
perhaps the noblest lines Marlowe ever wrote, goes on:

And then, at the end, comes the inevitable bathos. To what is all this
aspiration and hunger directed? 'To the ripest fruit of all' Marlowe tries
to persuade us:

'The sweet fruition of an earthly crown'

We do not believe him. We go back to the lines about the 'faculties' of
the soul and take care never again to link them with what follows. For
the fact is that Marlowe has suddenly—it may be all unconsciously—
broken faith with his idea. The instinct is there, magically defined and
passionate. The error, the inability to grasp in a weaker mood its full
significance, occurs when Marlowe attempts to give it a specific direction.

Muriel Bradbrook is equally definite:

Knowledge is infinite; that is given in the straight soaring of the
'mighty line', but the movement is not cumulative and flags to 'the
sweet fruition of an earthly crown'. In fact the whole passage about

the soul and knowledge occurs as a mere parenthesis in Tamburlaine's argument to justify attacking Cosroe: it is flanked with prudential matter.

Frederick Boas, more perceptive, sees that the passion for sovereignty has the same ultimate source as the insatiable scientific impulse and the quest for beauty. But he fails to see that not only have these passions the same source, they are in fact said to be the same passion. The argument is one argument, and only if it is taken as one argument has the play meaning and coherence. Marlowe is under no misapprehension, has no doubt that to be a king is a higher felicity and a greater aspiration than anything else, even the pursuit of knowledge infinite.

The notion that knowledge is the highest of human aspirations is perhaps peculiarly a scholar's delusion and, in an age which worships knowledge, it is natural for scholars to misunderstand the passage in question. And this is especially so since kings have now fallen into such disrepute that to aspire to sovereignty over others has come to be regarded as a disgraceful if not actually a criminal ambition. But Marlowe's contemporaries would have had no trouble in understanding Tamburlaine's drift, though they might not have understood the view of man and the world that underlies his argument. The humanism of this passage is in fact far removed from the humanism of the study or the laboratory. It is the humanism of war, a view in which all human values are determined by war alone.

What Tamburlaine says to Cosroe in effect is this: 'You think my conduct that of a barbarian and a greedy thief. On the contrary my action in making war upon my king and taking his crown was that of a god and made with the motive and the understanding of a god. For the gods may be assumed to know the nature of the world and they know that its principle is that of war. War is only incidentally destructive and disruptive. In essence it is the principle of order, the principle of beauty, and the principle of knowledge. The gods who established the world and their rule of it, did so by war. The whole state of Nature is one of perpetual strife. The elements of which our bodies are composed are in a state of constant strife and the order and growth of those bodies is the product of the strife. The same is true of the soul and its faculties, of the frame and structure of the world which the soul by its nature desires to comprehend, and of the social order in which each man has his place. That place is determined by strife and the highest human achievement is to become the master of men, the only being whose will is entirely free, the only being whose values are absolute in fact as well as in aspiration.'

The metaphysical conception on which the play is based is this theory of a universe in which order is the creation of strife and values are determined by strife. It is not a modern theory of 'might is right'; it is not a Nietzschean view of the will to power. It is based on the Aristotelian view that every creature strives towards the perfection of its nature. Man is the highest of the creatures and the perfection of his nature is to rule his world. Given the law of strife, the highest state of that perfection is to rule man himself. But those who actually rule usually do so, not by virtue of their absolute right to do so, for that right has not been tested by contest. This is where Tamburlaine differs from the hereditary kings. He has the natural genius for power and he actually tests it out against all possible contenders. He achieves the perfection of human nature in a world in which only one man can be perfect. This standard of values means that the man who imposes his will on all others is, in a sense, the only fully human being among them. For he alone has achieved the full possibilities of the human. He subsumes all values into himself. It means in fact that the man who can achieve this and maintain his position must have gifts and qualities above the human. He partakes of the divine, a claim that Tamburlaine makes more than once. Usumcasane remarks:

> To be a King, is half to be a god.

To be supreme King of Kings certainly requires it; and in this the sole meaning and the whole beauty of life consist. Knowledge has its part but it is only a subordinate part in this aesthetic notion of power, which links knowledge and beauty with political supremacy.

The key to Tamburlaine's speech to Cosroe is the mention of the war of the four elements. This is not the usual Elizabethan view which, in general, stresses the harmony and combination of the elements, under the rule of Nature; Nature, again, is under the rule of God. But Marlowe appears to have belonged to that group of daring minds which gathered round Sir Walter Raleigh, though he may not have been a member of the circle when he wrote *Tamburlaine*. Of this group Miss Bradbrook says that they

> . . . sought a 'Philosophic Theology' and for this purpose they turned to the classics for help in the synthesis. They were driven to those early writers whose sayings were most conveniently to be adapted to their own situation. They began with Stoicism . . . the stoicism of Plutarch and Seneca. But the Stoics had included a good deal of the doctrine of such esoteric writers as Heraclitus of Ephesus and his sayings can be divined behind the poetry of Marlowe, Chapman and Raleigh.

Marlowe's was a thoroughly original and independent mind, but if we do need to find a source for an unusual idea, it is very possible that he might have been struck by the remark in Plutarch's *Moralia*:

Heraclitus . . . says that Homer in praying on the one hand that strife might perish from among gods and men, was [on the other] unaware that he was praying against the occurrence of all things since from battle and antipathy they have their beginning.

He might also have come across a passage in Aristotle's *Eudemian Ethics* in which Heraclitus is made to comment on the same speech of Achilles with the statement that without opposites there would be no attunement or harmony in the universe, that is to say that order depends on strife. And in the same work of Plutarch he could have come on the statement, even more pertinent to the theme of *Tamburlaine*: 'Heraclitus named war, without reservation, father and king and lord of all things.' Marlowe's knowledge of Greek has been questioned, and there is little evidence that he read the Church Fathers, but, had these views of Heraclitus been in question, there were plenty of contemporaries who could have referred him to Origen's quotation from Celsus:

Celsus says that the men of old used to hint at a sort of divine warfare and that Heraclitus said as follows: We must know that war is common (to all) and justice is strife and that all things happen by strife and necessity.

But whether Marlowe thought of it for himself or caught a hint from Heraclitus, it is on some such theory that the Argument of Arms is based, and it is only if we see it based on this sort of theory that the play is whole and coherent and not a series of barbarities and absurdities relieved, but hardly redeemed, by great poetry.

I imagine that the reason why the view of life on which *Tamburlaine* is based has been overlooked is simply the fact that it is so strange and so repugnant to most minds that it would never occur to them to take it seriously. The mere notion of accepting, even for the sake of argument, a thorough-going morality of power, aesthetics of power and logic of power, with its implication that only one man can achieve the end of life and that society is entirely subordinated to producing and promoting that man, these are ideas which the mind boggles at entertaining. And when it does so, many of the events in the play are bound to appear senseless, extravagant or merely revolting.

Dr. Boas, for example, boggles at the massacre of the virgins of Damascus. It is, he says:

. . . a glaringly unsuitable prelude to the immediately following lyric invocation of 'fair Zenocrate, divine Zenocrate' mounting line by line to the superb rhapsody, in which the romantic impulse ever-yearning after an unrealizable perfection finds its expression once and forever.

This might be true if we were justified in taking the 'romantic impulse' as the source of the speech. But this is what Tamburlaine disclaims. What he is talking about is the *power* of beauty arising from its actual perfection, not from any unrealized ideal. It is this power which alone can conquer the conqueror of the world, and this disturbs him. It has, he says, 'troubled his senses with conceit of foil' more than any of his foes in the field of battle. He is driven to ask how beauty fits into the Argument of Arms:

> What is beauty, saith my sufferings, then?

And his reply is as follows:

> If all the pens that ever poets held
> Had fed the feeling of their masters' thoughts,
> And every sweetness that inspired their hearts
> Their minds and muses on admired themes;
> If all the heavenly quintessence they still
> From their immortal flowers of poesy,
> Wherein as in a mirror we perceive
> The highest reaches of a human wit—
> If these had made one poem's period,
> And all combined in beauty's worthiness,
> Yet should there hover in their restless heads
> One thought, one grace, one wonder, at the least,
> Which into words no virtue can digest.
> But how unseemly is it for my sex,
> My discipline of arms and chivalry,
> My nature, and the terror of my name,
> To harbour thoughts effeminate and faint!
> Save only that in beauty's just applause,
> With whose instinct the soul of man is touched,
> And every warrior that is rapt in love
> Of fame, of valour, and of victory,
> Must needs have beauty beat on his conceits,
> I thus conceiving, and subduing both,
> That which hath stopt the tempest of the gods,
> Even from the fiery spangled veil of heaven,
> To feel the lovely warmth of shepherds' flames,
> And march in cottages of strowed weeds,
> Shall give the world to note, for all my birth,
> That virtue solely is the sum of glory,
> And fashions men to true nobility.

The parallel between this speech on beauty and the previous speech on kingship is clear enough. In both, the precedent of the gods is invoked. In the one the war of nature within and without produces the harmony of the body and the soul and the universe which the mind cannot rest till it knows, and this same restless search for knowledge is what leads the soul to the highest felicity of all, the supremacy of power. Science and sovereignty are each part of the same process, but sovereignty is the crown of knowledge. In the other speech, it is the same thing that prompts the ever-restless poets and all men to aspire towards the beauty they celebrate. Poetry represents the highest achievement of human genius, but perfect beauty is something beyond that genius, as sovereignty is beyond knowledge. The end of the speech is ambiguous. Some scholars think the text corrupt. But it is plain enough that after we have placed sovereignty and beauty as the two supreme human aspirations, beauty has a power to subdue sovereignty, and this, Tamburlaine argues, would be shameful except that beauty only subdues sovereignty as a means to inspire and complete it. It is the completion of the man of power by the concept and possession of beauty in which the perfection of his nature, his *virtue*, consists. It is for this reason that Tamburlaine, who won Zenocrate at the beginning of his career, defers his union with her perfection until he has achieved his own. The Argument of Beauty completes and gives sense to the Argument of Arms.

There is of course nothing romantic in this, no yearning after an unrealizable perfection in the principal actor. Tamburlaine leaves that to the poets as he leaves the yearning after infinite knowledge to the scientists and the sages. In spite of the evocation of the beauty of Zenocrate in the exquisite speech that follows immediately on the slaughter of the Damascus virgins, there is no softness, no *gemütlichkeit*, in this conception. Tamburlaine is moved by Zenocrate's tears, but the moving itself testifies to the power of her beauty which the pleas of the youthfulness, innocence and beauty of the virgins have not possessed. It is appropriate for Tamburlaine to praise Zenocrate while the girls dangle on the spears of his soldiers before the eyes of their parents. The virgins perish in their lesser degrees of beauty and appeal as the other kings of the earth perish in their lesser degrees of force of character and genius for arms. In fact it is wrong to talk of degrees in this world, for it is a world in which what is not perfect is without meaning and without value. There is no middle way and no compromise in such a world. Beauty is the rival of beauty as force of force, and only the supreme and perfect survives. Defeat, like victory, is total, absolute, final.

Some such view makes the play in its two parts a single and

coherent whole, which on other views it is hard to maintain. The first part of *Tamburlaine* may appear coherent and complete even to those who do not see its theme. The hero sets himself a goal and that goal is achieved when he proves himself capable of defeating the greatest monarchs, and marries Zenocrate. It could be taken as a simple success story. It is the continuation in Part II which has often been criticized as a mere accumulation of battles, conquests, murders and disasters, ending arbitrarily when Tamburlaine dies. As his death has nothing to do with his conquests, and his conquests in this part of the play seem to have little to do with one another, Marlowe has been accused of filling out Part II with an unrelated series of sensational incidents for the edification of an uncritical audience. Actually it is contrived to carry the Argument of Arms to its conclusion.

The first part of *Tamburlaine* may be called the triumph of life—the triumph of life conceived as the fruition of human nature in the one man capable of achieving the perfection of the human in terms of power. The second part might be described as the triumph of death. It opens many years after the conclusion of Part I. Tamburlaine's sons are almost grown up. He has extended his conquests to a point where even his generals are now great emperors in their own right, carrying out their own careers of conquest; and all belongs to their master. But there are still combinations of enemies against him; there are still vast regions of the world unconquered and Tamburlaine knows that he cannot rest till he has conquered them. His neighbours know it too, and so war begets war as one combination of kings after another tries to crush him. The effect of the battles, sieges and campaigns of Part II is not meant to form, like those of Part I, a connected plot. They form instead a series like the waves of a slowly mounting sea, so that we feel that Tamburlaine's presence in the world and his purpose is to bring the world to a final crisis, a great Armageddon of the nations. In these wars, in this apparently senseless and wholesale slaughter, we are made to feel ever more and more strongly the picture of human history as seen from the point of view to the Argument of Arms. Individual human life ceases to have any meaning and the nations themselves rise, fight and are destroyed like individual men. The sole meaning of the process seems to be that it produces its Tamburlaine; for the significance of man, the significance of history is its Tamburlaines.

The fact that these wars have nothing to do with the death of Tamburlaine is precisely their point. Had he died in battle he would have lost his significance. He would simply have been one of the innumerable waves in their meaningless succession. Orcanes conquers Sigismund today. Tamburlaine conquers Orcanes tomorrow; Callapine revenges his father by conquering Tamburlaine the day after; and nothing has any permanent meaning or importance. The point about Tamburlaine is that he is and remains unconquerable. He is justified in claiming a superiority that is almost divine. But he is a mortal man for all that, and his servant death will turn on his master in the end. From the death of his joy, when Zenocrate dies, to the death of Tamburlaine himself we feel Fate waiting to strike. The prayers of his generals for his life are significant in their suggestion that if he perishes then all is meaningless, for he has taken all meaning into himself. If there is no morality, no beauty, no value but in absolute and supreme power, then the tragedy of Tamburlaine is the tragedy of man himself. It is here that we may wonder where Marlowe himself stands. Does he accept the argument or not? Tamburlaine the scourge of God must die, and Tamburlaine realizes that in spite of his defiance of the gods he can control neither them nor death. He realizes that he cannot live to complete his supremacy even in this world, and that his son Amyras is incapable of continuing and perfecting his work. His reference to Phaeton and to his disastrous attempt to guide the horses of the sun, shows it only too well. Even in his own terms, if Tamburlaine represents the perfection of the human, the result is failure and is bound to be failure. But Marlowe makes no comment. We are free to accept the Argument of Arms and regard this failure as the tragedy of man, or to reject it and take Tamburlaine's failure as evidence that it is unsound, the fatal flaw that makes the play the tragedy of Tamburlaine alone.

In one sense the coherence of the play resides in its poetry. Taken in terms of the action alone the play is not free of absurdity. If Tamburlaine were merely a supreme military genius, the argument which asserts his total superiority and perfection would be unconvincing. But Tamburlaine is a poet. He conceives poetry as concentrating in its highest conceivable form, the whole of beauty, imagination and music into 'one poem's period', just as he concentrates all power in himself. It is in this alliance of the poetic imagination with temporal power, in a sense their identity, that the magnanimity of Tamburlaine consists. Poetry is his medium, as power is his nature and his genius. Poetry shares the supremacy of nature, for it is the natural language of beauty, of intellect and of power, the three perfect things. It is poetry alone which makes all three comprehensible:

> Wherein as in a mirror we perceive
> The highest reaches of a human wit—

The poetry of *Tamburlaine* is indeed the poetry of power, and the absolute morality of power which the play exemplifies is allied to the absolute standards of poetry, which it recognizes. For poetry accepts only success, and grants lasting life only to absolute success. It recognizes no gradations and no second best. What Hazlitt, in a very curious passage for an avowed republican, says of Coriolanus, is even more apt of the poetry of *Tamburlaine*:

> The language of poetry naturally falls in with the language of power. The imagination is an exaggerating and exclusive faculty: it takes from one thing to add to another: it accumulates circumstances together to give the greatest possible effect to a favourite object. The understanding is a dividing and measuring faculty: it judges of things not according to their immediate impression on the mind, but according to their relations to one another. The one is a monopolizing faculty, which seeks the greatest quantity of present excitement by inequality and disproportion; the other is a distributive faculty, which seeks the greatest quantity of ultimate good, by justice and proportion. The one is an aristocratical, the other a republican faculty. The principle of poetry is a very anti-levelling principle. It aims at effect, it exists by contrast. It admits of no medium. It is everything by excess. It rises above the ordinary standard of sufferings and crimes. It presents a dazzling appearance. It shows its head turretted, crowned, and crested. Its front is gilt and bloodstained. Before it 'it carries noise, and behind it leaves tears.' It has its altars and its victims, sacrifices, human sacrifices. . . . It puts the individual for the species, the one above the infinite many, might before right.

Those who wish to understand *Tamburlaine* should read and re-read this passage for it represents the Argument of Arms translated into the Argument of Poetry. And those who wish to understand the real nature of poetry would do well to have *Tamburlaine* by heart, for the heart of the matter is that the Argument of Arms and the Argument of Poetry are in their essence the same.

WILBUR SANDERS

Dramatist as Realist: *"The Jew of Malta"*

'Marlowe's Jew', complained Charles
Lamb, 'is a mere monster brought in with a large painted nose to please
the rabble. He kills in sport, poisons whole nunneries, invents infernal
machines. He is just such an exhibition as a century or two earlier might
have been played before the Londoners "by the royal command", when a
general pillage and massacre of the Hebrews had been previously resolved
upon in the cabinet. In a sense this is no more than a just reaction to one
aspect of *The Jew of Malta*; at least Lamb diagnoses correctly the element
of pandering to a debased public taste which links the play with *The
Massacre at Paris*. Yet he does it less than justice; for there is also some
truth in Eliot's contention that it is a 'farce of the old English humour, the
terribly serious, even savage comic humour . . . which spent its last breath
on the decadent genius of Dickens', and in his claim that Marlowe
'develops a tone to suit this farce, and even perhaps that this tone is his
most powerful and mature tone'. We may grant the farce and the savagery,
but the very real critical question concerns the powerfulness, the maturity
and the seriousness of the comic humour. To my mind, *The Jew of Malta* is
neither as successful as Eliot would have it to be, nor as crude as Lamb
implies.

Perhaps it is best to begin by considering the 'mere monster' in
Barabas, whose radical deviation from the human is immediately regis‑
tered by the huge 'artificiall nose' to which Ithamore repeatedly draws our
attention:

O mistress! I have the bravest, gravest, secret, subtle, bottle-nosed knave
    to my master, that ever gentleman had!

(III. iii. 9)

The monster is a composite figure. Partly it is the ethnic stereotype of the
Jew—a stereotype all the more tenacious in England for the fact that it
went largely unchallenged by first-hand acquaintance with Jews; partly the
stock figure of the usurer who is intimately allied to the Vice Avarice in
such a play as Udall's *Respublica* (and this mixed ancestry traces back
further to an earlier forbear—the Judas-usurer-Jew of the mystery cycles);
but also, as Marlowe's Prologue makes explicit, the monster is an Italian
monster, a Florentine to be precise (II. iii. 23), and one of the earliest of a
long line of stage Machiavels. Barabas thus has his dramatic roots deep in
the soil of popular, not to say vulgar, folk-lore and superstition, and the
vulgar origins contribute much that is crudely superficial in the play—the
heavy-handed dramatic technique, for example, which has Marlowe continually drawing black lines under what he has already written in heavy
type—'I must dissemble', shouts Barabas when it is evident to the veriest
infant that this is what is happening (VI. i. 50). The explicitness is the
mark of a dramaturgy which can endure nothing unexplained, subtle or
ambiguous—'I am betray'd' (IV. v. 41); 'I must make this villain away'
(IV. v. 30); 'So now, I am reveng'd upon 'em all' (IV. vi. 42). Or there is
the melodramatic aside which works, if it works at all, by presenting the
humane in violently incongruous juxtaposition with the inhuman, undy-
ing love with inveterate malice—

Please you dine with me, sir;—*and you shall be most heartily poisoned.*

(IV. v. 30)

Here, take 'em, fellow, with as good a will—
As I would see the hang'd; O, love stops my breath.

(IV. v. 53)

Or there is the preposterous exaggeration of Barabas's egomania—

Nay, let 'em combat, conquer, and kill all.
So they spare me, my daughter, and my wealth.

(I. i. 150)

Down to the cellar, taste of all my wines . . .
And, if you like them, drink your fill and die;
For, so I live, perish may all the world!

(V. v. 7)

—or Ithamore's random destructiveness—'But here's a royal monastery
hard by; / Good master, let me poison all the monks' (IV. i. 13); this same

motiveless aggression is displayed against the friars who are the butts of endless lewdly unfunny jests about monastic lechery and conventual pregnancy. One is inclined to conclude from this kind of evidence that Marlowe is too childish-vicious for this world, and that *The Jew*, like *The Massacre*, merely reflects some of the least savoury aspects of Elizabethan society. Certainly this side of the play cannot be described as either mature or serious.

However, Lamb and those who accept his estimate of the play, would extend this judgment to the whole play, claiming perhaps that it is 'modern and romantic' to see in Barabas anything more than a monster held up for abomination, because 'his Jewishness defines his condemnation'. But this is to ignore the qualities to which Eliot has pointed, and in any case it is fairly easy to show that 'his Jewishness' actually defines nothing at all—it is, in fact, a subject the play investigates.

A stereotype like that of the Jew (or the Machiavel) is not something which is necessarily accepted in a simple unqualified way, but it implies by its very existence the possibility of modification. The fact that many Elizabethans felt in a certain way about (say) political order, so that it is moderately meaningful to talk about 'the Elizabethan concept of the State', did not, as we shall see, preclude other ways of feeling about the State. The Elizabethans were probably less prone to this sort of mass thinking than the literary historians at whose hands they have suffered. Neither did the existence of a Jew stereotype prevent individual Elizabethans from adapting, modifying or simply rejecting the stereotype. Thus we find in an undistinguished play of the 1580s a Jew, and a usurer at that, favourably contrasted with an unscrupulous Christian merchant who seeks to evade his financial responsibilities by turning Turk. His Jewish creditor, appalled at this mercenary apostasy, immediately cancels the debt, and the judge moralises, 'Jews seek to excel in Christianity and Christians in Jewishness.' The semantic implications of this interesting sentence will occupy me in a moment, but it might be noted now that the traditional anti-semitism of the Elizabethans could be not only modified, but stood on its head.

The truth of the matter is that the Elizabethan audience—that peremptory hangman so frequently called in to effect the execution of this or that critical judgment—is so nebulous an entity as to be useless in an operation calling for precise definition. In so far as there is an Elizabethan mind, it is as much moulded by the playwrights who sought to educate its sensibility and broaden its horizons, as it moulds those playwrights. The 'orthodoxy' of a period is not an ideological steamroller that subdues all humanity to its ruling passion for the horizontal, but itself the product of the delicate, breathing organism of human society, in which cause and effect are never very sharply distinguished. The play itself not only offers something concrete for us to get to grips with, but it also constitutes *prima facie* evidence for the state of mind of the audience to which it is addressed; so that the primary question is the critical one—What is actually there in the play? To ask this question, even about a play as superficially barren as *The Jew of Malta*, is to discover a great deal more than a vulgar anti-semitism and a melodramatic Machiavellism.

I

Take the Jew-component first. For many Elizabethans the very word 'Jew' was a term of miscellaneous abuse: thus Thomas Coryat reflects on 'our English prouerbe: to looke like a Jewe (whereby is meant sometimes a weather beaten warp-faced fellow, sometimes a phrenticke and lunaticke person, sometimes one discontented)'; or Gobbo puns, 'I am a Jew if I serve the Jew any longer', thus separating the ethnic and pejorative senses of the word for the sake of a joke. But it had other usages at once more precise and more derogatory—'Jews seek to excel in Christianity and Christians in Jewishness' (where the primary meaning of 'Jewishness' is almost certainly the avarice the Christian merchant had shown, and the word is used as an antonym for 'Christianity', meaning 'charitable self-sacrifice'). As a smug Antonio puts it, 'This Hebrew will turn Christian: he grows kind.' The connexion between the word 'Jew' and the practice of usury (recorded in the verb 'to judaise', one meaning of which was 'to lend at interest') was strengthened by the similarity of sound in Elizabethan pronunciation—Iew, iudaize, usurer; and the hard-hearted attributes of the money-lender were thereby fathered on the entire Hebrew race, so that Antonio, faced by the implacable Shylock, despairs of ever softening 'that—than which what's harder?—/His Jewish heart'. Add to this the implication of double-dealing reflected in the common linking of 'Iudas' and 'Iew' and we have a semantic complex of infidelity, treachery, inhumanity and rapacity informing the very use of the word 'Jew'.

This usage can be found in Marlowe's play, where the word is sometimes employed for purposes of comprehensive denigration—'Then, like a Jew, he laugh'd and jeer'd, and told me he lov'd me for your sake . . .' (IV. v. 116); in Ferneze's smug reference to Barabas's diabolical engine as 'a Jew's courtesy' (V. v. 108) or Ithamore's drunken imprecation, 'Hang him, Jew' (IV. iv. 88). But these references on the whole represent the ignorant hostility of the speaker better than they give the tone of the play. True, we get a few easy laughs at the expense of Jewish cupidity—'O, that I should part with so much gold!' (IV. v. 52) or Barabas's reaction when Ferneze brings the gratuity of £100,000: 'Pounds say'st thou, governor? well, since it is no more, / I'll satisfy myself with that' (V. v. 21)—but the strongest tendency in the play is to assail the facile and hearty complacency of Christian anti-semitism with persistent inversions and permutations of the Jew—Christian antithesis. Thus, when Barabas gives a parody version of the usurer-Jew—

> I have been zealous in the Jewish faith,
> Hard-hearted to the poor, a covetous wretch,
> That would for lucre's sake have sold my soul.
> A hundred for a hundred I have ta'en—
>   (IV. i. 54)

the context (he is being blackmailed by two avaricious and lecherous friars on the strength of information revealed in shrift) turns the ironic shaft back into the flank of the Christians for whose benefit he is performing: at the same time as the friars accept this preposterous confession of the Jewish faith, the audience sees that it is, for all practical purposes, the Christian creed as well.

This technique of ironically undercutting Christian superiority is supplemented by a whole series of inversions by which Barabas simply pays the Christians with their own bad coin. The affectation of sanctified hauteur, well caught in Katherine's 'Converse not with him; he is cast off from heaven' (II. iii. 159), is neatly parodied by the Jew:

> This offspring of Cain, this Jebusite,
> That never tasted of the Passover,
> Nor e'er shall see the land of Canaan,
> Nor our Messias that is yet to come;
> This gentle [Gentile] maggot, Lodowick, I mean,
> Must be deluded . . .
>   (II. iii. 302)

and again:

>   these swing-eating Christians,
> Unchosen nation, never circumcis'd;
> Such as (poor villains) were ne'er thought upon
> Till Titus and Vespasian conquer'd us . . .
>   (II. iii. 7)

Perhaps the most exquisite of these parody-revenges comes when the Jew takes the medieval libel of the *foetor judaicus* (a vile-smelling bodily secretion due to alleged menstruation in Jewish males, which good Christians found intolerable and which could only be obliterated by the waters of baptism) and maliciously re-applies it:

> LODOWICK: Whither walk'st thou, Barabas?
> BARABAS: No further: 'Tis a custom held with us,
>   That when we speak with Gentiles like to you,
>   We turn into the air to purge ourselves;
>   For unto us the promise doth belong.
>   (II. iii. 44)

The parody is exact and devastating.

It is by the same process that Barabas turns the Christian blank charter for aggression against heretics. ('To undo a Jew is charity and not sin'—IV. vi. 80) into a weapon in his own Jewish armoury:

> It's no sin to deceive a Christian;
> For they themselves hold it a principle,
> Faith is not to be held with heretics:
> But all are heretics that are not Jews;
> This follows well, and therefore, daughter, fear not.
>   (II. iii. 310)

Barabas here confronts his Christian assailants with their mirror-image: the syllogism is identical in form; only the major premiss has changed. By reversing the direction of the Christian morality of anti-semitism. Marlowe reveals the destructive potential of its thoroughly pernicious logic—and the reversal is the more telling for the fact that the accent of pert self-congratulation is authentic.

If we are to have any quarrel with Marlowe's treatment of the Jew-Christian theme, then, it cannot be because (as Lamb suggests) he has capitulated to vulgar anti-semitic prejudice. The objection is rather to this technique of ironic inversion—it is almost the basic poetic strategy of the play—and the limitations that it imposes on the play's grasp of human realities. I shall be returning to this matter, but perhaps I can observe at this point that when a writer contents himself with a parody-inversion of the attitude he is attacking he commits himself to the narrow categories of that attitude. The results of the inversion may be, as they are with Barabas, acidly witty and mordant; but there is a certain shallowness and constriction which is the consequence of a refusal to allow parody to deepen into exploration. One can be grateful to Marlowe for mounting a courageous attack on a powerful and particularly vicious social prejudice, without regarding it as a very profound contribution to the understanding of anti-semitism to turn on the Christians and cry, 'Woe unto you hypocrites; for you are villains every bit as unconscionable as the Jews you abominate.'

Nevertheless, within these self-imposed limits, Marlowe achieves a good deal. There are moments in the play which seem to sum up the whole tortured history of anti-semitism: as when Barabas, with a furious self-loathing, assumes the role the Christians have cast for him:

> We Jews can fawn like spaniels when we please;
> And when we grin we bite; . . .
> I learned in Florence how to kiss my hand,
> Heave up my shoulders when they call me dog,
> And duck as low as any bare-foot friar;
> Hoping to see them starve upon a stall,
> Or else be gathered for in our synagogue . . .
>   (II. iii. 20)

At the same time as we are given the whining, ingratiating Jew with an almost tactile concreteness (and note how lively and gestural the verbs are), we also feel the pull of an alarming logic of circumstance, feel the historical roots of his irremovable rancour in repeated and unceasing acts of Christian 'injury' (l. 19). We recognize the 'teachers' who have forced the Jew to 'learn' this degrading trade.

Throughout the play, there is a steady drive to undermine Christian complacency about the Jews, and to reveal the common ground of rapacious self-interest which perpetuates their mutual enmity. As Barabas puts it,

> This is the life we Jews are us'd to lead;
> And reason too, for Christians do the like.
>   (V. ii. 115)

His little joke about the 'golden cross' (a gold coin stamped with a cross and bearing a superscription—a 'posy'—round the perimeter) focuses these themes with a sly lucidity. Lodowick, he expects,

> would disdain
> To marry with the daughter of a Jew:
> And yet I'll give her many a golden cross,
> With Christian posies round about the ring.
>   (II. iii. 295)

The subtle identification of religious 'profession' with financial advantage—if the wooden cross divides Jew and Christian, the golden one unites them—is a central motif in the play, and gives rise to some quite delicious comedy. The method is again parody, but parody so consummate as momentarily to break out of the limitations of that mode. The repenting Barabas, for instance—

> A hundred for a hundred I have ta'en;
> And now for store of wealth may I compare
> With all the Jews in Malta; but what is wealth?
> I am a Jew, and therefore am I lost.
> Would penance serve for this my sin,
> I could afford to whip myself to death . . .
> To fast, to pray, and wear a shirt of hair,
> And on my knees creep to Jerusalem.
>
> (IV. i. 57)

But what is wealth? The answer is instantaneous: 'O good Barabas, come to our house!' 'O no, good Barabas, come to *our* house!' 'O Barabas, their laws are strict!' '*They* wear no shirts, and they go barefoot too.' 'Good Barabas, come to me.' The juxtaposition is brilliant, as is the comic insight which makes this sanctified haggling issue in Jacomo's attempted murder of an already dead Barnardine. The Friars sequence ends with an unctuously regretful Barabas feeling himself morally obliged to carry Jacomo to the magistrates:

> No, pardon me; the law must have his course:
> I must be forc'd to give in evidence,
> That, being importun'd . . .
>
> (IV. iii. 24)

and discovering that a new scruple has arisen in connexion with his proposed conversion:

> No; for this example I'll remain a Jew:
> Heaven bless me! what, a friar a murderer?
> When shall you see a Jew commit the like?
>
> (IV. iii. 34)

The comic texture is very dense, but one perception that hovers at the edges of laughter is that Barabas's use of the language of religion and piety as a weapon against his personal and commercial enemies is not different in kind from the uses of that language elsewhere. It is just more explicit and less self-deceiving:

> As good dissemble that thou never mean'st
> As first mean truth and then dissemble it.
>
> (I. ii. 290)

The one thing that none of these purveyors of religious platitude ever does is to turn the prescriptive edge of Christianity against his own breast.

The comic probing goes deep enough, too, to show up the subhuman nature of the acquisitive urge itself—as when, for instance, we watch

Barabas hugging his newly recovered bags and capering about in a grotesque travesty of joyous emotion:

> Now, Phoebus, ope the eye-lids of the day,
> And, for the raven, wake the morning lark,
> That I may hover with her in the air;
> Singing o'er these, as she does o'er her young.
> *Hermoso placer de los dineros.*
>
> (II. i. 60)

This kind of workmanship *does* merit the title of 'serious farce', and it also, incidentally, makes nonsense of that curious myth of a Marlowe who had no sense of humour. The unforced gaiety of some early Shakespearian comedy may be outside his range, but a critic who fails to find anything funny in these scenes is in no position to accuse others of lacking humour. Whatever one may think finally of *The Jew of Malta* as a whole, one must admit that it gives evidence at times of a very lively wit and intelligence in its creator.

II

Almost all these trends—the comic exposure of rapacity, of the politic abuse of religion, and the assault upon gentile complacency—run in one channel in the play's second scene, a passage that deserves detailed scrutiny, not least for its sharp exposure of the ruinous assumptions that have underlain the history of anti-semitism: the assumption for instance that the Jews, being alien and accursed, represent a kind of National Deficit Liquidation Fund which can be drawn upon in any crisis; the assumption that their very presence in the community is the cause of ill-fortune, and, conversely, that when a national disaster occurs, it may be directly traced to the activity of the Jews; that Christians, as the chosen people, are the divinely appointed scourge of the wickedness of the rejected people; and that the Jews are collectively accountable for the blood-guilt invoked by their forbears who crucified the Messiah (that this doctrine had to wait until 1963 for official repudiation by the Catholic Church indicates how deeply rooted it is in Western Christian consciousness). The assumption, in short, that to be a Jew is to be *ipso facto* inexcusable. At the same time the depiction of state extortion provides Marlowe with an opportunity for a more general investigation of the ethics of acquisition—another aspect of his subject in *The Jew of Malta*.

Part of the scene's mastery resides in the subtle gradations of tone—the elevation of moral sentiment varying directly with the speaker's rapacity, politeness being merely a function of greed, and innocence a preliminary affectation. Ferneze opens with suave urbanity—'Hebrews, now come near'—and expostulates mellifluously—'Soft, Barabas! there's more 'longs to't than so'. The Jew counters with a pretended ignorance of their drift which pierces the euphemistic mist, and the First Knight, enraged by Barabas's feigned belief that they are asking him to fight in the army, explodes,

> Tut, Jew, we know thou art no soldier;
> Thou art a Merchant, and a money'd man,
> And 'tis thy money, Barabas, we seek.
>
> (I. ii. 52)

The swift transition, from surly contempt to an oily servility before the personification of Mammon, represents dramatic economy of a high order. Barabas's tone undergoes a complementary series of transformations: at first affected innocence ('How, my lord! my money!'), it modulates through mock incredulity to moral indignation ('The man that dealeth righteously shall live'), dying away finally in stoical indifference ('take it to you, i' the devil's name'). Ferneze, on the other hand, preserves a uniformly lofty tone—extortion is no occasion for indecorum—and is at some pains to cloak his expediency in moral rectitude. He offers the Jew the kind of supercilious mock-explanation that comes naturally to the consciously impregnable when dealing with a helpless victim.

His sophistries, however, expose in a lucid syllogism the logic of anti-semitism: Barabas will contribute to the Turkish levy, not 'equally', but 'like an infidel':

> For through our sufferance of your hateful lives,
> Who stand accursed in the sight of heaven,
> These taxes and afflictions are befall'n.
>
> (I. ii. 63)

Ferneze's primary intention is to justify the levying of the entire tax upon a tiny fraction of the population, but he cannot resist the additional gratification of a moral, as well as economic, vaunt: Observe, O Jew, the self-sacrificial charity of the Christians who, even at the risk of incurring the divine wrath, have graciously permitted Jews to trade in Malta. The logical form, with its *post hoc propter hoc* fallacy, is also characteristic: Jews are under a curse; we are suffering under the curse of Turkish extortion; *ergo* our misfortune is due to your accursed presence. If there were no more here than this syllogistic expediency, the comment would be perceptive. But the factor that lifts it out of the field of social commentary, and elevates it to the comic plane, is the lofty moral tone in which Ferneze chooses to enunciate his logical travesty. It is the timeless voice of pious dissimulation.

Evidently, however, he fears a retort, for he hastily draws the naked sword of ordinance and waves it over Barabas's head. Only now do we discover that the regulations are already drawn up and that the preliminary discussion has been the merest façade. The proclamation follows the traditional formula for squeezing the Hebrew orange dry— either you pay, or you pay. When Barabas demurs, the Governor, who is clearly tired of the game, immediately dispatches his officers. 'Corpo di Dio!' exclaims the Jew, as if only a Christian oath could do justice to this Christian villainy.

Ferneze's next justification is pure Pharisee: 'Better one want for the common good, / Than many perish for a private man', and calls up the memory of Caiaphas dealing with another recalcitrant Jew. The indirect effect of this echo is to put Barabas in the place of Christ, as the innocent victim of pharisaical expediency—another parody of Christian self-righteousness.

The Knight, however, sees events in a dimly religious light: are there not signs of a divine hand in Barabas's downfall?

> If your first curse fall heavy on thy head,
> And make thee poor and scorn'd of all the world,
> 'Tis not our fault, but thy inherent sin.
>   (I. ii. 108)

The principle by which a person can proceed against his fellow-man, while complacently regarding himself as some kind of supra-moral scourge of God, is the principle of anarchy. On this basis the action is his, but he has not performed it: the left hand cannot be brought to justice because the right hand knows nothing of the crime. The function of religion in Malta is always like this—the introduction of the imponderable and the irrefragable in order to drive a wedge between the agent and the consequences of his own act; it 'hides many mischiefs from suspicion'. 'Villains', exclaims Friar Jacomo, 'Villains, I am a sacred person, touch me not' (IV. iii. 40). But of course the sophistical invocation of the moral order merely sets up reverberations which drown the protestations of sanctity.

Refusing, however, to be 'preached out of his possessions', Barabas makes his appeal against the Christian doctrine of corporate Jewish guilt, and to a principle of individual responsibility. In so doing he reaches the heart of his apology, for it is precisely this determination to think of the Jews *en masse* which makes the present extortion possible. Barabas turns

Christian totalitarian thinking in their own teeth, thus revealing its absurdity:

> Some Jews are wicked, as all Christians are;
> But say the tribe that I descended of
> Were all in general cast away for sin,
> Shall I be tried by their transgression?
> The man that dealeth righteously shall live:
> And which of you can charge me otherwise?
>
> (I. ii. 113)

Barabas has been somewhat carried away by the lofty tone of his opponents, and, forgetting for the moment that he is a Machiavellian, lays claim to a nobility of spirit which is rather incongruous, if not blasphemous (cf. Christ's claim—John viii. 46). It is too much for Ferneze, who splutters,

> Out, wretched Barabas!
> Sham'st thou not thus to justify thyself,
> As if we knew not thy profession?
>
> (I. ii. 119)

(there can be no justification for being a usurer-Jew) and proceeds to exercise his considerable dialectical skill in cutting the ground from under Barabas's feet: 'If worldly success is the inevitable result of righteousness' (this is not quite what the Jew had said, but it is a reasonable extension of it) 'and if you are, as you say, righteous, there is no possible cause for anxiety.' This leaves Barabas neatly impaled on the horns of his own dilemma, unless he is to confess that he thrives, not by righteousness, but by 'policy'—and the confession would be monstrously impolitic.

Having won this point, Ferneze goes on to his last and most extravagant casuistry, which he offers with a pompous fatuity that is truly heroic:

> Excess of wealth is cause of covetousness:
> And covetousness, O, 'tis a monstrous sin!
>
> (I. ii. 124)

The responsibility for the Christian lust for Jewish gold is thus laid squarely on Barabas's shoulders; a responsibility of which Ferneze has obligingly relieved him, by yielding to that lust. This is the height of Marlowe's mordant irony, which, despite its extravagance, has secure historical roots in the habitual Christian, and human, practice of laying the entire burden of moral responsibility at one's neighbour's door, and elevating oneself above the merely moral plane into a minister of abstract

justice. Later in the play, Barabas is to demolish Ferneze's affected righteousness, by the simple device of singing the same tune after him—and
doing it better. He is promising the Governor's son a 'diamond', which he
proposes to give him 'with a vengeance'; Lodowick insists on 'deserving'
it, which moves the Jew to an ecstasy of *double entendre*:

> Good sir,
> Your father has deserv'd it at my hands,
> Who, of mere charity and Christian ruth,
> To bring me to religious purity,
> And, as it were, in catechising sort,
> To make me mindful of my mortal sins,
> Against my will, and whether I would or no,
> Seiz'd all I had, and thrust me out a doors,
> And made my house a place for nuns most chaste.
>
> (II. iii. 69)

The scene is more than an essay in the dialectic of religious
intolerance. Neither party is, in any case, greatly moved by the events
that take place, both having taken the necessary decisions, and made the
necessary arrangements, before this encounter took place. What Marlowe
leads us to perceive behind the verbal and rationalistic fencing, is the
perennial comedy of acquisition and the substratum of universal Machiavellism which makes nonsense of the division into Jew and Gentile.

III

I have lingered over the second scene because, as one of the best and
most sustained pieces of writing in the play, it does indicate where the real
creative currents are flowing—into an exposure of the ferocious egocen-
tricity upon which the structures of material acquisition and temporal
power are erected. The method is a dialectical demolition of the moral
superstructure until the brute facts show their real nature.

Yet although the points are trenchantly made, and the satiric barbs
stick fast, there is a certain constriction and a certain emptiness attendant
on the dialectical method, just as there was on the ironic inversions I
have already discussed. The kind of laughter upon which it trades has a
hard, self-righteous timbre. It does not, like the wit of the best comedy,
get in behind the egotistic defences, and engage creatively an audience's
capacity for self-criticism and self-ridicule. It draws too heavily on contempt for that. It is demonstrative satire, inviting us to indulge the secret
guffaw; and the guffaw tends to swamp the genuinely exploratory satire as

the play moves to its conclusion. In the First Knight's sophistry, for example ('If your first curse fall heavy on thy head . . . 'Tis not our fault . . .'), there is an explicitness, an overplus of assertiveness, which passes judgment on the sentiment almost before it has been expressed. If one considers the sanctimonious Richard of Gloucester hypocritically excusing Margaret's hair-raising curses—

> I cannot blame her: by God's holy mother,
> She hath had too much wrong; and I repent
> My part thereof that I have done to her—

one senses a significant difference: though the didactic point is there, it is refracted through the enriching medium of Richard's character, and the utterance has a human weight and body behind it that may properly be termed dramatic. The implied dissimulation, and the notion of playing a part, are enacted in Shakespeare's verse—'by God's holy mother'—whereas for Marlowe this is merely a premiss appropriately expressed in melodramatic asides—'How! a Christian? Hum, what's here to do? (I. ii. 75). Marlowe's verse, that is to say, has the wrong kind of clarity—a clarity which permits us to see what is being done, instead of enabling that which is being done to act more immediately on the imagination.

Barabas's famous autobiographical sketch (II. iii. 175–202) is faintly unsatisfactory in the same way; not because it is shocking—it is far too frivolously and slyly enunciated to be that—but because we can see it is meant to be shocking. Barabas confesses to most of the criminal occupations with which anti-semitic polemists had credited the Jews—poisoning wells (the alleged origin of Bubonic plague), practising a murderous physic, working as a military engineer, as inventor of diabolical devices and as diplomatic traitor, besides the course the conventional occupational role of usurer—and on this level the speech is a quiet jibe at the Christians who can believe such tales. Barabas clearly makes no great effort to convince Ithamore or us of its accuracy: the syntax is of the 'throw-away' kind—'As for myself, I . . . sometimes I . . . and now and then . . . Being young I . . . And, after that . . . Then, after that . . . some or other . . .'—and he puts the lid on the whole performance by enquiring blandly, 'But tell me now, how hast thou spent thy time?'

Yet, for all the nonchalant airs, what is the speech included for at all, if not to shock? And what is this affectation of bland indifference, if not an oblique attempt to strengthen the effect? The understatement is a sop to our sophistication, but it is the eternal Machiavel monster who is being put on show for our wonderment.

'Machiavel' is an especially appropriate denomination if I am right in detecting the same equivocation in the Prologue. Certainly there is the same affected nonchalance—'I come not, I, / To read a lecture here in Britain . . .' (ll. 28–9)—the same casual and loose-limbed syntax, the same exaggeration of sentiment in the most equable of rhythms—'I count religion but a childish toy, / And hold there is no sin but ignorance'. And over it all there hangs a strong sense that Machiavel is rather aimlessly exhibiting himself and his intellectual emancipation; further, that behind him stands the figure of an iconoclastic young man, very much up with the latest intellectual fashions, trying to goad us into protest or reproof, so that he can then laugh in our faces and claim that he is only joking. But in fact he is half-committed to the very monster he invites us to ridicule. He is not so much teasing the audience as giving expression to his own ambigious liaison with Italianate vice. It is this immature and unacknowledged fascination, I suggest, which accounts for the persistent tendency to overstate villainy, or to write verse in which the organising principle is a systematic assault on all our normal moral expectations—'Do you not sorrow for your daughter's death?' 'No, but I grieve because she liv'd so long' (IV. i. 17); or this of Barabas—

> There is no music to a Christian's knell:
> How sweet the bells ring, now the nuns are dead,
> That sound at other times like tinkers' pans!
> I was afraid the poison had not wrought.
> (IV. i. 1)

This is the brutal schoolboy humour of the 'sick' joke, whose only charm is that of perversity; and it is clearly related to that drive for random destruction which is so dominant in *The Massacre* and *Tamburlaine*.

All of which would suggest that it is to the vulgarised Machiavel-myth, not to Machiavelli himself, that we must look for Barabas's genesis and for the origins of the peculiar moral climate of the play. It is true that Barabas displays a preoccupation with the techniques of power, divorced from a consideration of the ends of power, which is congruent with Machiavelli's discussion of princely *virtù*, true also that there is a preoccupation with the politic uses of religion (which 'hides many mischiefs from suspicion') and friendship ('he from whom my most advantage comes, / Shall be my friend'), and that this can be parallelled in *The Prince* and *The Discourses*. But Barabas as dissembler, as poisoner, as inveterate malice personified, owes more to the flourishing legend of the Machiavel than to whatever first-hand acquaintance with the Florentine Marlowe may have had. And what had been in Machiavelli a dispassionate contemplation of the wolvish habits of men, a clinical dissection, tends, in the myth, to degenerate into a predilection for drawing men who are precisely the reverse of what we would like to think them to be. When Marlowe indulges this predilection at any length, the result is just as unreal as the idealised version of man that he is attacking. Again he has been betrayed by the 'mere idea'.

Yet, as so often with this desperately uneven play, one must qualify. For it seems probable that the plot is deliberately organised with a view to offering a serious critique of a society founded on the free operation of individual power-lust. This surely is the point of showing us Barabas frying to death in his own Machiavellian engine. Although one may hesitate to ascribe his final foiling, as Ferneze does, 'to Heaven', it is clearly intended to exemplify a kind of poetic, if not divine, justice. It is the development of a theme Greene stated two years earlier, in his death-bed exhortation to Marlowe:

> What are his [Machiavelli's] rules but meere confused mockeries, able to extirpate in small time the generation of mankind. For if *sic volo, sic iubeo* hold in those that are able to command; and if it be lawfull *Fas & nefas* to do anything that is beneficiall; onely Tyrants should possesse the earth, and they striuing to exceed in tyrannie, should each to other be a slaughter man; till the mightiest outliuing all, one stroke were left for Death, that in one age mans life should end.

As a refutation of Machiavelli this is less than adequate. It ignores, amongst other things, the way in which morality, ejected by Machiavelli at the pragmatic front-door, re-enters at the utilitarian back-door as a practical necessity of existence in society. But we can grant it a certain limited kind of truth: universal Machiavellism, supposing it to be possible, would entail universal annihilation. On this basis there need be no divine intervention to wreak vengeance on these cynical opportunists, because, given time, they will destroy each other. This Marlowe sees clearly enough to be able to dispense completely with the transcendental order in this play. There is never the slightest suggestion that anything but terrestrial processes are involved in Barabas's downfall. It is a simple failure of 'policy'—he makes the fatal mistake of allowing another Machiavellian to 'partake' his policy (V. v. 24), and his fortunes are thereafter dependent on the good-will of an accomplice who is his bitterest enemy. And so the long, murderous jockeying for power reaches its inevitable, and morally meaningless, stasis. The mightiest outlives all, to make a final cynical appeal to what Miss Mahood calls 'those truths which are outworn from a materialist viewpoint, but which are retained for the commercial value of their respectability':

So, march away; and let due praise be given
Neither to Fate nor Fortune, but to Heaven.
(V. v. 123)

Having complacently accepted the fruits of 'a Jew's courtesy' while smugly deploring 'the unhallow'd deeds of Jews', having exploited the situation for its maximum financial and political yield, having cannily repudiated Calymath's disingenous offer to negotiate Malta's peace in person, and having generally shown himself superior to either Fate or Fortune, Ferneze, with acute theological impertinence, identifies his own Machiavellian *virtù* with divine justice. On this note of exquisite casuistry Marlowe ends, leaving his unconscionable prince in command of the situation, his dead hero quietly simmering in his own juice, and no sign that Heaven cares sufficiently about the affairs of men to repudiate the gigantic blasphemy.

That this is effective enough in its cynical way, I don't dispute. It is one way of confronting the contradiction between the conception of a morally ordered universe and the amoral realities of the power-game— namely, with a moral shrug. At least in this way Marlowe preserved his hard shell of sophisticated mockery intact in a way that Shakespeare, faced with the same contradiction in *Richard III*, failed to do when he opted for Providence in the teeth of the dramatic facts. Yet in a young writer ingenuousness is far less damaging than a premature cynicism. At least he can grow out of the ingenuousness; but cynicism is one of those galloping diseases that is exacerbated by time.

Furthermore, by accepting the premiss of universal Machiavellism— one which Machiavelli, who regarded perfection in evil as a very rare endowment, would certainly not have granted—Marlowe has cut the knot which a more scrupulous mind would have tried to untie. If all men were indeed devoid of scruple, the matter would be comparatively simple—we would at least know where we stood, and could take measures accordingly. But part of the difficulty of living in society stems from the fact that men are neither uniformly moral nor uniformly immoral. The total contempt for principle which prevails in Marlowe's Malta is simply not to be found in nature. The exaggeration which makes all the personages in *The Jew* either knaves or fools, though it has the charm of all such summary solutions to the uneasy doubleness of life, committed Marlowe to a kind of unreality which became increasingly damaging as the action moved to its melodramatic conclusion. At the level where it really matters, Marlowe was not serious.

In any case, the attempt to depict the self-destructive dynamic of Machiavellism involved Marlowe in difficult structural complication: the plot is necessarily the representation of a machine that is running down. It is a kind of anti-drama, a theatre of disintegration in which the moral emptiness of the characters is a premiss of the action. In the early scenes there is some attempt to foist the spurious splendours of mere wealth upon the audience—the 'infinite riches in a little room' phase—but as the action progresses there is less and less than can engage us imaginatively. Barabas, robbed of the very bread of his existence (for his Machiavel cannot operate without the assistance of Mammon), degenerates into that repellent curmudgeon which he played in jest in the earlier scenes: he squirms, he whines and he cajoles.

> 'Tis not five hundred crowns that I esteem;
> I am not mov'd at that: this angers me,
> That he, who knows I love him as myself,
> Should write in this imperious vein. Why, sir,
> You know I have no child, and unto whom
> Should I leave all, but unto Ithamore?
> PILIA-BORZA: Here's many words, but no crowns: the crowns!
> BARABAS: Commend me to him, sir, most humbly,
>   And unto your good mistress as unknown.
>   (IV. v. 42)

The cold-blooded ruthlessness of Marlowe's portraiture has a certain impressiveness, but it alienates the audience to such an extent that in the latter part of the play he is obliged to sustain the interest by a frenetic proliferation of intrigue and counter-intrigue. The alienation is complete by the time Barabas is in the cauldron breathing forth his 'latest fate':

> And, had I but escap'd this stratagem,
> I would have brought confusion on you all,
> Damn'd Christians, dogs, and Turkish infidels!
>   (V. v. 84)

One can see that this is one way of making the point that the Machiavellian deprived of success is grotesquely sub-human; but dramatically it is a cul-de-sac. The road *in* is completely logical—given the existence of this kind of villainy—but there is no road *out*. Perhaps it is some awareness in Marlowe of being trapped, that gives to Barabas's last speech a hysteric intensity which is not entirely explained by reference to the 'extremity of heat' and the 'intolerable pangs' he is suffering. It is not a poetic intensity, because the aggressive energies are not *in* the verse but erupting through it, so that one has the impression of a wounded beast lashing about in the dark, a beast for whom Barabas is no more than a vehicle.

IV

There is one further respect in which *The Jew of Malta* engages directly with the social environment in which it was reared—in its treatment of the new world of international mercantilism:

> Warehouses stuff'd with spices and with drugs . . .
> At Alexandria merchandise unsold;
> But yesterday two ships went from this town,
> Their voyage will be worth ten thousand crowns:
> In Florence, Venice, Antwerp, London, Seville,
> Frankfort, Lubeck, Moscow, and where not,
> Have I debts owing; and, in most of these,
> Great sums of money lying in the banco . . .
>
> (IV. i. 67)

From the first scene of the play onwards, this milieu is created. Barabas initiates us into the cosmopolitan freemasonry of the great plutocrats—

> There's Kirriah Jairim, the great Jew of Greece,
> Obed in Bairseth, Nones in Portugal,
> Myself in Malta, some in Italy . . .
>
> (I. i. 122)

—talks easily of 'mine argosy at Alexandria', bills of entry, seeing the freight discharged, custom houses, and so on, displaying that mastery of detail combined with expansive opulence that marks him as the Renaissance merchant-prince—

> Here have I purs'd their paltry silverlings,
> Fie; what a trouble 'tis to count this trash.
>
> (I. i. 6)

There is the concrete particularity of a real world in this opening scene—in such details, for instance, as Barabas's quizzical scrutiny of the weather-vane (in the later scenes, as his gestures become increasingly flamboyant and imprecise, we tend to forget that ships are dependent on mere winds); and at the same moment that he is expending his most opulent verse on the varnishing of the higher cupidity—

> Bags of fiery opals, sapphires, amethysts,
> Jacinths, hard topaz, grass-green emeralds . . .
>
> (I. i. 25)

—Marlowe is also subtly bringing our sense of moral constriction into play:

> Thus trowls our fortune in by land and sea,
> And thus are we on every side enrich'd:
> These are the blessings promis'd to the Jews,
> And herein was old Abraham's happiness.
>
> (I. i. 101)

In Barabas's world, the patriarch's flocks and herds weight more than the
divine promise: Messiah has already come in the guise of 'fiery opals' and
'grass-green emeralds'. Throughout the scene there is this continuous
appeal to the substantial facts of worldly prosperity, against the moral view
of what *ought* to prevail:

> They say we are a scatter'd nation:
> I cannot tell; but we have scrambled up
> More wealth by far than those that brag of faith.
>
> (I. i. 119)

Birds of the air will tell of murders past? Barabas is ashamed to hear such
fooleries. His own career of extortion had disproved these notions of a
natural moral order:

> But mark how I am blest for plaguing them;
> I have as much coin as will buy the town.
>
> (II. iii. 200)

The hard metallic glitter of Barabas's world is striving to outshine the
hidden riches of morality and religion.

> Happily some hapless man hath conscience,
> And for his conscience lives in beggary.
>
> (I. i. 117)

The Jew's is a Machiavellian realism for which moral sanctions have been
abolished by the hard facts of predatory human nature; the 'wind that
bloweth all the world besides' is simply 'desire of gold' (III. v. 3), and with
good reason: for 'who is honour'd now but for his wealth?' (I. i. 111). When
the half-strangled Friar Barnadine enquires, 'What, will you have my life?'
Barabas appeals to the (by now) axiomatic equivalence of life and material
prosperity—'Pull hard, I say. You would have had my goods' (IV. ii. 20).

Parallel with this opening of the sepulchre of universal cupidity
runs a study of the various moral whitewashes which are employed to
conceal the worms and the corruption. We have seen Ferneze's theological
sophistries performing this function, but the issue is continually cropping
up in the play. It is at its most blatant in the persons of the two
contractor-friars, offering rival tenders for Barabas's soul, and making it
plain in the process that even salvation can be had at cut rates if the

market is good and your credit stands high. Religion for Barnadine and Jacomo is simply a technique of spiritual blackmail.

The same sanctified rapacity is shown to be at work in Act II, Scene ii, where Ferneze finds himself caught in the cross-fire between Spaniard and Turk. It is an extremely embarrassing diplomatic crisis: he must either alienate Christian Spain by refusing trading rights to their vice-admiral, or incur the wrath of the Turk, who is only being held at bay by ruinous cash payments and a somewhat one-sided treaty. The solution proposed—a Spanish alliance, followed by war with the Turk—brilliantly satisfies security, self-esteem and fiscal considerations. The funds extorted to pay the Turkish levy can be diverted to the Department of Defence (l. 27); the threatened expulsion by Spain can be averted (ll. 37–41); the stain on the honour of the Knights Templar is expunged (ll. 28–33); Maltese resistance is buttressed by Spanish aid (l. 40); trade, the deity of the mercantilist cult, can proceed unhindered (l. 42); and Ferneze may again congratulate himself on being a good Christian as he and his 'warlike knights' sally forth 'against these barbarous misbelieving Turks' (l. 46). With so many offered advantages, moral and economic, the mere breaking of faith with an ally (and an infidel at that) could carry no weight at all. Marlowe sums up this fox's wisdom of the Governor in the resounding accents of triumphant nationalism:

> Claim tribute where thou wilt, we are resolv'd—
> Honour is bought with blood, and not with gold.
> (II. ii. 55)

(He nevertheless keeps the gold.)

There is a strain of tough honesty in *The Jew* which commands some respect; a refusal to be deflected by the moralistic smokescreen with which rapacity tries to conceal its activities, and as such it is an entirely healthy strain. I am reminded of some remarks of Eric Voegelin's on the subject of Machiavelli's 'realism'. Machiavelli's generation, he claims, was strongly moulded by the traumatic experience of the French invasion.

> The more intelligent and sensitive members of such a generation have seen the reality of power at the moment of its existential starkness when it destroys an order, when the destruction is a brute fact without sense, reason or ideas. It is difficult to tell such men any stories about morality in politics. With the experienced eye of the moraliste [sic] they will diagnose the moralist in politics as the profiteer of the status quo, as the hypocrite who wants everyone to be moral and peace-loving after his own power drive has carried him into the position he would retain . . . In this aspect a man like Machiavelli . . . is a healthy and honest figure, most certainly preferable as a man to the contractualists who try to cover the reality of power underneath an established order, by the moral . . . swindle of consent.

In so far as Marlowe's (or Machiavelli's) contemplation of economic and political power is 'realistic' in this sense, no one will cavil. For it is a potentially tragic vision in which the inalienable ideal is held in tension with the brutal reality, and man is torn between them. But the tragic way of confronting life was, as I shall argue in the next chapter, totally foreign to Machiavelli's cast of mind. And Marlowe wrote neither a tragedy nor a tragi-comedy: he wrote a farce. That is to say, he succumbed to the inevitable tendency of 'realism' to become so insensitive to the bitter truths it tells that it degenerates into self-indulgence. This 'realist's sentimentality' revels in the *sensation* of honesty that comes from resolutely contemplating hard facts, without ever paying the price of mental anguish that such a contem-plation should entail. Realism, from being a mental discipline, has become a mental habit, and leads eventually to neglect of the facts that gave rise to it—the characteristic failing of a social-critic-cum-dramatist like Bertolt Brecht, in whose early work particularly the unmasking of bourgeois vice became an end in itself, and the revelation of the power-structure behind the stately façade of morality a joyful mission. As with Marlowe and Machiavelli, there is something stunted about the humanity that emerges from Brecht's reductive analysis. The up-to-the-minute enlightenment is too brash, the traditional values too glibly surrendered. Indeed there are signs in all three writers that they derived positive satisfaction from scuttling the old hulk and watching it sink beneath the waves of history.

The sentimentality of realism is perhaps less vicious than the more immediately recognisable brutality of realism, but it has its roots in the same diversion of the energies of perception from object to subject. In *The Jew* we have both the sentimentality and the brutality; but they are simply two phases of the one process—the application (as distinct from the realisation) of an *a priori* tough-mindedness which, because it is *a priori*, can never sufficiently divest itself of the doctrinaire and the abstract to clothe itself in the human and the dramatic. The ideas Machiavel promul-gates in the Prologue (which are lively enough as ideas) are deprived of imaginative sustenance because they are not held by men, but by ideological constructs designed specifically for their ability to hold them. And the world within which the ideas are held is not a human world, but a diagrammatic representation of that world. The objection is not to the schematisation which is indispensable to comedy, but to a certain brittle and defensive hardness, which tries to hold the real world, as it were, at arms' length. When Marlowe tires of the didactic constriction of his satirical microcosm, he relieves his feelings with those outbreaks of de-structive violence with which the play is dotted: brutality masquerading as realism is the degenerate end-product of that subjugation of the human to the 'truth', in which realism begins.

DAVID DAICHES

Language and Action in Marlowe's "Tamburlaine"

The greatest drama demands poetry rather than prose, and the reason is not far to seek. In drama the total meaning must be carried by the speech of the characters; the author cannot, as he can in the more discursive form of the novel, allow himself to comment or explain or moralise or in any other way to comment on or interpret the action. The author disappears behind his characters, whose speech and action constitute the play. The novel, which allows of every variety of author's direct and indirect comment and manipulation, does not require a language rich enough to be capable of satisfying simultaneously both the needs of the plot and the full range of awareness of the author's imaginative understanding of all its implications and suggestions. There the author can always speak in his own person. But the drama needs poetry because it needs an extra dimension of meaning built in to the speech of the characters. Modern dramatists of any stature who have used prose have tended to insert bits of novels under the guise of stage directions, as Bernard Shaw did, giving detailed biographical and psychological information in explanatory prose before allowing any character to come on to the stage. But we could hardly imagine Shakespeare inserting a long stage direction before Hamlet's first appearance telling us that he was a sensitive young man who had recently had a severe shock and discussing the implications of his childhood relations with his dead father, his adored mother, and his smooth and resourceful uncle. In *Hamlet* all

From *More Literary Essays*. Copyright © 1968 by David Daiches. The University of Chicago Press.

this comes out in the speech of the characters, in the language they use, in the overtones, associations, suggestions, and explorations achieved by poetic dialogue and soliloquy.

If, then, drama always tends towards poetic speech—even when, as often in Ibsen, it is formally written in prose—because it is only through poetic speech that the dramatist can make us aware of the full implications of the action, we surely do right to seek for the dramatist's meaning, his personal sense of the significance of the action he is showing us, in patterns of imagery and other characteristically poetical aspects of his use of language. To put it crudely, one might say that it is the way in which the characters talk about the actions in which they are involved that shows us what those actions mean both to the characters and to the author. In Shakespeare we often find a most suggestive counterpointing between those aspects of the language which suggest a character's own view of the significance of his actions and those which suggest if not the author's then at least some more objective or inclusive vision. In Marlowe, especially in the early Marlowe (and though the chronology of Marlowe's plays is largely a matter of inference, there can be little real doubt as to which are the earlier plays), the situation is rather different: the poetry is used not so much to interpret the action as to embody it. In *Tamburlaine* particularly there is a kind of relationship between language and action which is not easily parallelled in other poetic drama and which clearly reflects something of Marlowe's own temperament and approach to the subject. Before developing this point, let me try and illustrate it by some examples.

The Prologue, as has often been noted, shows Marlowe repudiating the more popular modes of drama of his time: he announces that he will eschew equally the "jigging veins of riming mother wits" and "such conceits as clownage keeps in pay"—that is, jog-trot rhyming verse and rough-and-tumble comic scenes. Instead

> We'll lead you to the stately tent of war
> Where you shall hear the Scythian Tamburlaine
> Threatening the world with high astounding terms
> And scourging kingdoms with his conquering sword.

We are going to see Tamburlaine in action, and that action involves, first, his "threatening the world in high astounding terms" and then "scourging kingdoms with his conquering sword". His action, that is, involves his way of talking, and indeed we might almost say that in view of the way it is put here language and action are actually equated: threatening with words and scourging with swords are parallel and even equivalent activities. The high imagination that leads to the desire for great actions must always first prove itself in rhetoric. Rhetoric, indeed, is shown in this play to be itself a form of action. We move immediately from the Prologue to the opening scene, where we find the weak Persian king Mycetes expressing to his brother his incapacity to express in words what the occasion demands:

> Brother Cosroe, I find myself agriev'd;
> Yet insufficient to express the same,
> For it requires a great and thundering speech;
> Good brother, tell the cause unto my lords;
> I know you have a better wit than I.

It seems clear from these few lines that Marlowe is implying that the ability to take appropriate action is bound up with the ability to express forcibly in "a great and thundering speech" the nature of the action proposed and of the situation which provokes it. Cosroe, the stronger brother, replies to the weaker in a speech which attempts to recover in language something of the lost might and glory of Persia:

> Unhappy Persia, that in former age
> Hast been the seat of mighty conquerors,
> That, in their prowess and their policies,
> Have triumphed over Afric, and the bounds
> Of Europe where the sun dares scarce appear
> For freezing meteors and congealed cold.

This is Marlowe's first introduction of the vocabulary of power which so dominates the play. "Might", "conquerors", "prowess", "triumphed", "dares" —these potent words rise in the beat of the blank verse with a martial clang. Their force is feeble compared to the force of Tamburlaine's own speeches, but at this opening moment in the play they sufficiently express the difference between the two brothers—just as Tamburlaine's even more soaring speech will express *his* martial superiority to Cosroe.

Now this is not simply a question of Marlowe's realising the limitations of the stage, as Professor Harry Levin suggests. "Driven by an impetus towards infinity and faced with the limitations of the stage", Professor Levin writes, "the basic convention of the Marlovian drama is to take the word for the deed". This is true, and the point is acutely made, yet is seems to me wrong to suggest that "the limitations of the stage" represent a significant cause of this characteristic of Marlovian drama. It is not as though Marlowe were saying, "I cannot show you their actions, the limitations of the stage being what they are; I shall therefore have to content myself by letting you listen to them talking about their actions".

It is made clear in innumerable ways that for Marlowe the proper kind of talk is both the precondition for and in a sense the equivalent of action. Soaring talk is the sign of the soaring mind, and only the soaring mind can achieve spectacularly successful action. I am not altogether happy, either, about the other cause which Professor Levin gives for Marlowe's characters taking the word for the deed—"an impetus towards infinity". One needs to be more specific about what is involved here. The infinite ambitions which spur on the Marlovian hero represent the impulse to do something more than can ever be achieved or even defined, but which at best can only be suggested by a particular kind of poetic imagery and rhetorical splendour. There is never an objective correlative in action to the ambitions of such a hero. When Dr Faustus exclaims

> O what a world of profit and delight,
> Of power, of honour, of omnipotence
> Is promised to the studious artisan!

he is not merely giving expression to the Baconian concept of knowledge as power, as control over one's environment; both the abstractness and the variety of the words he chooses—"profit", "delight", "power", "honour", "omnipotence"—suggests that he seeks something greater than could be represented by any practical example. True, Faustus' trivial use of the power which he gets—playing practical jokes on the Pope and similar pranks—suggests the fatuity which overcomes man once he has achieved power through infernal help, and this is an important moral point: but it is also true that any given example of power in action must be trivial beside the exalted human imagination that aspires after it. The disparity between desire and achievement is for Marlowe part of the human condition, and, this being so, it is in the expression of the desire rather than in accomplishing the achievement that man reveals his most striking qualities.

To return to the opening scene of *Tamburlaine*. The first mention of the hero's name is deliberately reductive: the Persians are trying to diminish him by reducing his stature verbally, by denying his claims to a grand description. The initial description of him is as a highway robber, compared to a fox in harvest time:

> . . . that Tamburlaine,
> That, like a fox in midst of harvest-time,
> Doth prey upon my flocks of passengers, . . .

And Meander follows this up by describing him as

> that sturdy Scythian thief,
> That robs your merchants of Persepolis
> Trading by land unto the Western Isles,
> And in your confines with his lawless train
> Daily commits incivil outrages, . . .

Marlowe wants to give Tamburlaine a chance to build himself up from the lowest possible position. What could be more lowering than "sturdy Scythian thief" and "lawless train", and what a contemptuous and reductive phrase we have in "incivil outrages" when applied to Tamburlaine's deeds! When we first see Tamburlaine in the following scene, he does not immediately proceed to build himself up by magnificent rhetoric. When the Medean lords tell him that

> Besides rich presents from the puissant Cham
> We have his highness' letters to command
> Aid and assistance, if we stand in need,

he vaults over all intermediate ranks in a single quiet sentence:

> But now you see these letters and commands
> Are countermanded by a greater man.

Tamburlaine excels in the expression of the consciousness of superiority, and this is in fact one important reason why he *is* superior.

Consciousness and acceptance of mortality limits both speech and action. The weak Mycetes charges his captain Theridamas to destroy Tamburlaine and return swiftly:

> Return with speed, time passeth swift away,
> Our life is frail, and we may die to-day.

Like Tamburlaine, he can imagine destruction, but not with the intoxicating sense of being the "scourge of God" and acting in the spirit of divine wrath, rather merely as a more passive observer of his dead enemies:

> I long to see thee back return from thence,
> That I may view these milk-white steeds of mine
> All loaden with the heads of killed men, . . .

No sooner is Mycetes off the stage than his brother Cosroe asserts his power and is crowned king by Ortygius and Ceneus. The rhetoric begins to rise:

> Magnificent and mighty prince Cosroe,
> We, in the name of other Persian states
> And commons of this mighty monarchy,
> Present thee with th' imperial diadem.

This is followed shortly afterwards by the first of many speeches in which exotic geographical names sound trumpet-like, proclaiming pomp and power:

> We here do crown thee monarch of the East,
> Emperor of Asia and of Persia,
> Great lord of Media and Armenia,
> Duke of Africa and Albania,
> Mesopotamia and of Parthia,
> East India and the late discovered isles,
> Chief lord of all the wide vast Euxine Sea,
> And of the ever raging Caspian Lake.
> Long live Cosroe, mighty emperor!

Eventually, of course, Tamburlaine's trumpets out-blow all others; his rhetoric soars to heights unequalled by any other speaker in the play. But his first appearance, following immediately on Cosroe's magniloquence and Ortygius' cry, "Sound up the trumpets, then. God save the king!", shows him as relatively subdued. He is still merely the robber-shepherd, leading in his captured treasure and his fair captive Zenocrate, to whom he speaks at first rather as Comus speaks to the Lady in Milton's Masque:

> Come lady, let not this appal your thoughts;
> The jewels and the treasure we have ta'en
> Shall be reserv'd, and you in better state
> Than if you were arriv'd in Syria.

Zenocrate addresses him as "shepherd". Then, after Tamburlaine's second speech to Zenocrate, in which, as I have noted, he quietly raises himself above the "puissant Cham", Zenocrate addresses him as "my lord", adding significantly "for so you do import". Tamburlaine accepts the title, adding the characteristically Marlovian remark that it is his deeds rather than his birth that will prove him so. (It should be noted, in passing, that Marlowe was a rebel against a hereditary social hierarchy, and though his imagination revelled in all the ritual of power and rank—he several times makes great play, for example, with subordinate kings receiving their crowns from the chief of them all—he accepted it only when it was the reward of achievement rather than merely of birth. Thus Faustus was born of "parents base of stock" and Tamburlaine vaunts rather than denies his humble origin. The poverty of the University Wits bred a special kind of pride, which in Marlowe's case merged with one current of Renaissance humanism to produce a non-hereditary view of aristocracy.) Zenocrate's third address to Tamburlaine appeals to him as one who

> hop'st to be eternised
> By living Asia's mighty emperor.

It is an interesting and rapid progression—from "shepherd", to "my lord", to "mighty emperor"—and is produced entirely by Tamburlaine's way of speech.

It is perhaps surprising that Tamburlaine's first appearance should show him less as the warrior than as the lover. After all, the chief interest of the play centres on his power, whether of language or of action, and falling in love is a kind of submission rather than an exercise of power. But it is significant that Tamburlaine regards Zenocrate as someone precious whose possession signifies power. As the daughter of the Soldan of Egypt she represents a high and ancient lineage, as the betrothed of the King of Arabia she represents a challenge, and as having supreme beauty she is, like a supremely precious stone, of inestimable *value*. Tamburlaine manifests his growing power by talking about and by achieving the conquest of inexpressibly rich treasures and of kingdoms. Competitive speeches promising wealth and pomp to your favourites or to those who come over to your side, represent one of the recurring features of the play, one of Marlowe's ways of establishing relative greatness of character. In his wooing of Zenocrate Tamburlaine is outbidding all other kings and princes in the wealth and glory he can promise her and at the same time he is winning for himself something infinitely precious. His first speech of courtship both expresses his sense of Zenocrate's enormous value and promises her the highest possible style of living. Rhetoric is the art of persuasion: in putting a blazing rhetoric into Tamburlaine's mouth Marlowe expressly recognises that one of the roads to power is the ability to *win people over*. Great speech is not only both the guarantor and even the equivalent of great action; it is also in itself a means to power which takes precedence of naked physical aggression. On several occasions Tamburlaine is shown as using it first, as trying to seduce his enemies into his service or into unconditional surrender. Action, we are sometimes made to feel, is only to be resorted to when speech meets with stubbornness or deafness. Or rather, to make the point yet again, speech is presented as being the primary form of action, that form which corresponds most closely to man's actual ambitions.

We first hear the full sound of Tamburlaine's rhetoric when he encounters Theridamas, the Persian captain sent against him by Mycetes. Before Theridamas' arrival, Tamburlaine has his soldiers lay out in public view their captured gold treasure, "that their reflexions may amaze the Persians". Surrounded by this spectacular wealth, he is found by Theridamas and greets him with a huge elemental dignity:

> Whom seeks thou, Persian? I am Tamburlaine.

Theridamas is impressed by Tamburlaine's appearance, and takes fire from it to speak in Tamburlaine-like tones:

> His looks do menace heaven and dare the gods,
> His fiery eyes are fixed upon the earth,
> As if he now devis'd some stratagem,
> Or meant to pierce Avernas' darksome vaults
> To pull the triple headed dog from hell.

Tamburlaine responds at once to this kind of rhetoric: this is his way of talking, and he appreciates it. We may wonder perhaps why he takes it as a sign that Theridamas is "noble and mild", but I should think that we are to regard these adjectives as a general sign of approval of his worthiness on the one hand and his capacity for being won over on the other. Tamburlaine then returns the compliment paid by Theridamas to his appearance:

> With what majesty he rears his looks!

He then embarks on the greatest of all the several speeches of competitive promising in the play. The increasing abstractness of Tamburlaine's imagery in the opening lines is the measure of his rapidly soaring imagination. The difference between being "but captain of a thousand horse" and triumphing "over all the world" is more than a difference in degree; it is the difference between the paltriness of a realisable kind of power and the magnificence of an ambition too tremendous to be capable of concrete definition. The contrast is immediate:

> Art thou but captain of a thousand horse,
> That by characters graven in thy brows,
> And by thy martial face and stout aspect,
> Deserv'st to have the leading of an host?
> Forsake thy king and do but join with me,
> And we will triumph over all the world.

From this point—as though he has intoxicated himself with the phrase "And we will triumph over all the world"—Tamburlaine's speech moves into its full grandiloquence:

> I hold the Fates bound fast in iron chains,
> And with my hand turn Fortune's wheel about,
> And sooner shall the sun fall from his sphere
> Than Tamburlaine be slain or overcome.
> Draw forth thy sword, thou mighty man at arms,
> Intending but to raze my charmed skin,
> And Jove himself will stretch his hand from heaven

To ward the blow, and shield me safe from harm.
See how he rains down heaps of gold in showers,
As if he meant to give my soldiers pay,
And as a sure and grounded argument
That I shall be the monarch of the East,
He sends this Soldan's daughter rich and brave,
To be my queen and portly emperess.
If thou wilt stay with me, renowned man,
And lead thy thousand horse with my conduct,
Besides thy share of this Egyptian prize,
Those thousand horse shall sweat with martial spoil
Of conquered kingdoms and of cities sacked.
Both we will walk upon the lofty clifts,
And Christian merchants, that with Russian stems
Plough up huge furrows in the Caspian Sea,
Shall vail to us as lords of all the lake.
Both we will reign as consuls of the earth,
And mighty kings shall be our senators;
Jove sometimes masked in a shepherd's weed,
And by those steps that he hath scal'd the heavens,
May we become immortal like the gods.
Join with me now in this my mean estate,
(I call it mean, because, being yet obscure,
The nations far remov'd admire me not,)
And when my name and honour shall be spread,
As far as Boreas claps his brazen wings,
Or fair Bootes sends his cheerful light,
Then shalt thou be competitor with me,
And sit with Tamburlaine in all his majesty.

One has the feeling, here as elsewhere, that when Marlowe uses classical mythology it is not for decorative purposes or to make literary capital out of references to known legends, but in order to give the myths new meaning by showing their usefulness in illustrating the limitless nature of human ambition at its most magnificent:

Jove sometimes masked in a shepherd's weed,
And by those steps that he hath scal'd the heavens,
May we become immortal like the gods.

It is as though Marlowe is showing us for the first time what classical mythology is all about, what it is *for*: it helps to provide symbols for the undefinable ambitions of the unfettered human imagination. Similarly, the monstrous extravagance of

I hold the Fates bound fast in iron chains,
And with my hand turn Fortune's wheel about,

is not to be glossed simply by reference to the medieval notion of Fortune's wheel, though of course Marlowe depends here for his shock effect on his readers' and hearers' realising that this is a frontal attack on the common idea of the fickleness of fortune. That attack is not, however, as it has sometimes been taken to be, a sign of an almost blasphemous arrogance on Tamburlaine's or on Marlowe's part; it is a way of expressing what it feels like to have limitless ambition and limitless self-confidence. Once again one might say that the use of this kind of language is a kind of action: to be able to talk that way is half the battle. Marlowe does not present this kind of talk as *boasting*, and the actual boasting of lesser figures, such as Bajazeth, is clearly differentiated from this particular kind of abstract extravagance. Tamburlaine, when he speaks like this, has gone far beyond boasting: he is in an almost trance-like condition of relishing the significance of his own highest imaginings. Such talk carries its own conviction: a man who can talk like that is the man on whose side we want to be. Theridamas makes this quite clear:

> Not Hermes, prolocutor to the gods,
> Could use persuasions more pathetical.

This scene ends with Tamburlaine's creating around him an atmosphere of total loyalty and mutual trust. Here Tamburlaine is at his most attractive. Service on the one hand and protection on the other are subsumed in a common notion of soldierly friendship and faithfulness which has its own simpler eloquence:

> THERIDAMAS: But shall I prove a traitor to my king?
> TAMBURLAINE: No, but the trust friend of Tamburlaine.
> THERIDAMAS: Won with thy words, and conquered with thy looks,
>   I yield myself, my men, and horse to thee:
>   To be partaker of thy good or ill,
>   As long as life maintains Theridamas.
> TAMBURLAINE: Theridamas, my friend, take here my hand,
>   Which is as much as if I swore by heaven,
>   And call'd the gods to witness of my vow,
>   Thus shall my heart be still combined with thine,
>   Until our bodies turn to elements,
>   And both our souls aspire celestial thrones.
>   Techelles, and Casane, welcome him.
> TECHELLES: Welcome renowned Persian to us all.
> USUMCASANE: Long may Theridamas remain with us.
> TAMBURLAINE: These are my friends in whom I more rejoice,
>   Than doth the king of Persia in his crown: . . .

The next scene shows us Cosroe being swung round to Tamburlaine by Menaphon's description of his appearance. Like Shakespeare's Cleopatra, whose beauty is symbolised by its ability to inspire eloquence in hard-bitten military men when they describe it, so Tamburlaine's greatness lies partly in its capacity for being eloquently talked about. The language here has not Tamburlaine's passion of grandeur, his commitment through language to the genuineness of his own enormous ambitions, but it strikes effectively the note of compelled admiration:

> Of stature tall, and straightly fashioned,
> Like his desire, lift upwards and divine,
> So large of limbs, his joints so strongly knot,
> Such breadth of shoulders as might mainly bear
> Old Atlas' burthen; 'twixt his manly pitch,
> A pearl more worth than all the world is placed,
> Wherein by curious sovereignty of art
> Are fixed his piercing instruments of sight,
> Whose fiery circles bear encompassed
> A heaven of heavenly bodies in their spheres,
> That guides his steps and actions to the throne
> Where honour sits invested royally:
> Pale of complexion, wrought in him with passion,
> Thirsting with sovereignty and love of arms,
> His lofty brows in folds do figure death,
> And in their smoothness amity and life:
> About them hangs a knot of amber hair,
> Wrapped in curls, as fierce Achilles' was,
> On which the breath of heaven delights to play,
> Making it dance with wanton majesty:
> His arms and fingers long and sinewy,
> Betokening valour and excess of strength:
> In every part proportioned like the man
> Should make the world subdued to Tamburlaine.

This mediated persuasion does not work as effectively as the words of Tamburlaine himself work directly on Theridamas. Cosroe does not yield to Tamburlaine as a preliminary to gaining his true friendship; he tries to make the best of both worlds by asserting that Tamburlaine will be his regent in Persia. Where Cosroe goes wrong is made abundantly clear in a later scene, where he patronises Tamburlaine and indicates that he is using him to further his own ambitions. He addresses Tamburlaine jovially as 'worthy Tamburlaine' and asks, in the tone of a squire addressing a farm labourer,

> What thinkst thou, man, shall come of our attempts?

In answer to Tamburlaine's speech of boundless confidence, Cosroe simply reiterates that he expects that the efforts of Tamburlaine and his friends

> Shall make me solely emperor of Asia,

and proceeds to dole out promises of advancement in language that sounds very tame beside that of Tamburlaine in his promising mood:

> Then shall your meeds and valours be advanced
> To rooms of honour and nobility.

Tamburlaine replies with an irony of which Cosroe is totally oblivious:

> Then haste, Cosroe, to be king alone, . . .

We are prepared for Cosroe's ultimate rejection and destruction by Tamburlaine: he has not made the right response to Tamburlaine's language.

The scene in which the timid Mycetes, caught by Tamburlaine in the act of trying to hide the crown, is contemptuously given back the crown by Tamburlaine and then runs away, will be misconstrued by the modern reader if he reads Mycetes' opening line

> Accursed be he that first invented war!

as a serious pacifist argument. Those critics who see Marlowe here as showing a humanitarian feeling and voicing a proper horror of war, or as adding some subtle touches to his portrait of Mycetes, are not reading the play that Marlowe wrote. The point about Mycetes—one is tempted to add, the only relevant point—is that he can find neither language nor gesture to correspond to his royal state, and therefore his royal state is forfeit. A crown is a symbol of human aspiration; in great spirits it provokes to eloquence of speech and magnificence of action, or at least to some behaviour correlative to the symbol's significance. All that Mycetes can think of doing with it is to hide it, to prevent himself from being known as king:

> So shall not I be known; or if I be,
> They cannot take away my crown from me.
> Here will I hide it in this simple hole.

This is anti-rhetoric, one might say. To say of a crown "Here will I hide it in this simple hole" is the ultimate lack of response to the challenge of the symbol. Tamburlaine's words, "The thirst of reign and sweetness of a crown", spoken later, show the approved response. Mycetes tends to speak in monosyllables, "For kings are clouts that every man shoots at", "And far from any man that is a fool", and when he encounters Tamburlaine he is quite incapable of rising to the occasion. Even Tamburlaine in his presence speaks with an unwonted and contemptuous simplicity:

> Well, I mean you shall have it again.
> Here, take it for a while; I lend it thee,
> Till I may see thee hemm'd with armed men.
> Then shalt thou see me pull it from thy head;
> Thou are no match for mighty Tamburlaine.

And when Mycetes discovers that it was Tamburlaine himself speaking, he records the fact in the most deflating language possible:

> O gods, is this Tamburlaine the thief?
> I marvel much he stole it not away.

Everywhere it is language that provides the clue. Compare, for example, the Persian Meander cheering up his army, with Tamburlaine's speaking to *his* men. Here is Meander:

> Therefore cheer up your minds; prepare to fight.
> He that can take or slaughter Tamburlaine,
> Shall rule the province of Albania.
> Who brings that traitor's head, Theridamas,
> Shall have a government in Media,
> Beside the spoil of him and all his train.

The province of Albania or a government in Media is tame indeed beside the vaguer but infinitely more eloquent

> We'll chase the stars from heaven and dim their eyes
> That stand and muse at our admired arms.

Again, we find that for Marlowe what is realisable in precise terms cannot be the product of a truly inspired imagination. The greatest ambitions are undefinable save in terms of abstraction, mythology, or cosmic metaphor. The best that Meander can promise his soldiers is that they shall

> Share equally the gold that bought their lives,
> And live like gentlemen in Persia.

Live like gentlemen indeed! Tamburlaine's soldiers will live like gods:

> For fates and oracles of heaven have sworn
> To royalise the deeds of Tamburlaine,
> And make them blest that share in his attempts.

That Tamburlaine cannot enjoy his power unless he is talking about it or indulging in a gesture symbolical of it is not to be explained simply by the limitations of the stage: it is a paradox inherent in Marlowe's conception of human ambition. It is only after he has crowned Cosroe as emperor that Tamburlaine allows his imagination to batten on the thought of kingship. Menaphon promises Cosroe that he will "ride in triumph through Persepolis", and after he and Cosroe have gone out, leaving Tamburlaine, Theridamas, Techelles, and Usumcasane on the stage—that is, Tamburlaine and his most faithful officers—Tamburlaine repeats and savours the words:

> And ride in triumph through Persepolis!
> Is it not brave to be a king, Techelles?
> Usumcasane and Theridamas,
> Is is not passing brave to be a king,
> And ride in triumph through Persepolis?

Here for the first time we hear the note of pure incantation in Tamburlaine's language. What is in fact involved in being a king? If we think of it, limited things—limited functions, limited powers, above all, limited length of life. The idea of kingship as it kindles the aspiring mind is more significant than a king's actual rights and duties. The word suggests power and glory—"for Thine is the kingdom, the power and the glory"—of a kind more absolute than any given example of human power and glory can be. Human beings have the power of responding to this suggestion, and in this lies their especial capacity for tragedy. Macbeth and Lady Macbeth, captivated by the magic of the idea of kingship, destroyed themselves in order to obtain it and learned at the very moment of obtaining it that their imagination of it had had nothing to do with the reality. *Tamburlaine* however is not a tragedy: Marlowe is not concerned with the disparity between the magic of names and the true nature of things, between the imagination and the reality, or with the corruption of noble minds to which this disparity can lead. To this extent the play lacks a moral pattern, lacks any real core of meaning. There is no sense of the pity of it or the waste of it or even of the ambiguity of it, though Marlowe does show some awareness of some of the paradoxes involved in the relation between words and actions. Tamburlaine is held up to our admiration in the literal Latin sense of *admirari*. His cruelty, which can be appalling, has no real moral significance one way or the other; it is simply a mode of action appropriate to a soaring ambition, and to Marlowe a soaring ambition is a mode of feeling appropriate to man's restless desire to break out of the limiting bounds within which any given actions of his must be confined. The slaughtering of the virgins and the other inhabitants of Damascus is a *gesture*, like the change of Tamburlaine's colours from white to red to black, and gestures are attempts to find actions which, though inevitably limited, are at least symbolic of something larger than themselves. I am not here concerned with Part II, which raises some different questions, but I would remark that Tamburlaine's insistence on courage to bear wounds and so on, in his discussion with his sons in Part II, and the somewhat confused picture of Calyphas as part coward, part sensualist, part realist, and part pacifist, lead us into other realms altogether. Part I is the original play, and complete in itself: in continuing it Marlowe had to modify the purity of his original conception and introduce elements which if examined closely take us far from the essential play as first conceived and written.

Tamburlaine, then, in repeating the phrase about riding in triumph through Persepolis and building up from it into an incantatory speech on the joys of kingship, is demonstrating his superiority to more mundane imaginations and his capacity for enjoying speech as a mode of action. What a king actually does, how a king actually employs and enjoys his power, is not inquired into. The idea of kingly power is itself intoxicating. When he sounds the names of his followers in a litany of invoked kingship, he is trying to carry them with him in his imaginative conception of the sweets of power. But they are not Tamburlaine. All that Techelles can say is

> O, my lord, 'tis sweet and full of pomp!

Usumcasane tries to go one better with

> To be a king, is half to be a god.

But Tamburlaine brushes these tame expressions away impatiently:

> A god is not so glorious as a king:
> I think the pleasure they enjoy in heaven,
> Cannot compare with kingly joys in earth;
> To wear a crown enchas'd with pearl and gold,
> Whose virtues carry with it life and death;
> To ask and have, command and be obeyed;
> When looks breed love, with looks to gain the prize,
> Such power attractive shines in princes' eyes.

From now on he is to be chasing his language in his actions, and, in the nature of things, never catching up. I have said that the spectacle is not tragic. Tamburlaine's imagination vents itself in rhetoric which in turn re-kindles his imagination to still greater ambitions, and this process is shown as guaranteeing military success. But it is an amoral process. We get the point about the restless, limitless nature of human ambition and the impossibility of its being able to find any single correlative in action. But what does it all add up to in the end?

It is no use saying that it adds up to great poetry, even if not always great dramatic poetry, for the point at issue is just how great is this kind of poetry and why. Consider the speech in which Tamburlaine most fully equates kingship with limitless human aspiration:

> The thirst of reign and sweetness of a crown
> That caused the eldest son of heavenly Ops
> To thrust his doting father from his chair,
> And place himself in the imperial heaven,
> Mov'd me to manage arms against thy state.
> What better precedent than mighty Jove?
> Nature, that fram'd us of four elements
> Warring within our breasts for regiment,
> Doth teach us all to have aspiring minds:
> Our souls, whose faculties can comprehend
> The wondrous architecture of the world,
> And measure every wandering planet's course,
> Still climbing after knowledge infinite,
> And always moving as the restless spheres,
> Wills us to wear ourselves and never rest,
> Until we reach the ripest fruit of all,
> That perfect bliss and sole felicity,
> The sweet fruition of an earthly crown.

Critics have differed as to whether the conclusion of this passage is an anti-climax or a supreme climax. At the beginning of the speech, characteristically, Marlowe presses a new meaning on a Greek myth to make it serve as an illustration and an illumination of the inevitability of continuously aspiring ambition among men. The line "What better precedent than mighty Jove?" rings out as an arrogant challenge. He next goes on to say that the four elements of which man's physical nature is composed (according to medieval and Aristotelian physiology), since they are in continual conflict with each other, teach us all to have aspiring minds. We might say that the relation between conflict and aspiration is not made clear and there seems to be no reason why the former should suggest the latter, but there is a suppressed middle term, emulation, which might bridge the logical gap here. In any case the argument is not essentially rational, but rhetorical: Tamburlaine is seeking mythological, cosmic, and natural sanctions for human aspiration: human ambition forms part of the total wonder of nature. The Faustian lines

> Our souls, whose faculties can comprehend
> The wondrous architecture of the world,
> And measure every wandering planet's course,
> Still climbing after knowledge infinite,

are very impressive in their rising eloquence and the fine, steady abstraction of "Still climbing after knowledge infinite". We are made to feel the *insatiable* nature of human curiosity. The search is never-ending—

> Until we reach the ripest fruit of all,
> That perfect bliss and sole felicity,
> The sweet fruition of an earthly crown.

The play itself, of course, belies this. Tamburlaine collects crowns as a philatelist collects stamps and remains unsatisfied. The extraordinary force of the abstract words "perfect bliss and sole felicity", suggesting a theological conception of heavenly beatitude, and, reminding us of Milton's "When everything that is sincerely good and perfectly divine", hardly prepares us for what they are leading up to, "the sweet fruition of an earthly crown". Yet I do not think the passage ends in anti-climax. The *ripest fruit* of all, that *perfect bliss* and *sole felicity*, turns out to be the *sweet fruition* of an earthly crown. The crown in this context is made, by its culminating position, into a symbol of ultimate human ambition. *This is what Tamburlaine (and Marlowe) mean, then, when they talk of a crown.* It is not the usual meaning of the word "crown" that limits the totality of meaning achieved by these lines; on the contrary, it is the meaning set up by the preceding lines that determines in what sense we are to take the word "crown" when we come to it in its climactic position. Contemplated by the imagination, an earthly crown seems to be the guarantee of what a heavenly crown is conventionally assumed to promise—"perfect bliss and sole felicity". It is the imagination which invests words and objects with symbolic meaning. The word "crown" literally "means" a circle placed on the head of a king. But the word, like the word "king", can be used to contain an idea or an emotion. This is what Shakespeare does with the words in *Richard II*. But with Marlowe the idea and the emotion are larger than any practice of kingship would warrant. Acting out kingship in language or in coronation ceremony thus becomes a way of pointing to the nature of human aspiration. Indeed, language and gesture become the best kind of action because they can bear all that the imagination puts into them and are therefore not limited as even the greatest ordinary actions are bound to be. A coronation ceremony is always more moving than a king giving laws or in any other way exhibiting his power. And in the last resort it is in the ceremony of language that human aspiration finds fullest satisfaction. This is the point so splendidly made by—or rather embodied in—the passage quoted.

What, then, does it all add up to in the end? *Tamburlaine* is a play in which the virtuosity of the actor is more important than the moral nature of his actions. The hero tells us what he is going to do before he does it; tells us what he is doing when he is doing it, and after he has done it tells us what he has done—and all in language whose grandiloquence makes almost every speech a ritual of aspiration. Successful action follows on the speech almost automatically, for speech of this kind can only spring from an irrepressible energy, a perpetual hunger for always going further and doing more, which *must* be satisfied. Those who fail are those with limited aims—contrary to the vulgar view that to limit one's aim is to make success more probable. Tamburlaine's antagonists are not only those with pettier minds; they are also those—like Bajazeth, his most formidable opponent—whose aim is complacently to maintain their achieved power, which they take for granted as part of the permanent state of things. The language of Bajazeth is not unlike that of Tamburlaine: he must be an opponent to challenge Tamburlaine's imagination and also one whose overthrow marks a significant step in Tamburlaine's pursuit of his words by his actions. One difference between the language of Bajazeth and that of Tamburlaine is that Tamburlaine's tends to be directed towards the future—what he wills to do and what he therefore will do, "For Will and Shall best fitteth Tamburlaine"—whereas the language of Bajazeth is more a complacent vaunting of what he is. When Bajazeth does talk of the future, it is in terms of intention—

> —We *mean to* take his morning's next arise
> For messenger he will not be reclaim'd,
> And *mean to* fetch thee in despite of him—

which sounds tentative beside Tamburlaine's

> I that am term'd the Scourge and Wrath of God,
> The only fear and terror of the world,
> Will first subdue the Turk, and then enlarge
> Those Christian captives which you keep as slaves.

In the verbal duel between Bajazeth and Tamburlaine this difference disappears, and both speak in terms of "will" and "shall". The event shows which is the boaster. It is however worth noting that Bajazeth projects his images of power in terms of number and quantity rather than in the cosmic and mythological imagery characteristic of Tamburlaine.

The scene immediately preceding the exchange of words between Tamburlaine and Bajazeth shows us Zenocrate, now deeply in love with Tamburlaine, being urged by Agydas to give up Tamburlaine in favour of her original Arabian king. Agydas, significantly, has no appreciation of Tamburlaine's language. When Zenocrate looks for "amorous discourse", he tells her, Tamburlaine

> Will rattle forth his facts of war and blood.

Marlowe is deliberately playing a dangerous game here, allowing us to hear this brilliantly contemptuous description of Tamburlaine's speech in the very middle of the play. But he is confident that once we hear Tamburlaine's voice sounding again we shall dismiss this belittling description. Even before this, he has Zenocrate reply, in language that echoes Tamburlaine's own,

> As looks the sun through Nilus' flowing stream,
> Or when the Morning holds him in her arms,
> So looks my lordly love, fair Tamburlaine;
> His talk much sweeter than the Muses' song
> They sung for honour 'gainst Pierides,
> Or when Minerva did with Neptune strive;
> And higher would I rear my estimate
> Than Juno, sister to the highest god,
> If I were matched with mighty Tamburlaine.

Tamburlaine discovers Agydas trying to tempt Zenocrate away from him, and to this man who belittles his language he addresses no words but only sends a dagger as an invitation to him to kill himself. Agydas gets the point:

> He needed not with words confirm my fear,
> For words are vain when working tools present
> The naked action of my threatened end.

There is a fine irony in Tamburlaine's refusal to use words to the man who cannot appreciate them. One is reminded of a dialogue, earlier in the play, between Mycetes and Meander.

> MYCETES: Was there such brethren, sweet Meander, say,
>   That sprung of teeth of dragons venomous?
> MEANDER: So poets say, my lord.
> MYCETES: And 'tis a pretty toy to be a poet.

Miss Ellis-Fermor, in her note on this line in her edition, drew attention to what she considered its "biting irony", seeing it as a bitter comment by Marlowe on the reputation and fate of poets. But surely the irony does not lie here at all, but in the man who can neither speak nor act both doubting mythology and despising poetry. Mythology is the very stuff of much of Tamburlaine's speech, and his poetic utterance is bound up with his aspiration and thus with his capacity for action. Mycetes, incapable of poetic utterance and equally of effective action, shows his lack of understanding of the relation between language and action by his contemptuous remark about poets.

The slanging match between Zenocrate and the Turkish empress Zabina is a rather crude acting out of this same correlation between speech and action that is so important in the play: while their husbands fight it out on the field, they "manage words" in mutual taunting. Tamburlaine's humiliation and degradation of Bajazeth and Zabina and his complete victory over the Turkish forces is another acting out of his soaring ambition, yet it cannot be denied that there is an element of sadism in the detailed presentation of this cruel treatment. Bajazeth has counted on Mahomet to save him, and appeals desperately to the prophet for succour: but none comes. Man stands alone in Marlowe's universe and draws his strength from his own aspiring imagination. When Tamburlaine uses Bajazeth as a footstool and mounts on him to his throne, the gesture itself is striking—a gesture of overweening ambition and aspiration; he is not content, however, to leave it at that, but breaks out into a speech whose rhetorical extravagance gives full meaning to his symbolic act:

> Now clear the triple region of the air,
> And let the majesty of heaven behold
> Their scourge and terror tread on emperors.
> Smile, stars that reign'd at my nativity,
> And dim the brightness of their neighbour lamps;
> Disdain to borrow light of Cynthia,
> For I, the chiefest lamp of all the earth,
> First rising in the east with mild aspect,
> But fixed now in the meridian line,
> Will send up fire to your turning spheres,
> And cause the sun to borrow light of you.
> My sword struck fire from his coat of steel,
> Even in Bithynia, when I took this Turk;
> As when a fiery exhalation,
> Wrapt in the bowels of a freezing cloud,
> Fighting for passage, makes the welkin crack,
> And casts a flash of lightning to the earth.
> But ere I march to wealthy Persia,
> Or leave Damascus and th' Egyptian fields,
> As was the fame of Clymene's brainsick son
> That almost brent the axletree of heaven,
> So shall our swords, our lances and our shot
> Fill all the air with fiery meteors;
> Then, when the sky shall wax as red as blood,
> It shall be said I made it red myself,
> To make me think of naught but blood and war.

CLEANTH BROOKS

The Unity of Marlowe's "Doctor Faustus"

In his *Poetics*, Aristotle observed that a tragedy should have a beginning, a middle, and an end. The statement makes a point that seems obvious, and many a reader of our time must have dismissed it as one of more tedious remarks of the Stagirite, or indeed put it down to one of the duller notes taken by the student whom some suppose to have heard Aristotle's lectures and preserved the substance of them for us. Yet the play without a middle does occur, and in at least three signal instances that I can think of in English literature, we have a play that lacks a proper middle or at least a play that *seems* to lack a middle. Milton's *Samson Agonistes* is one of them; Eliot's *Murder in the Cathedral*, another; and Marlowe's *Doctor Faustus*, the third. Milton presents us with Samson, in the hands of his enemies, blind, grinding at the mill with other slaves, yet in only a little while he has Samson pull down the temple roof upon his enemies. There is a beginning and there is an end, but in the interval between them has anything of real consequence happened? *Murder in the Cathedral* may seem an even more flagrant instance of an end jammed on to a beginning quite directly and without any intervening dramatic substance. Thomas has come back out of exile to assume his proper place in his cathedral and act as shepherd to his people. He is already aware of the consequences of his return, and that in all probability the decisive act has been taken that will quickly lead to his martyrdom and death.

Marlowe's *Doctor Faustus* may seem to show the same defect, for

From *A Shaping Joy*. Copyright © 1971 by Cleanth Brooks. Methuen & Co., Ltd.

very early in the play the learned doctor makes his decision to sell his soul to the devil, and after that there seems little to do except to fill in the time before the mortgage falls due and the devil comes to collect the forfeited soul. If the consequence of Faustus's bargain is inevitable, and if nothing can be done to alter it, then it doesn't much matter what one puts in as filler. Hence one can stuff in comedy and farce more or less *ad libitum*, the taste of the audience and its patience in sitting through the play being the only limiting factors.

In what I shall say here, I do not propose to do more than touch upon the vexed problem of the authorship of *Doctor Faustus* in either the A or B version. But I think that it is significant that the principal scenes that are confidently assigned to Marlowe turn out to be the scenes that open and close the play. To other hands is assigned the basic responsibility for supplying the comedy or sheer wonder-working or farce that makes up much of the play and is the very staple of Acts III and IV.

For their effectiveness, *Doctor Faustus, Samson Agonistes* and *Murder in the Cathedral*, all three, depend heavily upon their poetry. One could go further: the poetry tends to be intensely lyrical and in the play with which we are concerned arises from the depths of the character of Faustus himself; it expresses his aspirations, his dreams, his fears, his agonies, and his intense awareness of the conflicting feelings within himself. The poetry, it ought to be observed, is not a kind of superficial gilding, but an expression—and perhaps the inevitable expression—of the emotions of the central character. If there is indeed a "middle" in this play—that is, a part of the play concerned with complication and development in which the character of Faustus becomes something quite different from the man whom we first meet—then the "middle" of the play has to be sought in this area of personal self-examination and inner conflict, and the poetry will prove its most dramatic expression. One observes that something of this sort is true of *Samson Agonistes*. The Samson whom we meet at the beginning of the play is obviously incapable of undertaking the action that he performs so gloriously at the end. Something very important, I should argue, does happen to Samson in the course of the play, and his awareness of some "rousing motions" after Harapha has left him is no accident—that is, the rousing motions did not simply happen to occur at the propitious moment. I should argue that the encounter between Samson and his father, his wife, and the giant, all have had their part in transforming the quality of his response to the world about him, and that the sensitive auditor or reader will, if he attends to the poetry with which Milton has invested the play, come to see that this is true.

I think that a similar case can be made for Eliot's *Murder in the*

Cathedral, though I must concede that Eliot has cut it very fine. An attentive reading or a good production of the play will make the reader aware that the Thomas who is presented early in the play is not yet ready for martyrdom. True, Thomas thinks he has prepared himself. He has foreseen the three tempters. But the Fourth Tempter is indeed, as he tells us, unexpected, and Thomas himself is clearly shaken by the encounter and does not experience *his* rousing motions until after a further conflict.

But before attempting to get deeper into the problem of whether *Doctor Faustus* has a proper middle, it will be useful to make one or two general observations about the play. *Doctor Faustus* is a play about knowledge, about the relation of one's knowledge of the world to his knowledge of himself—about knowledge of means and its relation to knowledge of ends. It is a play, thus, that reflects the interests of the Renaissance and indeed that looks forward to the issues of the modern day. There is even an anticipation in the play, I should suppose, of the problem of the 'two cultures'. Faustus is dissatisfied and even bored with the study of ethics and divinity and metaphysics. What has captured his imagination is magic, but we must not be misled by the associations that that term now carries for most of us. The knowledge that Faustus wants to attain is knowledge that can be put to use—what Bertrand Russell long ago called power knowledge—the knowledge that allows one to effect changes in the world around him. When Faustus rejects philosophy and divinity for magic, he chooses magic because, as he says, the pursuit of magic promises "a world of profit and delight, / Of power, of honour, of omnipotence." He sums it up in saying: "A sound Magician is a mighty god." But if one does manage to acquire the technical knowledge that will allow one to "Wall all Germany with brass" or to beat a modern jet plane's time in flying in fresh grapes from the tropics, for what purpose is that technical knowledge to be used? How does this knowledge of means relate to one's knowledge of ends? Marlowe is too honest a dramatist to allow Faustus to escape such questions.

This last comment must not, however, be taken to imply that Marlowe has written a moral tract rather than a drama, or that he has been less than skilful in making Faustus's experiments with power-knowledge bring him, again and again, up against knowledge of a more ultimate kind. Marlowe makes the process seem natural and inevitable. For example, as soon as Faustus has signed the contract with the devil and has, by giving himself to hell, gained his new knowledge, his first question to Mephistopheles, rather naturally, has to do with the nature of the place to which he has consigned himself. He says: "First will I question with thee about hell, / Tell me, where is the place that men call hell?" In his reply, Mephistopheles explodes any notion of a local hell, and defines hell as a state of mind; but Faustus cannot believe his ears, and though getting his information from an impeccable source, indeed from the very horse's mouth, he refuses to accept the first fruits of his new knowledge. He had already come to the decision that stories of hell were merely "old wives' tales"—one supposes that this decision was a factor in his resolution to sell his soul. Yet when Mephistopheles says that he is an instance to prove the contrary since he is damned, and is even now in hell, Faustus cannot take in the notion. "How? Now in hell? / Nay and this be hell, I'll willingly be damned here. . . ."

The new knowledge that Faustus has acquired proves curiously unsatisfactory in other ways. For instance, Faustus demands a book in which the motions and characters of the planets are so truly set forth that, knowing these motions, he can raise up spirits directly and without the intervention of Mephistopheles. Mephistopheles at once produces the book, only to have Faustus say: "When I behold the heavens, then I repent / . . . Because thou has deprived me of those joys." Mephistopheles manages to distract Faustus from notions of repentance, but soon Faustus is once more making inquiries that touch upon the heavens, this time about astrology; and again, almost before he knows it, Faustus has been moved by his contemplation of the revolution of the spheres to a more ultimate question. "Tell me who made the world," he suddenly asks Mephistopheles, and this thought of the Creator once more wracks Faustus with a reminder of his damnation. Marlowe has throughout the play used the words *heaven* and *heavenly* in a tantalizingly double sense. *Heavenly* refers to the structure of the cosmos as seen from the earth, but it also has associations with the divine—the sphere from which Faustus has cut himself off.

Thus, technical questions about how nature works have a tendency to raise the larger questions of the Creator and the purposes of the creation. Faustus cannot be content—such is the education of a lifetime —or such was Marlowe's education, if you prefer—cannot be content with the mere workings of the machinery of the universe; he must push on to ask about ultimate purposes. Knowledge of means cannot be sealed off from knowledge of ends, and here Faustus's newly acquired knowledge cannot give him answers different from those he already knew before he forfeited his soul. The new knowledge can only forbid Faustus to dwell upon the answers to troubling questions that persist, the answers to which he knows all too well.

To come at matters in a different way, Faustus is the man who is all dressed up with no place to go. His plight is that he cannot find anything to do really worthy of the supernatural powers that he has come to possess. Faustus never carries out in practice his dreams of great accomplishments. He evidently doesn't want to wall all Germany with brass, or make the swift Rhine circle fair Wittenberg. Nor does he chase the Prince of Parma from Germany. Instead, he plays tricks on the Pope, or courts favour with the Emperor by staging magical shows for him. When he summons up at the Emperor's request Alexander the Great and his paramour, Faustus is careful to explain—Faustus in some sense remains to the end an honest man—that the Emperor will not be seeing "the true substantial bodies of those two deceased princes which long since are consumed to dust." The illusion is certainly life-like. Faustus has gone beyond a mere cinematic presentation to the feelings of Aldous Huxley— the Emperor is invited to go up and touch the wart on the Grecian paramour's neck—but even so, Alexander and his paramour are no more than apparitions. This magical world lacks substance.

With reference to the quality of Faustus's exploitations of his magical power, one may point out that Marlowe is scarcely answerable for some of the stuff that was worked into the middle of the play. Yet to judge only from the scenes acknowledged to be Marlowe's and from the ending that Marlowe devised for the play, it is inconceivable that Faustus should ever have carried out the grandiose plans which he mentions in Scene iii—such matters as making a bridge through the moving air so that bands of men can pass over the ocean, or joining the hills that bind the African shore to those of Spain. Faustus's basic motivation—his yearning for self-aggrandisement—ensures that the power he has gained will be used for what are finally frivolous purposes.

I have been stressing the author's distinction between the different kinds of knowledge that Faustus craves, and his careful pointing up of the inner contradictions that exist among these kinds of knowledge. I think that these matters are important for the meaning of the play, but some of you may feel that in themselves they scarcely serve to establish the requisite middle for the play. To note the confusions and contradictions in Faustus's quest for knowledge may make Faustus appear a more human figure and even a more modern figure. (I am entirely aware that my own perspective may be such as to make the play more "modern" than it is.) Yet, if Faustus is indeed doomed, the moment he signs, with his own blood, his contract with the devil, then there is no further significant action that he can take, and the rest of the play will be not so much dramatic as elegiac, as Faustus comes to lament the course that he has taken, or simply clinical, as we watch the writhings and inner torment of a character whose case is hopeless. Whether the case of Faustus becomes hopeless early in the play is, then, a matter of real consequence.

On a purely legalistic basis, of course, Faustus's case *is* hopeless. He has made a contract and he has to abide by it. This is the point that the devils insist on relentlessly. Yet there are plenty of indications that Faustus was not the prisoner of one fatal act. Before Faustus signs the bond, the good angel twice appears to him, first to beg him to lay his "Damned book aside" and later to implore him to beware of the 'execrable art' of magic. But even after Faustus has signed the bond, the good angel appears. In Scene vi he adjures Faustus to repent, saying: "Repent, yet God will pity thee." The bad angel, it is true, appears along with him to insist that "God cannot pity thee". But then the bad angel had appeared along with the good in all the early appearances too.

There are other indications that Faustus is not yet beyond the possibility of redemption. The devils, in spite of the contract, are evidently not at all sure of the soul of Faustus. They find it again and again necessary to argue with him, to bully him, and to threaten him. Mephistopheles evidently believes that it is very important to try to distract Faustus from his doleful thoughts. The assumption of the play is surely that the devils are anxious, and Mephistopheles in particular goes to a great deal of trouble to keep Faustus under control. There is never any assumption that the bond itself, signed with Faustus's blood, is quite sufficient to preserve him safe for hell. At least once, Lucifer himself has to be called in to ensure that Faustus will not escape. Lucifer appeals to Faustus's sense of logic by telling him that "Christ cannot save thy soul, for he is just, / There's none but I have interest in the same." But Lucifer employs an even more potent weapon: he terrifies Faustus, and as we shall see in Scene xiii, a crucial scene that occurs late in the play, Faustus has little defence against terror.

In Scene xiii, a new character appears, one simply called "an Old Man". He comes just in the nick of time, for Faustus, in his despair, is on the point of committing suicide, and Mephistopheles, apparently happy to make sure of Faustus's damnation, hands him a dagger. But the Old Man persuades Faustus to desist, telling him: "I see an angel hovers o'er thy head, / And with a vial full of precious grace, / Offers to pour the same into thy soul: / Then call for mercy, and avoid despair".

The Old Man has faith that Faustus can still be saved, and testifies to the presence of his good angel, waiting to pour out the necessary grace. But Faustus has indeed despaired. It may be significant that Faustus apparently does not see the angel now. At this crisis when, as Faustus says, "hell strives with grace for conquest in my breast", Mephistopheles accuses him of disobedience, and threatens to tear his flesh piecemeal. The threat is sufficient. A moment before, Faustus had addressed the Old Man as "my sweet friend". Now, in a sudden reversal, he calls Mephistopheles sweet—"Sweet Mephistopheles, intreat thy lord / To pardon my unjust presumption, / And with my blood again I will confirm / My former vow I made to Lucifer." The answer to Mephistopheles is interesting and even shocking. He tells Faustus: "Do it then quickly, with unfeigned heart, / Lest greater danger do attend thy drift." There is honour among thieves, among devils the appeal to loyalty and sincerity. "Unfeigned heart" carries ironically the very accent of Christian piety.

Faustus, for his part, shows himself, now perhaps for the first time, to be truly a lost soul. For he suddenly rounds upon the Old Man and beseeches Mephistopheles to inflict on him the "greatest torments that our hell affords". The pronoun is significant. Faustus now thinks of hell as "our hell", and the acceptance of it as part of himself and his desire to see the Old Man suffer mark surely a new stage in his development or deterioration. The shift-over may seem abrupt, but I find it credible in the total context, and I am reminded of what William Butler Yeats said about *his* Faustian play, *The Countess Cathleen*. The Countess, as you will remember, redeemed the souls of her people from the demons to whom they had sold their souls by selling her own. Many years after he had written the play, Yeats remarked that he had made a mistake, he felt, in his treatment of the Countess. As he put it in his *Autobiography*: "The Countess sells her soul, but [in the play] she is not transformed. If I were to think out that scene to-day, she would, the moment her hand has signed, burst into loud laughter, mock at all she has held holy, horrify the peasants in the midst of their temptations." Thus Yeats would have dramatized the commitments she had made. The comment is a valid one, and I think is relevant here. Yeats, in making the signing of the bond the decisive and effective act, is of course being more legalistic than is Marlowe, but he vindicates the psychology of the *volte face*. When Faustus does indeed become irrecoverably damned, he shows it in his conduct, and the change in conduct is startling. Faustus has now become a member of the devil's party in a sense in which he has not been before.

I think too that it is a sound psychology that makes Faustus demand at this point greater distractions and more powerful narcotics than he had earlier required. In the scene before this, it was enough for Faustus to call up the vision of Helen. Now he needs to possess her. And if this final abandonment to sensual delight calls forth the most celebrated poetry in the play, the poetry is ominously fitting. Indeed, the poetry here, for all of its passion, is instinct with the desperation of Faustus's plight. Helen's was the face "that launched a thousand ships and burnt the topless towers of Ilium". If the wonderful lines insist upon the transcendent power of a beauty that could command the allegiance of thousands, they also refer to the destructive fire that she set alight, and perhaps hint at the hell-fire that now burns for Faustus. After this magnificent invocation, Faustus implores Helen to make his soul immortal with a kiss, but his soul is already immortal, with an immortality that he would gladly—as he says in the last scene—lose if he could.

It may be worth pointing out that the sharpest inner contradictions in Faustus's thinking are manifest in the passage that we have just discussed. Faustus is so much terrified by Mephistopheles's threat to tear his flesh piecemeal that he hysterically courts the favour of Mephistopheles by begging him to tear the flesh of the Old Man. Yet Mephistopheles in his reply actually deflates the terror by remarking of the Old Man that "His faith is great, I cannot touch his soul". He promises to try to afflict the Old Man's body, but he observes with business-like candour that this kind of affliction amounts to little—it "is but little worth".

Perhaps the most powerful testimony in the play against any shallow legalistic interpretation of Faustus's damnation occurs in one of the earlier speeches of Mephistopheles. If Mephistopheles later in the play sees to it, by using distractions, by appealing to Faustus's sense of justice, by invoking terror, that Faustus shall not escape, it is notable that early in the play he testifies to the folly of what Faustus is proposing to do with his life.

When Faustus asks Mephistopheles why it was that Lucifer fell, Mephistopheles replies with complete orthodoxy and with even Christian eloquence: "Oh, by aspiring pride and insolence." When Faustus asks him "What are you that live with Lucifer?" Mephistopheles answers that he is one of the "unhappy spirits that fell with Lucifer", and that with Lucifer he is damned forever. It is at this point that Faustus, obsessed with the notion that hell is a place, expresses his astonishment that Mephistopheles can be said at this very moment to be in hell. Mephistopheles's answer deserves to be quoted in full:

> Why, this is hell, nor am I out of it:
> Think'st thou that I who saw the face of God,
> And tasted the eternal joys of Heaven,
> Am not tormented with ten thousand hells,
> In being deprived of everlasting bliss?
> Oh Faustus, leave these frivolous demands,
> Which strike a terror to my fainting soul.

Faustus is surprised that great Mephistopheles should be, as he puts it, "so passionate" on this subject, and the reader of the play may himself wonder that Mephistopheles can be so eloquent on the side of the angels—of the good angels, that is. But Marlowe has not been careless nor is he absent-minded. The psychology is ultimately sound. In this connection, two points ought to be observed. Though there is good reason to believe that Marlowe expected his audience to accept his devils as actual beings with an objective reality of their own and not merely as projections of Faustus's state of mind, in this play—as in any other sound and believable use of ghosts, spirits, and other such supernatural beings—the devils do have a very real relation to the minds of the persons to whom they appear. Though not necessarily merely projections of the characters' emotions, they are always in some sense mirrors of the inner states of the persons to whom they appear.

The second point to be observed is this: Faustus does learn something in the course of the play, and in learning it suffers change and becomes a different man. At the beginning of the play, he does seem somewhat naïve and jejune. He is fascinated by the new possibilities that his traffic with magic may open to him. Mephistopheles's use of the phrase "these frivolous demands" is quite justified. But in a sense, the very jauntiness with which he talks to Mephistopheles is proof that he is not yet fully damned, has not involved himself completely with the agents of evil. As the play goes on, he will lose his frivolousness: he will learn to take more and more seriously the loss of heaven. Yet at the same time, this very experience of deeper involvement in evil will make more and more difficult any return to the joys of heaven.

At any rate, there is a tremendous honesty as the play is worked out. Faustus may appear at times frivolous, but he is honest with himself. With all of his yearning for the state of grace that he has lost, he always acknowledges the strength of his desire for illicit pleasures and powers. At one point in the play, before he signed the fatal bond, Faustus says to himself that he will turn to God again. But immediately he dismisses the notion: "To God?" he asks incredulously, and then replies to himself: "He loves thee not, / The God thou servest is thine own appetite."

Most of all, however, Faustus is the prisoner of his own conceptions and indeed preconceptions. It is not so much that God has damned him at that he has damned himself. Faustus is trapped in his own legalism. The emphasis on such legalism seems to be a constant element in all treatments of the Faustian compact. It occurs in Yeats's *The Countess Cathleen*, when the devils, trusting in the letter of the law, are defeated and at the end find they have no power over the soul of the Countess. Legalism is also a feature of one of the most brilliant recent treatments of the story, that given by William Faulkner in *The Hamlet*.

Faustus's entrapment in legalism is easily illustrated. If the devils insist that a promise is a promise and a bond is a bond that has to be honoured—though it is plain that they are far from sure that the mere signing of the bond has effectively put Faustus's soul in their possession—Faustus himself is all too easily convinced that this is true. Apparently, he can believe in and understand a God of justice, but not a God of mercy. If Faustus's self-knowledge makes him say in Scene vi: "My heart's so hardened, I cannot repent," his sense of legal obligation makes him say in Scene xiii: "Hell calls for right, and with a roaring voice / Says, Faustus come, thine hour is come / And Faustus will come to do thee right." Even at this point the Old Man thinks that Faustus can still be saved. The good angel has reiterated that he might be saved. The devils themselves would seem to fear that Faustus even at the last might escape them: but Faustus himself is convinced that he cannot be saved and his despair effectually prevents any action which would allow him a way out.

In one sense, then, this play is a study in despair. But the despair does not paralyze the imagination of Faustus. He knows constantly what is happening to him. He reports on his state of mind with relentless honesty. And at the end of the play, in tremendous poetry, he dramatizes for us what it is to feel the inexorable movement toward the abyss, not numbed, not dulled with apathy, but with every sense quickened and alert. (Kurtz, in Conrad's *Heart of Darkness*, shows these qualities. He is damned, knows that he's damned, indeed flees from redemption, but never deceives himself about what is happening, and mutters, "The horror, the horror.")

One may still ask, however, whether these changes that occur in Faustus's soul are sufficient to constitute a middle. Does Faustus act? Is there a sufficient conflict? Is Faustus so incapacitated for choice that he is a helpless victim and not a conscious re-agent with circumstance?

Yet, one must not be doctrinaire and pedantic in considering this concept of decisive action. As T.S. Eliot put it in *Murder in the Cathedral*, suffering is action and action is suffering. Faustus's suffering is not merely passive: he is constantly reaffirming at deeper and deeper levels his original rash tender of his soul to Lucifer. Moreover, if Faustus's action amounts in the end to suffering, the suffering is not meaningless. It leads to knowledge—knowledge of very much the same sort as that which Milton's Adam acquired in *Paradise Lost*—"Knowledge of good bought dear by knowing ill"—and through something of the same process. Early in the play, Mephistopheles told him: "Think so still till experience change thy mind." Perhaps this is the best way in which to describe the "middle" of the play: the middle consists of the experiences that do change Faustus's mind so that in the end he knows what hell is and has become accommodated to it, now truly damned.

My own view is that the play does have a sufficient middle, but this is not to say that it is not a play of a rather special sort—and that its dependence upon its poetry—though a legitimate dependence, I would insist—is very great.

There is no need to praise the poetry of the wonderful last scene, but I should like to make one or two brief observations about it. The drama depends, of course, upon Faustus's obsession with the clock and his sense of time's moving on inexorably, pushing him so swiftly to the final event. But this final scene really grows integrally out of the play. The agonized and eloquent clock-watching matches perfectly the legalism which has dominated Faustus from the beginning of the play. What Faustus in effect tries to do is to hold back the hand of the clock, not to change his relation to God. Incidentally, what Faustus does not notice is that like Mephistopheles earlier, he himself is now already in hell. The coming of the hour of twelve can hardly bring him into greater torment than that which now possesses him and which the poetry he utters so powerfully bodies forth.

Everybody has commented on Marlowe's brilliant use of the quotation from Ovid: "O lente, lente, currite noctis equi," in the *Amores* words murmured by the lover to his mistress in his wish that the night of passion might be prolonged, in this context so jarringly ironic. But the irony is not at all factitious. The scholar who now quotes the lines from Ovid in so different a context is the same man who a little earlier had begged the phantasm of Helen to make his soul immortal with a kiss. Now, in his agony, he demands of himself: "Why wert thou not a creature wanting soul? / Or, why is this immortal that thou hast?"

Again, the great line, "See, see where Christ's blood streams in the firmament," echoes a significant passage much earlier in the play. (I do not insist that the reader has to notice it, or that Marlowe's audience would have necessarily been aware of the echo, but I see no reason why we should not admire it if we happen upon it ourselves or if someone calls it to our attention.) When Faustus prepares to sign the document that will consign his soul to the devil, he finds that he must sign in blood, and he pierces his arm to procure the sanguine ink. But his blood will hardly trickle from his arm, and he interprets his blood's unwillingness to flow as follows: "What might the staying of my blood portend? / Is it unwilling I should write this bill? / Why streams it not, that I might write afresh?" His own blood, in an instinctive horror, refuses to stream for his damnation. Now, as he waits for the clock to strike twelve, he has a vision of Christ's blood *streaming* in the firmament for man's salvation. But in his despair he is certain that Christ's blood does not stream for his salvation.

In short, the magnificent passage in the final scene bodies forth the experience of Faustus in a kind of personal *dies irae*, but it is not a purple patch tacked on to the end of a rather amorphous play. Rather, the great outburst of poetry finds in the play a supporting context. It sums up the knowledge that Faustus has bought at so dear a price, and if it is the expression of a creature fascinated with, and made eloquent by, horror, it is still the speech of a man who, for all of his terror, somehow preserves his dignity. Faustus at the end is still a man, not a cringing wretch. The poetry saves him from abjectness. If he wishes to escape from himself, to be changed into little water drops, to be swallowed up in the great ocean of being, he maintains to the end—in spite of himself, in spite of his desire to blot out his personal being—his individuality of mind, the special quality of the restless spirit that aspired. This retention of his individuality is at once his glory and his damnation.

A. BARTLETT GIAMATTI

The Arts of Illusion

George Sabellicus was pleased to call himself, a contemporary tells us in 1507, "the younger Faust, the chief of necromancers, astrologer, the second magus, palmist, diviner with water and fire, second in the art of divination by water." But even this billing did not smooth the way, for Dr. Faust, as Sabellicus came to be called, was constantly forced to move on. City after city, nervously or defiantly, expelled him. It had always been so for the man called to the arts of illusion.

From antiquity through the seventeenth century, if no farther, the mummer, the mime, the juggler, the actor, the mountebank, the magician, even the scientist as astrologer or alchemist—all were suspect for their solitary or their irregular lives. But even more, they were profoundly distrusted for ther varying and various capacities for irreverence. By irreverence, I mean not only their blasphemous conditions and conversation; I mean essentially their abilities to imitate and to transform, their gifts for changing shape and surpassing limits in ways which seemed to threaten Divine plan or Divinity itself. The historical Faust played to all these fears. By the time he disappears as an actual figure, around 1540, even his name has changed from George to Johann Faust—a harmless image within the historical records of his alleged sinister powers to manipulate appearances.

The Faust story is a product of the Protestant Reformation when, in Germany, men saw clearly the price of sin, the power of evil, and above all the limits of man. It was a time when the religious impulse, always ambiguous and now obsessed with purity and reform, precipitated out and identified its own darker side, the urge to magic and deformation.

From *The Yale Review* (1972). Copyright © 1972 by Yale University Press.

The Faust story is a Reformation story because it implies deformation as the result of any human impulse beyond or outside the strictly interpreted norm.

The Faust story sees both reformation and deformation as springing from the same source: the impulse to be at one with God—the difference being that the former results from submission to God, the latter from trying, like Faust, to assume Godhead. But the Faust story has even deeper roots than the Reformation. It draws its radical potency from that great Renaissance (and hence modern) myth which says that spiritual reformation and deformation derive from man's innate power of formation, the capacity of the self to shape the self. The Faust story is firmly rooted in Renaissance man's profound conviction that he is a Proteus, that he can remake or change or transform himself.

The problem in this attitude, a problem crystallized by the Faust story, is this: Given man's basic urge and potential for transformation, would man re-form himself in a good sense and be one of the blest, or would he de-form himself and become a monster? What shape would he fashion for himself? Would he be Hyperion, or a satyr? Both were in him. Finally, once he unleashed the process of transformation, could he stop it? This was the most haunting question of all, and is the issue in *Doctor Faustus*.

> we must now perform
> The form of Faustus' fortunes, good or bad.

So the chorus to Marlowe's play. And here Renaissance art offers itself as one solution to the massive ambiguities of Renaissance life. Performing is one way of forming, for the theatre can safely release the human desire for new shapes. It provides an arena for limitless aspiration and multiple shapes while containing this impulse within the physical limits of the theatre and the arbitrary structure of art. This is no final answer, because now the theatre becomes simply a public image, a public language, for man's private agonies. "The great Globe" is a theatrical place and an individual's head, and both are reservoirs in their way for the energy to change and to remake human form. Both are dangerous places. The final solution is to purify the mind and the place; it is to have another Reformation, a Puritan Revolution, and close down the theatres. You return to radical principles, write a poem justifying the ways of God to man, and go back to calling Faustus Satan or Eve. But that was all ahead. In the early 1590's, the theatre was still being fashioned as the medium for manageable metamorphosis. And Marlowe takes a giant step when he transforms the material from the English translation (1592) of the German

Faustbuch (1587) into a play about how the splendid urge to aspire to new form can deform past salvation if the shape you want is that of God Himself.

Renaissance man felt he had the power to transform himself because he had the power of language. Words were units of energy. Through words man could assume forms and aspire to shapes and states otherwise beyond his reach. Words had this immense potency, this virtue, because they were derived from and were images of the Word, the Word of God which made us and which was God. Used properly, words could shape us in His image, and lead us to salvation. Through praise, in its largest sense, our words approach their source in the Word and, therefore, we approach Him.

Because words, like men, were fallen, however, they contained, as we do, shapes of evil within them. Fallen words, like men, are unstable elements; thus they are, as we are, such dangers to us. As we must always check that impulse to deformation in ourselves, so we must constantly be aware of the beast in language—Spenser calls it the Blatant Beast, whose rabid bite is vicious slander—and we must know that when we unleash a word and let it soar, we run the risk of loosing an evil force as well, one that we cannot control. We, as men using words, must stay within our limits, or what we master may master and misshape us.

This is simply to say that the power of words and the power in words reflect our fallen state—above the beasts, below the angels, and capable of assuming either form. As a power, language is neither good nor bad. It all depends upon how we convert this energy, upon how we transform this power, in the mind with the mind. We are what we are depending upon how we shape ourselves with words; depending on whether we use words as God intended us to use them, or we use words to set ourselves up in His place and assume His knowledge and power.

Because all men are users of the magic power, language, because all men are performers with words and transformers through words, the Renaissance could figure all men under the single image of the *magus*, the magician. And as there were two ways of using language to project new shapes, a good and a bad, the Renaissance distinguished two kinds of *magus*. One is the "goetic" or black magician. This is Faustus, or Spenser's Archimago, or—in his own fashion—Iago, who imposes a nightmare on the island of Love, Cyprus, and who transforms the shape of Desdemona in the head of Othello. The other kind of *magus* and magic is represented by the "natural" or white magician. In harmless form, this is Puck, who can take whatever shape he wants—"Sometime a horse I'll be, sometime a hound, / a hog, a headless bear, sometime a fire"—but whose power to transform finally will amend and harmonize all the divisions of love and the law. In Spenser's *Faerie Queene*, opposed to Archimago, there is Merlin in Book III who can project in his magic glass the true shape of love in Britomart's Artegall. Finally, there is the great white magician of Elizabethan literature, Prospero, who controls not only form and substance in Ariel and Caliban, and fashions justice and love, but who also can recognize the limits of his art and drown his book. This knowledge of white Prospero—where his knowledge stops—is acquired by black Faustus much too late.

In the black and white magicians, the Renaissance poets and thinkers saw concentrated the black dangers and the white glories of that single power, language, and that single urge, self-transformation. In the *magus*, they saw man; through the One, they perceived the Many. Therefore Renaissance Faustus differs from all those other magicians who stand behind him in grand and receding array, Roger Bacon and Piero d'Albano (*Doctor Faustus* I. i. 155), the medieval Virgil (III. i. 13), the sinister sorcerer Simon Magus, who offered to buy the power of the Holy Ghost (Acts viii:9–24; the apocryphal Acts of Peter), for Faustus is not simply doing tricks or trying to buy magic power. Faustus is any of us, any man using (and misusing) power in the quest for all knowledge and total control. Faustus is no trickster; he is modern man who would play the role of God.

In our play, the warring impulses for good and evil in the mind of everyman are visualized by the Good and Bad angels which hover around Faustus. Again, the single human head is the source for the double drive. And when we first meet those angels, the first words of the Good angel are:

> O, Faustus, lay that damnèd book aside,
> And gaze not on it. . . .
> Read, read the Scriptures. That is blasphemy.
> (I. i. 71–74)

Here, at the outset, is an indication of the way the play is a battle of books. We see how the deepest issue in the play is words, the language of black magic versus the language of Scripture. We see how the power of words to shape for good or ill, and how that power is used and how that power can use you, is the pivot on which the play turns. We see how, at bottom, the problem of language remains.

Throughout his career, as he struggled to shape a new idiom for the nascent English stage, Marlowe wrestled with the multiform angel (or demon) of language. He made his problem as a playwright the subject of his plays. He expanded the limits of the stage by writing of the human mind in its battle to surpass human limitation. He used soaring words as symbols of man's aspiring mind. And he used the lurking dangers in words to image the terrors of aspiring too far.

Only *Doctor Faustus* fully exploits the glories and terrors in language to illuminate the full ambiguity of the human condition, though even as early as *Hero and Leander* one can hear Marlowe exploring through words the terrain of human potential, its mountain peaks and dark ravines:

> And fruitful wits that in aspiring are,
> Shall discontent, run into regions farre.
>
> (I. 477–278)

In the earlier days, however, the emphasis is heavily on man's mind as it soars beyond human limits—the dangers are not at issue yet—and thus the emphasis is on what language can do and not yet on what it can do to you. So we hear of the "aspiring mind" of Tamburlaine, and of his "conquering mind," whose foil is Bajazeth's "conquered head." Marlowe's great heroes all live in the present participle and the future tense. So in *Edward II* we hear of Mortimer's "virtue that aspires to heaven," but because we hear of it as he goes to prison, the ambiguities begin to emerge. And the ambiguities of the human condition are fully clear when we hear the Duke of Guise, whose "aspiring thoughts aim at the crown" (*The Massacre at Paris*, xix.24):

> That I like best that flies beyond my reach.
> Set me to scale the highest pyramidès
> And thereon set the diadem of France;
> I'll either rend it with my nails to naught
> Or mount the top with my aspiring wings,
> Although my downfall be the deepest hell.
>
> (ii. 42–47)

There is what the Marlovian hero always knows: that his superb urge to transcend may also damn him deep.

Even more interesting is the image of Icarus submerged in the metaphor of flight in the last two lines. This myth fascinated Marlowe all his life, for like winged words themselves, it was another way of imaging the glories and terrors of transcendence. We first meet Icarus in Marlowe's earliest play, *Dido Queen of Carthage*, when Dido passionately laments Aeneas' parting:

> I'll frame me wings of wax like Icarus,
> And o'er his ships will soar unto the sun,
> That they may melt and I fall in his arms.
>
> (v. i. 243–245)

Dido will be Icarus so that she may fall, but later in the words of the Duke of Guise Marlowe exploits the myth as an image of the act of reaching per se and he comes back to Icarus one last time—if *Doctor Faustus* is his last play—in the chorus' description of Faustus, who excelled in theological disputes:

> Till swoll'n with cunning of a self-conceit,
> His waxen wings did mount above his reach,
> And melting, heavens conspired his overthrow.
>   (Prol. 20–22)

To say the Icarus myth has informed the substance of Marlowe's plays all along is a way of suggesting that Faustus, under various guises, has been all Marlowe's study. I am not implying Marlowe knew about Faust before he wrote of Faustus, though he may have, nor that Marlowe writes the same play over and over, for in crucial ways they are different. What I am suggesting is that in *Doctor Faustus* Marlowe's life-long obsessions with the language of aspiration found their perfect vehicle. However, there is another sense in which *Doctor Faustus* reveals Marlowe's life-long absorption in problems of language, and that emerges throughout the plays not in a Faust-like figure, but in a Faust pattern.

By Faust pattern, I mean that the crucial act in the Faust story is the consummation of a pact which promises a soul for twenty-four years of omnipotence. And in all the plays a pact or pledge has a critical role by representing that limit which the hero either rejects or overreaches. In *Dido*, it is the marriage pledge (Marlowe makes much of what his Virgilian source says is only a figment of Dido's imagination), which Aeneas superhumanly ignores to Dido's despair; in *I Tamburlaine*, there are Zenocrates' letters of safe conduct from the Great Cham himself which Tamburlaine, as his first act before us, countermands to prove himself "a greater man"; in *The Jew of Malta*, there are two pacts: the decrees Barabas refuses to sign which then deprive him of his goods (and goad him on) and the pledge between him and the Governor to betray the Turk, which both plan to break. In *Edward II*, the King is forced to sign a document banishing Gaveston, and in *The Massacre at Paris*, various pacts in the form of letters propel the Duke of Guise to his excesses, but none so much as the pledge of marriage—the "union and religious league"—between the King of Navarre and Margaret.

It would serve no purpose to push this pattern, if pattern it is, too hard. Still it is striking that in each play the hero defines himself and his role (or roles), his form and his performance, in terms of what for a better term we can call a verbal institution—some pact or pledge, letter, contract, or decree, whose validity as binding the hero at some point denies and which he tries to overcome. In all the plays, words supply a limit which the heroes' language attempts to supersede, an image of the mind trying to surpass our human limitations.

In *Doctor Faustus*, the verbal institution Faustus wants to overcome is language itself, language as it codifies, regulates, controls. And simply with his words, he can do this. He can send his words past the limits of other men's knowledge and control. But while his words are soaring, what about his deeds? What about the issue, the shapes, created by those flying words? If language is the power to form new realities, what are they? At the beginning of his career, with *Tamburlaine*, Marlowe saw no problem. "Go stout Theridamas; thy words are swords," says Mycetes. We change words to swords by prefixing an *s*, and for Tamburlaine things were almost that easy. He needed only to say he was a King to be one. In *Tamburlaine*, there is no gap between word and deed, no tragic lag between what you want and what you can have. But Tamburlaine is a figure of romance, the shepherd who becomes a knight and gets the girl. By the end of his career Marlowe had thought hard on our fallen state, and language; and tragedy, not romance, is the result.

In *Doctor Faustus*, the gap between word and deed widens and widens until it yawns like the mouth of Hell. As Faustus' language soars higher, the products of language—events, shapes, actions—become lower and lower, in the sense of trivial, in the sense of approaching Hell. What his words express and what they effect could not be more tragically separated. As we witness the widening gap between the mental spectacle the words conjure and the theatrical spectacle actually unfolding, between the way one thing is said and a very different effect is communicated or results, we see how Marlowe dramatizes the terrible ambiguities in the power of self-transformation through the magic of words.

First, the difference between what Faustus' words say and what his words actually do. In I.i. we find Faustus alone in his study, about to "settle" his studies. He then speaks for some sixty-five lines. Now, according to his own words, he is a most learned man and very deep thinker; but according to what we see as a result of his words, Faustus has very patchy learning and a superficial mind. For while his words tell us he has soared above all organized human knowledge, they actually show us deep ignorance, particularly in the simple and central matters of the soul.

For instance, when Faustus dismisses Philosophy at line 10—he has attained its end; when he considers Medicine, finds it wanting, and dismisses it at line 27; when he says Law is all "paltry legacies," "external trash," and waves it away at line 36; and when he regards Theology and then, in the first of many unintentionally sinister puns (and there resides the issue of the play) bids it "adieu" at line 49—when he is saying all this, what do we actually see? When he says Philosophy is limited, we see a man who confounds Aristotle and Peter Ramus, a man who treats the deep questions of being and not being and the technique of disputing well as if they were the same. When he says Medicine is limited, we see a man who confuses gold and health, alchemy and physic, and who finds medicine wanting because it is not miracle, a lack he will remedy by turning to magic, miracle's parody. The soaring language does not offer us an ennobling spectacle; rather, the opposite.

When Faustus dismisses Law, something more sinister commences. To prove Law is really only legalism, Faustus quotes Justinian twice in Latin. In the first citation, Faustus misquotes Justinian. But if the ironic spectacle of misquoting what you claim is far beneath you were not enough, further ironies attend the second citation, which is: "The father cannot disinherit the son except . . ." (line 31). Faustus leaves the citation unfinished, but the rest of the play completes it. God the Father cannot disinherit man His son except when the man chooses to will his soul to Satan. What Faustus considers legalistic trash far beneath his soaring mind is in reality an abiding principle which eludes his grasp.

Nowhere does Marlowe's technique of having Faustus dismiss a body of knowledge by a partial quotation have more devastating effect than in Faustus' denial of Theology. Faustus says Theology only teaches that we must sin and die, thus *che serà, serà*, and he wants no part of a doctrine whose lesson is that necessity hangs over us. Nowhere do we see his limitations through his statements of mastery more clearly than here and in his citations from Scripture. He cites, in Latin, Romans vi:23, "The wages of sin is death," but as with Justinian's words he fails to finish the line: "But the gift of God is eternal life through Jesus Christ our Lord." He cites the first Epistle of John, "If we say we have no sin, we deceive ourselves, and there is no truth within us," but he fails to finish the passage, "If we confess our sins he is faithful and just to forgive us our sins, and to cleanse us from all unrighteousness." It is certainly to convert, and abuse, the power of the Word through one's own words when the Bible is misshaped to justify turning to "heavenly" "necromantic books." The play's techniques and issues are concentrated in this first speech and projected into the rest of the drama. The more Faustus transforms himself into a god through language, looking down on all human experience and knowledge, the more we see his very words transform him into something foolish, ignorant, superficial; the more Faustus tells of total mastery, the more we see a process of enslavement. Finally, we begin to understand how

Marlowe's irony operates through the techniques of partial citation; for when Faustus only partially quotes Justinian or the Bible, language releases a meaning which Faustus does not pursue but which throughout the action of the play pursues Faustus. That is the problem with language, and is the issue Marlowe probes.

Faustus has dismissed Philosophy, Medicine, Law, and Theology. He has embraced the "metaphysics of magicians." Then he exclaims:

> A sound magician is a demi-god.
> Here try thy brains to get a deity!
> Wagner—

Here are those crucial lines where Faustus says in effect that through magic he will assume powers only God has. Immense and potent lines. Then, "Wagner"—and Wagner, his servant and disciple, enters. The joke is verbally juxtaposing "deity" and "Wagner"; the joke is visually juxtaposing mighty Faustus and foolish Wagner, calling upon godhead and getting a goon. The terrifying implications of this process (and scene) develop in Act II.ii, when Faustus cries out to Christ, and Lucifer springs up. But that is tragedy, and later. This is still funny—challenging Heaven and getting Wagner—and here, in I.i, we really initiate the subplot.

The function of a subplot is to burlesque the concerns of a main plot by mirroring those concerns in lower form; not simply to reduce mighty concerns to absurdity but also to show us that no man's mighty self is immune to human fallibility, to foolishness, to flaw. The subplot is the great equalizer, savagely reducing or gently jesting the main concerns as the dramatist sees fit. The subplot's ironic spectacle and perspective make it a crucial element in *Doctor Faustus*, and in Act I, Marlowe introduces us to its uses. In Scene ii, Wagner and the two scholars, but mostly Wagner, burlesque Faustus and his two accomplices in magic in Scene i; in Scene iv, the actions of Wagner and Robin, the clown, provide farcical, shrewd commentary on Faustus and Mephistophilis in Scene iii. In Act II, the subplot begins to provide more than burlesque.

Scenes i and ii of Act II show us Faustus assuming the awesome powers of the devil, and at the end of Scene ii Lucifer gives Faustus a gift: "peruse this book and view it thoroughly, and thou shalt turn thyself into what shape thou wilt." But we really only understand the implications of this Satanic gift of words which shape when immediately in the following scene, Robin and Dick enter with one of Faustus' conjuring books. They mumble and jumble, parodying what has just preceded, and then make for a tavern where we meet them again three scenes later at Act III.iii. There, the Vintner searches them for a stolen cup. Robin decides to conjure. And Mephistophilis appears. This is suddenly no joke. As Mephistophilis is the first to say:

> To purge this rashness of this cursèd deed,
> First be thou turned to this ugly shape,
> For apish deeds transformed to an ape. . . .
> Be thou transformed to a dog, and carry him upon thy back.
>
> (40–42, 45)

The two clowns go off chattering and baying: in the devil's word, and by his word, transformed.

Here in the midst of farce, something serious has happened. The subplot's burlesque of the main plot's mighty concerns has been gradually acquainting us, in visual terms, with the way foolish shapes are latent in Faustus' aspiring words. But with the appearance of Mephistophilis at Robin's conjuring, this larger issue is clarified. We suddenly see clearly the way language releases meaning the user—here the clown—cannot control, and the way this meaning—here Mephistophilis—shapes or transforms the user. We see the transformer transformed, precisely what was suggested on the basis of Faustus' opening speech would happen to Faustus by the end. The seemingly simple contrast of subplot and main plot leads back to the central problem of the play: how the power to shape—language—can also misshape. And we have been led to this because the clown, transformed, is only a version of what Faustus, mighty magician, will become.

Or, indeed, what Faustus is rapidly becoming before our eyes. For there is that ever-growing split between Faustus' mighty words and his trivial deeds, between the shapes his language envisions and the shapes it actually creates. This larger movement, like the subplot which it parallels and meets in Act IV, begins in Faustus' second long speech in Act I.i, just after Wagner has appeared.

Beginning at line 79, we see the way Faustus' words fly up while their effects remain below. Faustus says he will create spirit servants. They will fly to India—for gold; ransack oceans—for pearls; search the corners of the earth—for fruits and delicacies. His servants will read him strange philosophies—and tell him royal secrets; they will dress schoolboys in silk, and invent new war machines. Here indeed is the language of aspiration— and the spectacle of naked appetite. Superb words—which show a taste for jewels, food, gossip, fashion, grim destruction. While we hear the flying words, we also see a man changing himself, through those words, from a magician to a dabbler in luxury to a general agent of death.

And when, over the course of the play, we see what Faustus does with those splendid powers; when we see how Faustus only uses them to vex the Pope and his retinue (III.i–ii), produce a dumbshow and put horns on a courtier (IV.ii), fool a fop with a false head (IV.iii) and a horse-courser with a false horse and leg (IV.v), and gather grapes for a pregnant Duchess (IV.vii)—then we see that what Faustus does with his power totally undercuts what we heard Faustus claim for his power. But not only does the power to be a god make trivia; much worse, that very power makes Faustus trivial. Over the play, the magician metamorphoses himself to a court jester, a fool. The process dramatized in the language of Act I.i is dramatized in the spectacle of the whole play.

The overall effect of this process is to trivialize everything, finally to trivialize main plot to the level of subplot. We see this happening when the characters of the subplot begin to enter the main plot—Wagner entering after Faustus gulls the horse-courser; Robin and Dick talking to the horse-courser and carter about Faustus' mighty deeds, like turning horses to hay. This merging of the two levels of life is completed in IV.vii when, after Faustus brings off his last piece of tremendous trivia—grapes for the Duchess—Robin, Dick, and Company burst in and one by one Faustus charms them dumb. Now subplot is main plot; there is no difference. With his power to gain a deity, Faustus has reduced the world to its lowest level. Instead of learning the secrets of the universe, he has turned reality to farce. Finally, even the power of language, the power of transformation, is itself dramatically trivialized before our eyes when, without a word, Faustus denies the gulls the power of speech. That mighty power of language is so abused it no longer even communicates on a simple level; it only produces silence in the mouths of fools.

When we ponder the spectacle of the last scene, V.ii, in comparison with the statement of I.i, we notice that we see at the end precisely what we heard at the beginning. In both scenes, a universe, an unlimited existence, is unfolded. But, of course, similarities only underscore differences, and here the difference between the scenes is all the world. Where at the outset Faustus was a creator, at the end he is a creature; where before he dreamed of unlimited power and glory, now he is assured of limitless torment.

The words by which he reshaped himself into a demi-god at the beginning have now exploded into horror all about him. What we see on stage are the contents of his head—the Hell he will possess forever, the Heaven he will shortly lose. He brought it on himself, this deformed world, when he converted, when he turned to magic from God, when he turned the power of words from God's praise to his own. It does him no good to shriek "I'll burn my books" at the very end. The power in his books has swallowed him, and he is now himself only a misshapen symbol, another occult sign, in Satan's ledger.

More than any other play, Marlowe's *Doctor Faustus* celebrates that God-like power of language, and shows us how words can soar, and tempts us to dizzying heights within our heads. But all the time, Marlowe is in control. He knows too much about the shaping power of words to be a Faustus. Marlowe is a *magus* too, all poets are, but one who tells us in this play to use that awesome power of words to fashion ourselves in God's image. Else, like his hero, we will be deformed by the servant we abuse.

ERICH SEGAL

Marlowe's "Schadenfreude": Barabas as Comic Hero

A broad-shouldered man clubs a scrawny cripple. The victim staggers in pain, bleeds, begins to weep. Far from being a police report of felonious assault, this is an objective account of the first stimulus to human laughter in the history of Western literature. Though the modern sensibility may recoil at the thought of such brutality as "comedy," Homer is unequivocal in reporting the delight of the Greek leaders when Odysseus beats Thersites: "Though sad and homesick, they laughed with pleasure at him" (*Iliad* 2.270).

Several theorists of the comic could explain this laughter from a psychological standpoint, but it is important to recognize that not a few would decry it from a moral standpoint. We think immediately of Plato, an enemy of laughter in general and Homeric laughter in specific. How wrong of the gods to enjoy "unquenchible laughter" at the sight of the crippled Hephaistos. Cruelty should never be a laughing matter, argues Socrates in the *Philebus* (49D) and Aristotle in the *Nichomachean Ethics* (IV.8.3). In the *Poetics* (V.1–2), Aristotle draws the line at what is properly ludicrous: we may laugh at a kind of ugliness which is "neither painful nor harmful." And yet Aristotle's own prescription might well justify the amusement at Thersites' expense, since he was "the ugliest man who came to Ilium" (2.216). Besides, even Socrates allows that we may rejoice at the misfortunes of those we hate. And barely hidden beneath the moralizing in both Plato and Aristotle is the implicit concession that, however ethically reprehensible, people *do* laugh at their friends' misfortunes.

It is almost universally accepted that comedy provides an inward release for various antisocial instincts; even Plato grants this. But one finds less willingness to acknowledge that among the instincts satisfied is man's inherent thirst for cruelty. That man is innately hostile has always been a more difficult notion to accept than the idea that he is innately erotic. Alfred Adler first posited the "agression drive" in 1908 ("every individual really exists in a state of permanent agression"), but Freud fought the concept for twenty years until, in *Civilization and Its Discontents*, he finally conceded its validity: "The bit of truth behind all this— one so eagerly denied—is that men are not gentle, friendly creatures wishing for love, who simply defend themselves if they are attacked, but that a powerful measure of desire for aggression has to be reckoned as part of their instinctual endowment . . . *homo homini lupus*." Later in the essay, Freud restates this even more emphatically: "The tendency to aggression is an innate, independent, instinctual disposition in man, and . . . it constitutes the most powerful obstacle to culture."

Considering how difficult this was for modern psychologists to accept, one more readily understands the moral indignation of the ancient philosophers at the raising of brutal laughter. Moreover, Aristotle's position was distorted by subsequent misinterpretations. Sir Phillip Sidney saw the philosopher as forbidding "laughter in sinful things," and Ben Jonson even argues that Aristotle was against laughter of any kind: "[it is] a kind of turpitude, that depraves some part of man's nature without a disease." We are but one small step from the ultimate agelastic attitude, which Chesterfield urges upon his son—that he never laugh at all in his entire life.

But Sidney notwithstanding, the very essence of laughter is "sinful things," the more hostile the better. Freud observes that the closer we are to the original aggression, the greater the comic delight. Of course none of this is new. The modern view of laughter-as-aggression subtends the Hobbesian "sudden glory" theory which, by the nineteenth century, as W. K. Wimsatt recounts, "became crudified through various physiological, psychological and primitivistic analogies." Mr. Wimsatt questions the worth of inquiries along these lines:

> Why do I laugh . . . when an old peddler stumbles and spills his pencils all over the street? I don't know. Maybe I don't laugh. But a Fiji Islander would! He will laugh when a prisoner is being roasted alive in an oven! Confident proclamations about the nature of anthropoid laughter are invested with importance by equally confident assumptions that reduc-

tion to the lowest common factor is the right way of proceeding. . . .
Are such theories of hidden elements and forgotten origins supposed to
increase my appreciation of jokes or comic situations?

The argument of the present essay dissents somewhat from Wimsatt's
view, believing that there can be value in recalling "forgotten origins" of
ancient stimuli to laughter. The answer to "why they laughed" may
provide many insights to literatures of the past. There is a ready case in
point right from Wimsatt's essay. His example of the blind peddler recalls a
famous incident in Spanish literature, when Lazarillo de Tormes tricks his
blind master into jumping into a post, causing very painful injury: "da con
la cabeza en el poste, que sonó tan recio como si diera con una gran
calabaza, y cayó luego para atrás medio muerto y hendida la cabeza."

However it may affect us today, this episode was enormously
popular in sixteenth-century Spain and was imitated by other writers in
prose and song. It may even have been a part of the folklore well before it
found its way into the Lazarillo novel. Suffice it to say that at the time,
this cruel trick earned as much admiration for Lazarillo as the beating of
Thersites did for that proto-picaro, Odysseus.

Naturally times change, and likewise objects of laughter. Our
greater "civilization" may come to reject certain brutalities as too painful
to be risible, and the Lazarillo incident may be one of them. Emotion is
ever and always the foe of laughter. And yet every age produces new
cruelties and new possibilities for comic *Schadenfreude*. In the preface to
Joseph Andrews, Fielding discusses the limits, in fact, the *ne plus ultra* of the
Ridiculous: "What could exceed the Absurdity of an Author who should
write 'The Comedy of Nero, with the *merry* Incident of ripping up his
Mother's Belly'; or what would give a greater shock to humanity . . ." But
in 1742 de Sade was still in swaddling clothes, the childish brutalities of
Jarry's King Ubu were more than a century away, and the Absurdity of
"The Comedy of Nero" would be exceeded in 1959 by *Oh Dad, Poor Dad,
Mamma's Hung You in the Closet and I'm Feelin' So Sad*. Martin Esslin
recently observed that the spirit of von Masoch has become increasingly
congenial to modern comedy. And who could have imagined a comedy
that would invite us to relish the annihilation of the human race? But
then who could have imagined that the absurd optimism of Dr. Pangloss
would be surpassed by the insouciant glee of Dr. Strangelove?

But since our concern is cruelty in comedy past, it will be useful to
examine several stories which are told in a "framed" context and include
the reaction of a fictive audience. The Eighth Day of Boccaccio's *Decameron*
contains many tales of brutality, much of it perpetrated by two rogues,

Bruno and Buffalmacco, "uomino sollazzevoli molto, ma per altro avveduti e sagaci." In the third story, they dupe Calandrino, hit him with stones till he whines in pain, and then abandon him, "con le maggior risa del mondo." The victim then vents his frustration by brutally beating his wife. Boccaccio's fictive listeners welcome this story with great delight. Their reaction is even more enthusiastic for the ninth tale, in which Bruno and Buffalmacco victimize one Maestro Simone, a dimwitted doctor, finally hurling him down a latrine. This malodorous mayhem evokes enormous laughter: "Quanto la novella . . . facesse le donne ridere, non è da domandare: niuna ve n'era a cui per soperchio riso non fossero dodici volte le lagrime venute in su gli occhi."

And yet there are limits. The seventh tale of this same Day, the cruel revenge wrought by the scholar Rinieri on a woman who scorned him, evokes icy silence. Unlike Panurge's revenge upon the haughty Parisienne, this tale engages our pity. As Bergson explains, "to produce the whole of its effect . . . the comic demands something like a momentary anesthesia of the heart. Its appeal is to the intelligence, pure and simple."

The *Canterbury Tales* afford another opportunity to study the success or failure of comic *Schadenfreude* on an audience. For example, Oswald the Reeve tells a lusty tale which involves aggressive sexuality: two scholars "swyve" the wife and daughter of a miller as revenge for his having shortchanged them. At the end there is much physical violence:

> And on the nose he smoot hym with his fest
> Doun ran the blody streem upon his brest.
> (4275–4287)

As a final coup, the miller's wife accidentally smashes him with a staff "on the pyled skulle":

> That doun he gooth and cride, "Harrow I dye!"
> Thise clerks beete hym weel and lete hym lye.
> (4307–4308)

And yet, although the Reeve can tell such a story, he is the only pilgrim who did *not* laugh at the Miller's tale just preceding his. In fact, Chaucer describes him as being angry and upset. Surely it is not due to the grossness of the Miller's tale (which involves some hostile flatulence), or even its explicit brutality:

> The hoote kultour brende so his toute
> And for the smert he wende for to dye.
> (3812–3813)

Actually, the scatology and cruelty help to explain the near universal laughter with which the pilgrims greet the tale. Oswald the Reeve is discomfited not because the young student was branded, but because the old carpenter was cuckolded. As he himself explains his ill humor:

> But ik am oold, me list not pley for age
> Gras tyme is doon, my fodder is now forage . . .
> We olde men, I drede, so fare we . . .
> (3867–3868,3874)

Schadenfreude is delight at someone else's misfortune. For Oswald the Reeve, the cuckold in the Miller's tale was too close to himself. He sympathized; he feared ("We olde men, I drede . . ."). Clearly, this is *Schade* without *Freude*. Successful comedy must subliminally reassure us that the victims could not possibly be ourselves. How curious, though, that Chaucer's Reeve could tell of cuckoldry and yet not listen to it. One thinks of how Molière could transmute the pain of his personal life into the joy of such plays as *Ecole des femmes*.

This brief detour has demonstrated that what might today be considered excessive cruelty was greatly enjoyed in times past. The entire discussion began with Homer, and to Homer it now returns. We can only speculate on what sort of effect the Thersites episode had upon the bard's audience. And yet it is not unreasonable to think that Homer's listeners would laugh much the way the Greek leaders did. They too might even regard Odysseus' manhandling of Thersites as "the very best thing Odysseus had done since he got to Troy" (*Iliad* 2.274). Homer's audience knew well that Odysseus would go on to better things, but it is significant to note that his actions here attract so much attention and comment among his fellow warriors. This episode is especially important as presaging the Odysseus we will come to know, the comic hero who will "live up to his name."

For the essence of Odysseus is in his name, as George Dimock has emphatically demonstrated. The newborn son of Laertes was named by his grandfather, Autolycus ("Lone Wolf"), who said: "I have odysseused many in my time, up and down the wide world, men and women both; therefore let his name be Odysseus." As Dimock argues: "In the Odyssey *odyssasthai* means essentially 'to cause pain (*odynē*) and to be willing to do so.'" Thus from birth, by name and by nature, the first comic hero in Western literature is an inflictor of pain. In a certain sense, the Thersites episode in the *Iliad* anticipates the entire epic devoted to the satisfaction of comic *Schadenfreude* through the agency of a wily aggressor. And, as Dimock also notes, there is not always rational provocation for Odysseus' behavior. Not all his wild actions can be attributed to a *force majeure* like the Wrath of Poseidon. More often than not, Odysseus is merely following his own instinct "to plant evils," κακὰ φυτενείκ: "So let us think no more of 'wrath' which implies provocation and mental perturbation, but rather of a hand and mind against every man, by nature, or as a matter of policy."

Odysseus is a rogue by nature and heredity. We should never seek psychological explanations *for* his behavior. Rather, we should acknowledge the psychological appeal *of* his behavior. Cedric Whitman sees Odysseus as the antecedent of the crafty Aristophanic protagonist, "the self militant, and devil take the means." Whitman uses *poneria*, the modern Greek word for wiliness, to describe not only the amoral Aristophanic hero, but the essential characteristic of a popular Greek folk hero whose appeal through the ages has never diminished.

Throughout the comic tradition, the hero's attitude may be called by different terms, but its essence is childish aggression, a behavior pattern noted even by Socrates. Suzanne Langer cites Punch as "the most forthright of these infantilists," but in great comedy we are never very far from "givers of pain" in the Odyssean sense.

Take the Aristophanic hero, an insouciant breaker of laws, jaws, and his own mind. Hostility incarnate. This aspect of his character has not always pleased the scholars. Gilbert Norwood, for instance, objected to *The Knights* for being too much "an anthology of verbs meaning 'to kick in the stomach.' " But Aristophanes' art merely lyricizes the cruelty of his characters. Philocleon in *The Wasps*, one of the playwright's "rejuvenated" heroes, gets drunk at the final *kosmos*, grossly insults the guests (adding flatulence to verbal hostility), steals his son's flute-girl, and heads homeward, punching people in the street (1292ff). It should be noted that the word *hubris* or its compounds is used four times in the account of Philocleon's antisocial behavior.

In *The Clouds*, there is the famous finale in which a young man beats up his father and threatens to do likewise to his mother (1321ff); the psychology of this *Schadenfreude* is obvious. Grosser—and less comprehensible to the modern sensibility—is the joy described by the chorus of *The Birds* as being one of the added pleasures of possessing wings: airborne excretion (790ff). Psychologists have established the relation between hostility and defecation. In the *Ecclesiazusae* the fantasy of beating one's parents makes this duality explicit. Blepyros objects to the formation of a communistic state envisioned by his wife, Praxagora. Among the many reforms she proposes is that children be raised by the state. This, argues Blepyros, would invite mass murder. Youngsters would regard all old people as their parents, strangle them . . . and excrete upon them (637ff).

As mentioned above, the word *hubris* is common in the works of Aristophanes, often in the literal sense of violent physical assault. Per contra, in the tragic authors, *hubris* is almost always something mental. Aristotle, advocate of restrained laughter, defines wit as educated *hubris*, doubtless implying that the activities of the comic hero should not transcend the verbal assault. But Aristophanes is not the only comic author who sees physical *hubris* as a comic virtue. One thinks immediately of Restoration comedy, cruel and cynical, whose prime weapon was called "wit," a word less refined in the usage of that time than in ours. "Wit" can be almost any antisocial act, as described, for example, in Wycherly's *Plain Dealer* (V.ii):

> NOVEL: I wonder . . . that young fellows should be so dull, as to say there's no humor in making a noise, and breaking windows! I tell you there's wit and humor too in both . . .
>
> OLDFOX: Pure rogue! There's your modern wit for you! Wit and humor in breaking of windows; there's mischief, if you will, but no wit or humor.
>
> NOVEL: Prithee, prithee, peace old fool! I tell you, where there's mischief, there's wit.

In this case, and indeed as a rubric of comedy, one might define wit as what has oft been thought but ne'er so well repressed. There is often wit in *hubris*. There is always *hubris* in wit.

Aristophanes is also replete with verbal aggression. Every *agon* begins with an exchange of insults, and not every *agon* rises above his level. But Greek New Comedy, infused with Menandrian *philanthropia*, substituted *ethos* for *gelos*. Laughter was not its aim. In fact, the famous Menandrian-Terentian maxim about nothing human being alien explains why there could be no laughter in this sort of comedy. Feeling is fatal; *qui pense rit, qui sent pleure*. *Philanthropia* is admirable, but uncomic. Even Terence, notoriously lacking *vis comica* (which might here be rendered "comic violence"), is best remembered for a character who delights in physical assaults:

> PHORMIO: quot me censes homines iam deverberasse usque ad necem, hospites, tum civis? quo mage novi, tanto saepius.

Why does Phormio beat people to death, especially since he claims to be living only for the pleasure of life (338ff)? The question is its own answer. He is a descendent of the Autolycan-Odyssean rogue, an inflictor of pain for pleasure.

Of course the Plautine slave is an Odyssean hero, as both he and the playwright are wont to remind us:

CHRYSALUS: ego sum Vlixes quoiius consilio haec gerunt.
(Bacchides 940)

SIMO: superauit dolum Troianum atque Vlixem Pseudulus.
(Pseudolus 1244)

He delights in mischief for its own sake, and his aggressive attitude is that expressed by Epidicus: apolactizo inimicos omnis (678), "I kick the hell out of all who oppose me." There is no need to go into great detail, for clearly one factor unites Aristophanic poneria, Plautine malitia, and Rabelasian panourgia. And the machinations of the commedia dell'arte Brighella and the massacres of Père Ubu are part of the same phenomenon. For the baton with which Scapin beats Géronte is no different from the club with which Odysseus beats Thersites. The effect in each case is comic Schadenfreude.

The argument thus far has been but a prologue to a discussion of Marlowe's Jew of Malta. T. S. Eliot pointed out the essential truths: the play is not tragedy but farce. Marlowe, like Ben Jonson, writes that Eliot calls "savage comic humour." But Jonson's brutality has been discussed far more often than Marlowe's cruelty, though it is everpresent in his plays. As in Tamburlaine's torture of Bajezeth and sack of Babylon; in Faustus' willingness to "offer luke warme blood of new borne babes." And in Barabas' entire raison d'étre.

Bernard Spivak has recently demonstrated Barabas' relation to the Vice of morality plays, "a single intriguer, a voluble and cunning schemer, an artist in duplicity, a deft manipulator of human emotions." But Barabas existed long before medieval drama, before Christianity, and even before morality as Socrates "invented" it. Before he was called Vice, he was called Odysseus.

To best understand the Jew of Malta, we must seek not ancestors, but analogues. Dimock's description of Homer's wanderer is quite as apt for Marlowe's Jew: "a hand and a mind against every man, by nature, or as a matter of policy." Harry Levin has pointed out that "policy" is a key word for Barabas, and Mario Praz has pointed out that "policy" enters the English language in 1406—associated wth Ulysses.

By now the Romanticized views of Marlowe's hero have lost currency, although at least one critic in the last decade has referred to Barabas as "a sensitive and helpless victim" for whom the Elizabethan audience might have felt "genuine sympathy." But rationalism dies even harder than Romanticism. There are still critics who try to argue cause and effect for Barabas' behavior. But one does not have to explain Harpagon's greed or Volpone's acquisitiveness; that's the "humour of it." And Barabas is also a humourous character. No doubt the earnest attempts to "understand" the Jew of Malta were influenced by the dimensions Shakespeare later added to his Jew of Venice. But Barabas is not Shylock; if you prick him, he will not bleed.

Barabas' humor is the *poneria* of the Aristophanic hero, and he too is essentially "the self militant." All of Marlowe's heroes are what Levin calls "monomaniac exponents of the first person" (p.157), but none as much as Barabas, for he contains multitudes, a cast of thousands in a malevolence of one. He is not only every *thing* orthodox Elizabethans were against, he is every *one*. A Jew was a gargoyle much the same as a Turk. In fact, an Elizabethan writing in 1590 remarks: "Turcismus enim Judaismo cognatus admodum et affinis est." And both Turk and Jew were associated with the Devil. The Devil-Jew-Vice was a familiar stage figure, but surely never was there an ambiance of villainy to match that of Marlowe's Malta. The prologue sets the tone. It is Machiavelli's first appearance on the English stage.

> Albeit all the world thinke *Macheuill* is dead,
> Yet was his soule but flowne beyond the *Alpes*,
> And now the *Guize* is dead, is come from France . . .
>
> (1–3)

Here is yet another Elizabethan bugbear: atheism and villainy incarnate. Interestingly, Machiavelli too was frequently considered an incarnation of the Devil. Moreover, his soul (unlike Faustus') enjoys Pythagorean metempsychosis, and after having visited that infamous Protestant-killer the Duke of Guise, he now flies across the Channel to present "the Tragedy of a Iew" (30). To Machiavelli, of course, Barabas' ultimate fall *is* a tragedy, "because he fauours me" (35). To add to his innate sins, the Jew is also a Machiavellian, and it should be noted that when he boasts of his successful co-religionists throughout the Mediterranean world, he specifically points out that there are "many in France" (165).

But of course the Maltese are more or less Italians. No need to emphasize what that nation evoked in the Elizabethan imagination. In *Pierce Penilesse* Thomas Nashe calls Italy "the Academie of man-slaughter, the sporting place of murther, the Apothecary-shop of poyson." And worst of all, these men are Catholics. Here again we confront the diabolical, for the Pope is in league with the Devil, as Satan himself admits in the morality play, *The Conflict of Conscience* (1581): ". . . the Pope, who is my darling dear, / My eldest Boy in whom I do delight." Indeed, Marlowe's Malta is a kind of Devil's Island.

The name Marlowe chooses for his protagonist makes it perfectly clear: he is the antithesis of Christ. And as Anouilh says of one of his mythological heroines, "Elle s'appelle Antigone et il va falloir qu'elle joue son rôle jusqu'au bout." Quite simply then, Barabas plays "hate thy neighbor." And this primary humour is not miserliness. He does not even share Volpone's enthusiasm for lucre. Even for silver the fox of Venice would not say, "Fye, what a trouble 'tis to count this trash" (42). To Barabas, fantastic wealth is only useful "to ransome great Kings from captiuity" (67); money is equated only with policy. Since the real essence of Barabas is motion, the instant he has told us the sole value of "infinite riches in a little roome" (72), he asks the first question of the play: "But now how stands the wind?" (73). Barabas will always be moving—and shifting with the wind. The importance in what follows is not so much that his ships immediately arrive laden with goods, but rather the interesting revelation that he is always taking risks. When he asks about his argosy at Alexandria, a merchant replies:

> . . . we heard some of our sea-men say,
> They wondred how you durst with so much wealth
> Trust such a crazed Vessell, and so farre.
> (115–117)

But Barabas realized his ship was damaged: "Tush . . . I know her and her strength" (118). And four lines later, the "crazed Vessell" arrives safely in Malta port. Barabas will risk sinking more than once in this play.

When his co-religionists tell him that the Turk has arrived in Malta, Barabas implies his concern for them all. But he immediately tells the audience in an aside:

> Nay, let 'em combat, conquer, and kill all,
> So they spare me, my daughter, and my wealth.
> (191–192)

We cannot take too much stock in his affection for his daughter, since he has already told us he loves her "As *Agamemnon* did his *Iphigen*" (176). And by the same token that he is richer than Job (414ff) Barabas surely owns more than a thousand ships. His first love is not even Volpone's for gold, "far transcending . . . children, parents, friends" (I.i.16–17). Rather, Barabas salutes his co-religionists, "Assure your selues I'le looke vnto [*aside*] my selfe" (212).

Barabas' true policy is selfmanship—which he indulges immediately after the departure of "these silly men" (218). He is not concerned with the Jews' problem or even Malta's:

> How ere the world goe, I'le make sure for one,
> And seeke in time to intercept the worst,
> Warily garding that which I ha got
> *Ego mihimet sum semper proximus.*
> Why let 'em enter, let 'em take the Towne.
> (225–229)

And he is always against the universe, even in moments of prosperity. This is not the only time Barabas wishes the rest of humanity dead. In act five he exclaims "For so I liue, perish may all the world" (2292). Marlowe's Faustus is tempted with a Deadly Sin who says much the same. This unchained aggression is also evident in Jarry's unchained infantilistic hero:

> PÈRE UBU: Vous vous fichez de moi! Dans la trappe, les financiers. *On entoure les financiers.*
> MÈRE UBU: Mais enfin, Père Ubu, quel roi tu fais, tu masacres tout le monde!
> PÈRE UBU: Eh merdre!

Those who would have us feel for the plight of Barabas inevitably point to his "persecution" in the scene of the confiscation of his wealth. But there is no reason why Barabas should refuse to pay something in order to keep much more than half his property (remember what he has hidden away). He could, in fact, keep all his wealth merely by the application of a little holy water. After all, to a Machiavellian, religion is "but a childish Toy" (14); and he will immediately persuade his own daughter to feign conversion, arguing that

> A counterfet profession is better
> Then vnseene hypocrisie.
> (531–532)

When Abigail tells him his house (with hidden horde) has already been occupied, it becomes a challenge to outfox the little foxes, or as Barabas himself says in more Odyssean Language:

> No, I will liue; nor loath I this my life:
> And since you leaue me in the Ocean thus
> To sinke or swim, and put me to my shifts,
> I'le rouse my senses, and awake my selfe,
> (501–504)

With the full awakening of his militant self, his splendid creative malice will now be fully displayed. He will epitomize his last advice to his daughter, "be cunning *Abigail!*" (539).

Marlowe's "balcony scene" (640ff) ends with Barabas and his gold reunited and his ecstatic effusion: "hermoso placer de los dineros" (705). Why in Spanish? It could be a tag in any one of the many languages he knows, but Marlowe is ironically anticipating the arrival (in the next line) of one more Elizabethan devil, the Spaniard del Bosco, "Vizadmirall vnto the Catholike King" (712). In granting del Bosco permission to sell his slaves, the Maltese governor is breaking faith with his ex-allies, whom he now calls "these barbarous mis-beleeuing *Turkes*" (751). This note of international treachery sets the stage for the most memorable confrontation in the play; between the Jew Barabas and the Turk Ithamore.

Barabas enters brimming over with sweet hostility, for he is not really bitter or vengeful. He is already as rich as he ever was (772) and now can devote himself entirely to mischief. To Lodowick, his hostility is but thinly veiled:

> . . . 'tis custome held with vs,
> That when we speake with *Gentiles* like to you,
> We turne into the Ayre to purge our selues
> (805–807)

He speaks of the "burning zeal" with which he regards the nuns who live in his former home, adding in an aside, "Hoping ere long to set the house a fire" (851); but then he must excuse himself to buy a slave. We need seek no emotional reason for Barabas' wanting a new servant. It is not, as some critics would have it, that he feels lonely, for Barabas does not *feel* anything. He has always been alone; there has never been a Leah to whom he gave a ring. He lives in a continuum of active aggression. And Ithamore will merely be a weapon.

At their first meeting, Barabas and the lean Turk each sing an aria of evil, an amoebean song of cruelty. This is a set piece with much precedent in comic literature. In Aristophanes' *Knights*, for example, there is perpetual rivalry between the Sausage Seller and the Paphlagonian, a "super-panurgist and super-diabolist." They constantly exchange threats of violence and scatalogical attack. The Chorus enjoys the prospects of the Paphlagonian being bested (or worsted):

> But we are delighted to say that a man has
> come on the scene, far more corrupt than you, and it's
> clear he'll harass you and surpass you in villainy,
> boldness, and dirty tricks.
> (328–332)

The *agon* here is nothing less than a bragging contest of crimes past and better crimes to come. At the end, the Paphlagonian must concede defeat, with a uniquely Aristophanic play on words: "Aieeh, bad luck—I'm absolutely ab-rogue-ated!" (1206).

But the "aria of evil" which can best be compared with Barabas' occurs in Boccaccio. While, strictly speaking, it is prose narrative, we everywhere sense the speaker's delight in presenting the achievements of Ser Ciapelletto:

> Testimonianze false con sommo diletto diceva, richesto e non richesto . . .Aveva oltre modo piacere, e forte vi studiava, in commettere tra amici e parenti e qualunque altra persona mali ed inimicizie e scandali, de' quali quanto maggiori mali vedea seguire, tanto più d'allegrezza prendea. Invitato ad uno omicidio o a qualunque altra rea cosa, senza negarlo mai, volonterosa-mente v'andava, e più volte a fedire e ad uccidere uomini con le proprie mani si ritrovò volentieri . . . Perchè mi distendo io in tante parole? Egli era il piggiore unomo, forse, che mai nascesse.

Ciapelletto is like Molière's Dom Juan, according to Sganarelle "le plus grand scélérat que la terre ait jamais porté." But Barabas is more than a match for the grandest rogues of comedy, and his outrageous brag bears quoting at length:

> As for my selfe, I walke abroad a nights
> And kill sicke people groaning under walls:
> Sometimes I goe about and poyson wells . . .
> Being young, I studied Physicke, and began
> To practise first vpon the *Italian*;
> There I enric[h]'d the Priests with burials,
> And alwayes kept the Sexton's armes in vre
> With digging graues and ringing dead mens knels:
> And after that was I an Engineere,
> And in the warres 'twixt *France* and *Germanie*,
> Vnder pretence of helping *Charles* the fifth,
> Slew friend and enemy with my stratagems.
> Then after that was I an Vsurer,
> And with exorting, cozening, forfeiting,
> And tricks belonging vnto Brokery,
> I fill'd the Iailes with Bankrouts in a yeare,
> And with young Orphans planted Hospitals,
> And euery Moone made some or other mad,
> And now and then one hang himselfe for griefe.
>   (939–941, 946–961)

There are, of course, aspects of Barabas' "career" which derive from medieval stereotypes of the Jew. In any case, we are not meant to take any of his words at face value or believe that he has actually traveled to all the places he mentions. Marlowe's style is always one of exaggeration, especially in this play. We note in Barabas' brag, which begins significantly, "As for my *selfe*," that his interest is always in malice, not money. As a doctor his delight was enriching the priests (with burials). As a usurer, his joy was in the pain he caused (suicides, insanity, and so on). Most interesting is his behavior while "helping" Charles the fifth, for here he slew friend as well as enemy. This delight in totally indiscriminate cruelty is exactly like Ser Ciapelletto's in stirring pain and trouble among relatives and friends. Both Boccaccio's and Marlowe's descriptions are intended to arouse the laugh of *Schadenfreude* through a comic hero who unabashedly relishes the inflicting of pain, "o qualunque rea cosa."

Whereas Barabas' exploits may be imaginary, before the play is out, he will have committed almost all the atrocities of which he boasts. And Ithamore, who begins as one of Barabas' dupes, will end as one of his victims. For the Jew merely baits his slave with the Volpone-trick. Whereas he may flatter him as "my second self" (1317), and chant litanies of "I here adopt thee for mine onely heire" (1345), Barabas wastes no time in telling the audience that he is but guiling Ithamore:

> Thus euery villaine ambles after wealth
> Although he ne're be richer then in hope . . .
> (3154–3155)

How little veiled is the hostility in Barabas' expression of gratitude to his collaborator in the poisoning of the nuns: "Ile pay thee with a vengeance, Ithamore" (1418). In fact, Barabas buys Ithamore to enlarge his own scope of hate.

Barabas' purchase is followed by a crescendo of comic cruelty. First, the Jew schemes to set Lodowick against Mathias in a heartless perversion of what Sir Toby stirs up between Viola and Sir Andrew Aguecheek. But in Shakespeare the trick adds to the midsummer madness; here it adds to Maltese murder. And there is so much gusto on the part of the murderer that we feel no sympathy at the death of the two young men.

It is even difficult to grieve for Abigail. For as she gasps her last breath, we cannot help but think of an offstage chorus of her fellow nuns, all dying at the same time. The many other murderous pranks of Barabas which have analogues on the comic stage cannot be listed here. Sometimes Ithamore will lend a helping hand—to strangle a friar, for example (Boccaccio's Ser Ciapelletto was likewise generous when it came to killing people). But he is a mere zany to his master, who has no real need of him.

In fact, after Ithamore's defection, the speed and scope of villainy actually increase. Here, as throughout the play, Barabas' single aim is to outdo himself in evil:

> Now I haue such a plot for both their liues,
> As neuer Iew nor Christian knew the like . . .
> (1626–1627)

That is why he persists in scheming even after he becomes governor, which could be ambition's *ne plus ultra*. He must continue in malice; it is his humour. This is that Odyssean quality in Barabas (and we cannot ignore how he led the Turk through the city walls in Ulysses-like fashion). Just as when Mosca believes that he and Volpone have achieved "our master-peece: We cannot thinke, to goe beyond this"—and Volpone immediately comes up with yet another scheme to "torture 'em rarely" (V.i.30–31,128). So too Barabas' instinct urges him to undo others till he himself is undone.

Thus, immediately following the brutal sack of Malta, Barabas switches sides. We need seek no explanations in reason or *Realpolitik*. The motive is far more basic: are there not Turks to kill? Barabas is a man who could laugh at the annihilation of the world. He cares no more for Turk than for Christian (2213); he cares for himself. And at the end, he is quite the same person he was at the outset, ever risking, shifting, testing the wind, and delighting in his villainy:

> . . . why, is not this
> A kingly kinde of trade to purchase Townes
> By treachery, and sell 'em by deceit?
> Now tell me, worldlings, vnderneath the sunne,
> If greater falshood euer has ben done.
> (2329–2330)

His opening monologue had already explained his views on "the policy" of riches.

His last trick is both his best in quantity of victims and his worst—since he is one of them. Shakespeare's Jew ends at the baptismal font, but Marlowe's ends in hotter water. Barabas' cauldron is also an ancient comic prop (it rejuvenated Demos in *The Knights*). Surely the last glimpse of Barabas, boiling mentally and physically, and cursing the "damn'd Christians, dogges, and Turkish Infidels" (2370) was intended to raise a "heartless laugh." It must have, for audiences packed Henslowe's playhouses to see Marlowe's wildly successful play. Today we may find such laughter as foreign as that of Wimsatt's Fiji Islander delightedly watching a prisoner roast. But that was in another country. Yet so was

Barabas, and as Baudelaire wrote in his essay on laughter: "Pour trouver du comique féroce et très féroce, il faut passer la Manche et visiter les royaumes brumeux du spleen."

Schadenfreude is a childish pleasure, say the psychologists, and Marlowe often displays a rather adolescent delight in cruelty. It is perhaps difficult to accept this as a laughing matter, but the beast in man does not always evoke pity and terror—as in the case of Lear's pelican daughters or that Spartan dog Iago. There is also Jonson's fox of Venice, and Marlowe's snake of Malta, both of whom make laughter of what Freud had to concede was a basic human trait: *homo homini lupus*. Did Freud know he was quoting Plautus?

JACKSON I. COPE

Marlowe's "Dido" and the Titillating Children

Most critical commentary upon Elizabethan drama directs itself toward the play as poem rather than production. This is properly so because we know so much about the poetic and rhetorical bent of the education received by playwrights and their auditors alike, know that it *was* a poetic drama. Boys trained "to turn the prose of the Poets into the Poets owne verse, with delight, certainty and speed, without any bodging," trained to listen to the drone against the hourglass on Sundays "in order to make a repetition of the whole Sermon without book . . . rehearsing the severall parts . . . distinctly & briefly"—such were the boys trained by Shakespeare's exact contemporary John Brinsley in Leicestershire, and many another schoolmaster less pedagogically articulate. They were not so likely as our contemporaries to feel it a ludicrous assumption that the ear could catch, the mind maintain those intricate schemes and tropes and trains of metaphor through which play becomes poem. But it is not only proper to read early plays as poems, it is unhappily too often necessary to read them only as poems because we know so relatively little about contemporary productions. At lucky moments staging and significance converge in strokes we cannot miss. The blind and despairing Gloucester of *Lear* cries out to the gods that he can bear no longer "and not fall / To quarrel with your opposeless wills," enacts a farcical pratfall from the illusory cliffs of Dover in good vaudeville tradition, and so is cured of incurable despair (as Edgar comments, "Ten

From *English Literary Renaissance* (1974). Copyright © 1974 by University of Massachusetts Press.

masts at each make not the altitude / Which thou hast perpendicularly fell: / Thy life's a miracle"). Poetry and performance converge, eye and ear, to tell us that we are once again in the presence of that great Christian myth of miracle, the Fortunate Fall.

Such triumphant moments of the playmaker's control of his media are most easily discernible when, as in this case, they fuse. That control can be as productive, however, when the theatrical *frisson* is embodied in words and scenes which mirror the psyche's pleasure in hosting conflicting systems, mutually irreverent senses of the nature of things. When this conflict emerges in the drama we, as critics, often hasten to apologize for the dramatist with the good intention of protecting the poet; better half a play than none. Such, I think, has been the case in our miscalculations about *Dido, Queen of Carthage*, Marlowe's only text written not for the public theater, but for the Queen's Children of the Chapel. Having listened too intently to the siren song of its sweet verse, we have ship-wrecked its fine farce. Doing so, we have relegated what is perhaps Marlowe's best piece of total theater to the status of apprentice work.

Trollope went too far in labeling *Dido* "pretty quaint, and painful" and a "burlesque," but he moved in the right direction. Harry Levin and Clifford Leech have noted a comic element in some scenes, but only as fragmented compromise with the limitations of boy actors. Don Cameron Allen alone has taken the humor seriously, and that only as it affects the play's deities: "In his poetic philosophy men are surely better than their gods and have only one mortal weakness: they lend their ears . . . to the advice and direction of the silly hulks they have themselves created." The case is not, I think, quite so metaphysical. It is not its conclusions, but the play's potential for laminating conflicting sensibilities which Marlowe wishes to impose upon his audience's imagination.

The Children of the Chapel ranged in age roughly from eight to thirteen, and were, of course, chosen for their voices, not their ability as realistic "actors." Such ability could scarcely be very maturely developed even in an age of rhetorical education. But with that rhetorical training, the sweet-singing boys were ideally prepared to declaim complex verse. And it is to this ability that Marlowe directed his serious adaptation (in many long passages a close translation) of Vergil. The Vergilian elements of *Dido* are much less dramatic than declamatory, and what the Queen's Children's audience heard was an expert professional declamation of parts of the best English *Aeneid* before Dryden, Marlowe's challenge to Stanyhurst, Surrey, and his other predecessors.

But, no matter how able verse and voices, poetic declamation was not drama in the 1580's. So Marlowe made several additions to the

Vergilian narrative, the principal being a framing induction, a comic nurse, and multiple suicides at the close. All of these additions are interpolated to exploit the self-conscious theatrical situation vectored by sexually romantic love matter, a literate adult audience, and the little boy players.

The first addition is an induction in which Jupiter is revealed dandling Ganymede upon his knee. This Ganymede is Plato's (*Laws*, I, 636c) and Lactantius' glorified catamite. "Hold here, my little love! / . . . I'll hug with you an hundred times" (I.i.42–48), Jupiter cajoles, and Venus, entering upon the scene, is disgusted: "Ay, this is it! You can sit toying there / And playing with that female wanton boy, / Whiles my Aeneas wanders on the seas" (50–52). This unexpected and broadly homosexual opening would not have failed, of course, as a joke for those friends and scandal-seekers who knew Marlowe's (at least, alleged) personal predilections. Richard Baines's note on Marlowe's beliefs reported that he had said "That St John the Evangelist was bedfellow to Christ and . . . that he vsed him as the sinners of Sodoma." Thomas Kyd was more succinct upon his roommate's blasphemy: "He wold report St John to be our savior Christes *Alexis*." These were neither entirely negative nor random remarks, perhaps, because according to Baines, Marlowe felt "That all they that love not tobacco & Boyes were fooles."

But this was only a private joke at best, riding upon the inevitable recognition that the boys and their masters were mirroring and mocking their own public reputations. The reflexive satire is a reflection less upon the poet and the gods than upon children's theater itself. I have said that the boys were *chosen* for the singing company; in many cases that was a euphemism for impressment or even kidnapping. Richard Edwardes, William Hunnis, and other Masters of the Chapel were given royal *carte blanche* by Elizabeth to search out and "take as manye well singinge children as he or his sufficient deputie shall thinke mete . . . within this our realme of England whatsoever they be." Parents, guardians, or church authorities were obligated not only to surrender the boy to the Chapel Master, but to provide transportation of the child to London. The degree to which the Master's privilege could be extended into flagrant arrogance is revealed in the angry litigation over the carrying off of little Thomas Clifton from Christchurch grammar school to the Blackfriars headquarters of the Chapel Children in 1600, and the subsequent taunting of father and son with threats of beating and such. That this case should have surfaced publicly is owing to the father's having been a gentleman from Norfolk with high government connections, but it is unlikely to have been singular in the child companies' history. The potential for private as well as public abuse of the boys in a context which made them chattel became part of their public image. Gabriel Harvey taunted Lyly as "the Vicemaster of Poules" when he was associated with the boys, and Middleton ironically informed would-be gallants later that they could "see a nest of boys able to ravish a man" at Blackfriars. Stephen Gosson worried about boys who put on "the attyre, the gesture, the passions of a woman," and Phillip Stubbes found the theaters bringing mate to mate where "in their secret conclaues (couertly) they play the *Sodomits*, or worse." Cocke's character of an actor asserted that "if hee marries, hee mistakes the Woman for the Boy in Womans attire, . . . But so long as he lives unmarried, hee mistakes the Boy . . . for the Woman."

Before the Englishing of Vergil's poem begins, then, the metamorphosis of the boys and their Master into the luxurious pagan gods provides self-conscious satire. This dimension will broaden into farce as the play develops. But it will not reduce *Dido* to travesty; rather, it will interlace farce with poetry in an atmosphere where both can survive. Indeed, it would seem that acting of serious romantic matter by little boys could *only* survive as *tour de force* rather than parody if a presenter occasionally winked over the performers' shoulders to indicate awareness of the suspension of disbelief imposed upon and enjoyed by the audience. A case in point is Lyly's story of unconsummated love written for the boy singers of St. Paul's in which Endymion, classical Rip van Winkle, just before the denouement "finds means to part with his white beard and other signs of age." The illusion can withstand the light of exposure only if it anticipatorily underlines the paradox which is its base: this seems the dramatic lesson of such interplay between auditor and immature actor.

Let us return to *Dido*, then, with a pertinent theatrical question: who played Jupiter? Perhaps it was the Master or another adult, thus emphasizing the boys' imposed predicament. Perhaps, on the other hand, it was an older boy (between eight and thirteen, inches are enhanced as rapidly as sophistication), in which case the older boy himself became publicly privy to the adults' supposedly salacious secret. In any case, this initial play upon sexual maturity and immaturity was incorporated from the induction into the body of the play by Marlowe's other additions to the Vergilian narrative.

Let us consider the frequently criticized psychology of Dido's scene of mixed emotion as she holds Cupid, supposed Ascanius, upon her lap. Venus has come upon the true Ascanius, drugged him to sleep, and carried him into the forest while metamorphosing Cupid into Ascanius' shape. Cupid's instructions from his mother are to get upon Dido's lap, "Then touch her white breast with this arrow head, / That she may dote upon Aeneas' love" (II.i.26–27)—a golden arrow dipped in magic love juice such as that with which (upon Oberon's instructions) Puck anointed the eyes of Titania that she might look dotingly upon Bottom the Ass. Seductively teasing, Cupid does gain Dido's lap as she is speaking with her suitor Iarbas (whose role has been expanded by Marlowe from small Vergilian hints). Then, through the magic of Venus' potion, Dido becomes a whirligig of emotion:

> DIDO: O stay, Iarbas, and I'll go with thee.
> CUP.: And if my mother go, I'll follow her.
> DIDO [to Iarbas]: Why stay'st thou here? thou art no love of mine.
> IAR.: Iarbas, die, seeing she abandons thee!
> DIDO: No, live, Iarbas; what hast thou deserv'd,
>   That I should say thou art no love of mine?
>   Something thou hast deserv'd—Away, I say,
>   Depart from Carthage, come not in my sight! . . .
> IAR.: I go to feed the humour of my love,
>   Yet not from Carthage for a thousand worlds.
> DIDO: Iarbas!
> IAR.: Doth Dido call me back?
> DIDO: No, but I charge thee never look on me.
>   . . . his loathsome sight offends mine eye,
>   And in my thoughts is shrin'd another love.
>
> (III.i.37–57)

Such crude psychology and strident verse are not failures of either dramatic or poetic modulation; to hypothesize that is to assume sudden deafness in the ear which a few lines later could lead Marlowe to write:

> I'll give thee tackling made of rivell'd gold
> Wound on the barks of odoriferous trees;
> Oars of massy ivory, full of holes,
> Through which the waters shall delight to play;
> Thy anchors shall be hew'd from crystal rocks,
> Which if thou lose shall shine above the waves. . . .
>
> (III.i.115–20)

It is more reasonable to assume that what seems an unaccountably abrupt falling off upon the printed page is a deft shift of theatrical tone when the little boys must begin to talk of love. As the scene opens, Cupid sings a "pretty song," then provides some innuendos which would remind the viewer of Jupiter's homosexual toying with Ganymede: "Will Dido let me hang about her neck?" the one boy asks the other and Dido responds: "Ay, wag, and give thee leave to kiss her too" (III.i.30–31). Climbing upon her lap, Cupid produces the arrow from his sleeve and by its magic induces the improbable oscillations in Dido's attitude toward Iarbas which have been cited above. Marlowe is titillating us again with the boys' interesting limitations: instead of declaiming sentiments, he elects to have them enact a farce of love. Before our eyes one small boy crawls into the arms of another and draws a conspicuously golden arrow stealthily into view (the stage direction is built into the dialogue as the scene begins: "Now, Cupid, . . . Convey this golden arrow in thy sleeve, / Lest she imagine thou art Venus' son" [III.i.1–4]). This he periodically jabs into Dido's paps at each bewildered, wavering turn she makes back toward her old interest in Iarbas, paps either non-existent or stuffed out and painted in parody of the life this play never intends to imitate. Any doubt of Marlowe's intentions should have been laid to rest by the repetition of Cupid's game an act later with that other boy who, in female guise as a gabbling old nurse, could challenge Salomon Pavy's alleged talent at playing old men. She scoops him into her arms and, under his influence, immediately turns lecherous: "That I might live to see this boy a man! / How prettily he laughs! Go, ye wag, / You'll be a twigger when you come to age" (IV.v.18–20).

The same scene is repeated three times, a scene drawing the boys to the edge of their reputation and talents. In the Jupiter-Ganymede induction the homosexual potential of the troupe is exploited with a leer of mock acknowledgement for the scandalmongers. In the Dido-Cupid version the paradox of love's absurdity is mocked by the parody of boys playing it absurdly. In the nurse's scene with Cupid, the boy company triumphantly reclaims its reputation for charming the imagination by making us laugh at yet another boy lover because he is so obviously disqualified for love, not this time primarily because he is a boy but because he is an old woman. All three scenes are, of course, among Marlowe's additions to his Vergilian undertext. They are his answer to the challenge of making the limitations of boy players into theatrical strengths. But, beyond that, they force demands upon the audience's imagination, demands that it consciously react to that "doubleness" which is the theatrical experience, the ability to hold simultaneous consciousness of actor and role, story world and stage world, to be aware of the psyche's separate life as a fantasy in the midst of its engagement with reality.

But let us now return to look at the action with an eye on the boys' physical size rather than their sexual immaturity or precociousness, states so closely allied in this prematurely sophisticated theater. Leaving the character Jupiter aside because of the possibility that he might have been played by an adult, we find that Venus, Dido, and the Nurse were all larger boys. Venus carries Ascanius on-stage in her arms in order to place him in a grove; Cupid (Ascanius' double) sits in Dido's lap; the Nurse carries Cupid off-stage at the close of Act Four. The female figures are older, larger boys than Ascanius and Cupid. But what of Aeneas?

The assumption that would seem most natural is that he was played by an older, larger boy, equal if not superior in size to Dido. And this assumption appears to be supported by little Ascanius when, immediately after Aeneas' initial heroic rhetoric, the son emphasizes his minority in pleading: "Father, I faint; good father, give me meat" (I.i.163). But if Ascanius is small enough to be scooped up and carried by a boy of twelve or thirteen, there is a sufficient range of potential physical size in a group of pre-pubescents to allow for an Aeneas large enough to play Ascanius' father, yet smaller than his lover Dido. If we assume that to have been the case in the staging by the Chapel Children, certain other disturbing elements in the play cease to seem puzzling lapses.

Marlowe, as might be expected in a dramatization, expands the meeting at a cave which brings about the admission and consummation of Dido's love for Aeneas, a meeting only briefly reported by Vergil. But here Marlowe's verse again falters. Rhythms are truncated as line after line becomes independent sentence, exclamation, question. Monosyllables march across the page, false semi-rhymes abound internally, and schemes dominate tropes to produce flagrantly obvious conceits with which Dido attempts to reveal her love dilemma, as in "The thing that I will die before I ask, / And yet desire to have before I die" (III.iv.8–9), or "And yet I'll speak, and yet I'll hold my peace; / Do shame her worst, I will disclose my grief" (26–27). But Aeneas is incapable of penetrating her messages: "What means fair Dido by this doubtful speech?" (30), "What ails my Queen, is she fall'n sick of late?" (23). Such inexplicably obtuse blunting of the climactic love scene becomes comic irony, merging staging and verse, if we project a child Aeneas being uncomprehendingly seduced by a teenage Dido. When he has freely stripped all pretensions from this boy-as-hero being bullied into improbable love by his bigger boy "queen" in skirts, Marlowe caps the farce with a closing embrace. But as he does so, he forces admiration out of fun, reinforces our awareness of the doubleness available to art when he returns to lyric rhythms graceful enough for the tongue of any Shakespearean *inamorata*:

> What more than Delian music do I hear,
> That calls my soul from forth his living seat
> To move unto the measures of delight?
> Kind clouds that sent forth such a courteous storm
> As made disdain to fly to fancy's lap!
> Stout love, in mine arms make thy Italy.
> (III.iv.51–56)

It will be a decade before the stage again will chance such stylistic juxtapositions of the lyric and the laughable, when Bottom responds to Titania's "Thou art as wise as thou art beautiful" with, "Not so, neither. But if I had wit enough to get out of this wood, I have enough to serve my turn," and invokes in reply: "I'll give thee fairies to attend on thee, / And they shall fetch thee jewels from the deep, / And sing while thou on pressèd flowers dost sleep" (III.ii.151–62).

The assumption that Aeneas was a smaller boy than Dido and that Marlowe was playing a double game as lyric poet and comic playwright further aids us in understanding Marlowe's addition to the Vergilian story in Act Four, an addition in which the point is Aeneas' wooden helplessness in the ambience of Dido. No sooner has Aeneas declared his resolve to depart and manned his ships than he allows himself to be called back and lies about his intentions like the shuffling schoolboy which he, in fact, is: "O princely Dido, give me leave to speak; / I went to take my farewell of Achates" (IV.iv.17–18). Dido crowns him, dissipates his resolution, and regains his weathervane allegiance: "O Dido, patroness of all our lives, / When I leave thee, death be my punishment!" (55–56). The little hero is toyed with by the bigger queen, as she will remind us with a little irony which points back to the induction as Dido and Marlowe mock Aeneas under the Carthaginian crown he has just accepted: "Now looks Aeneas like immortal Jove: / O where is Ganymede, to hold his cup [?]" (45–46).

The metaphoric play with Aeneas' hapless bandying among physically as well as psychically greater powers is carried into Act Five. The action opens with his announced decision, induced by Dido, to establish the new Troy in an expanded Carthage, but no sooner has he finished than Hermes leads in Ascanius by the hand, emphasizing his own stature by scorning Aeneas' concern "about this little boy" (V.i.51) while Jove is anxiously desiring that he get on to Italy. Hermes scolds crossly, and Aeneas quails querulously as his deity's messenger departs in a huff: "How should I put into the raging deep / Who have no sails nor tackling for my ship?" The cause for his lack of equipment is Dido who, after recalling him from his first attempt to leave, has "ta'en away my oars and masts, / And left me neither sail nor stern aboard" (55–61). Iarbas overhears his rival's complaint, promises to equip his ships to be rid of him, and the helpless Aeneas sadly agrees to be manipulated by god and man: "How loth I am to leave these Libyan bounds" (81). The queen sees the new preparations and girds herself for one more seduction of the boy hero ("Dido, try thy wit" [86]), but Vergil and history have denied her, if Marlowe has not in his providing her with a fluid and lyric tongue which

Aeneas can confront only with acknowledgment of his puppet-like role as a boy among men, women, and poets. All argument silenced, his last words are Marlowe's self-tribute: "In vain, my love, thou spends't thy fainting breath: / If words might move me, I were overcome" (153–54).

Then comes the close. Dido madly imagines Aeneas' return, Anna disabuses her, and Marlowe writes his psychologically soundest scene. But having done so, he adds the suicides of Iarbas and Anna to that of Dido, telescoping them all within the last fifty lines of the play. This constitutes Marlowe's final departure, not only from Vergil but from tradition, it having been observed that all the other numerous Renaissance plays on the Dido story devote the entire last act to the queen's death. Nothing in the first four acts has suggested a tragic tone, and Marlowe's playfulness with the dramatic limitations of the boys should have encouraged his audience until this penultimate moment to expect a denouement in the tradition which would become known as *Vergile travestée*. Such a denouement is denied as Dido throws herself upon the pyre with a dignity literally borrowed from Vergil's epic:

> Now, Dido, with these relics burn thyself,
> And make Aeneas famous through the world
> For perjury and slaughter of a queen. . . .
> *Litora litoribus contraria, fluctibus undas*
> *Imprecor; arma armis; pugnent ipsique nepotes:*
> Live, false Aeneas! Truest Dido dies;
> *Sic, sic iuvat ire sub umbras.*
>> (V.i.292–313)

In this unexpected recovery of passionate seriousness, Marlowe defies anticipation by imitating the full resonances of his source. But to end upon such a reserve of lyric power would be to deny the theatrical game he has been playing with the children, and he has no intention of doing so. It is in this context that he appends the final dozen lines:

> Enter Anna.
> O help, Iarbas! Dido in these flames
> Hath burnt herself! Ay me, unhappy me!
>> *Enter Iarbas running.*
> Cursed Iarbas, die to expiate
> The grief that tires upon thine inward soul!
> Dido, I come to thee: ay me, Aeneas! [*Kills himself.*]
> ANNA: What can my tears or cries prevail me now?
> Dido is dead, Iarbas slain, Iarbas my dear love! . . .
> Now, sweet Iarbas, stay, I come to thee!
>> (V.i.314–28)

Having evaded the expectation of farce, Marlowe injected high feeling into the death of Dido. But, looking over the talented little boy actors' shoulders and winking at their triumph and his own, he added a fillip to that conclusion and followed up with what he had teasingly promised all along: a silly story hastily superimposed upon the realities of passionate love and death. Doing so, he prepared the mind of at least one contemporary to gather superficially incompatible forces into a play which has dogged and dodged our imaginations in its happy combination of improbabilities. I implicitly have been arguing, of course, that the mixed farce and romance of *Dido, Queen of Carthage* is Marlowe's most significant gift to Shakespeare, progenitor of that strange crossbreeding of Puck and Oberon and Theseus and Bottom's players, *A Midsummer Night's Dream*.

WILLIAM KEACH

"Hero and Leander"

Hero and Leander seems to have been written at the same time as *Venus and Adonis*. Although Marlowe's epyllion was not entered in the Stationers' Register until 28 September 1593, almost five and a half months after Shakespeare's (18 April), and of course not published until 1598, it must have been written by the spring of 1593, since Marlowe was killed at Deptford on 30 May of that year. The plague of 1592–1593 had interrupted Marlowe's career as a dramatist much as it had Shakespeare's; he probably worked on *Hero and Leander* during his stay at Sir Thomas Walsingham's house at Scadbury, near Chislehurst in Kent, where he had gone to wait for the plague to subside in London and the theatres to reopen. He may well have contemplated a poem like *Hero and Leander* during his Cambridge days, when he was translating Ovid's *Amores*. But the confident virtuosity of the couplets of his epyllion suggests that the stylistic development manifested in the plays intervened between *All Ovids Elegies* and *Hero and Leander*.

Marlowe, like Shakespeare, set himself the challenge of treating a familiar myth with distinctive originality. The story of Hero and Leander was, if anything, even more familiar in the sixteenth century than the story of Venus and Adonis. As Abraham Fraunce observed in 1592, "Leander and Heroes love is in every mans mouth." Fraunce was probably thinking of the numerous Continental versions of the Alexandrian epyllion attributed to the writer known as Musaeus (fifth century A.D.): Clément Marot's French translation (1541), Bernardo Tasso's Italian version (c. 1540), or possibly the Spanish *Leandro y Ero* of Juan Boscán (1543), based mainly on the elder Tasso's Italian version and quoted by Fraunce in his *Arcadian Rhetoric* (1586). English readers were even more likely to have known the Latin translation of Marcus Musurus, which from 1518 on was widely available in *Aesopi Phrygis, Fabellae Graece et Latine*. The story had been told or alluded to in other sources, but its remarkable popularity in the sixteenth century centered around Musaeus's poem, in its various versions.

It is impossible to know for certain whether Marlowe used the Greek text of Musaeus, the Latin translation of Musurus, or one of the sixteenth-century Continental translations. He may very well have used a combination of these. If, for example, he employed the Musurus translation included in the collection of Aesop's fables, he would have had parallel Greek and Latin texts before him and could have consulted the original in key passages. What needs to be emphasized at this point, however, is Marlowe's response to those aspects of the overall structure and theme of Musaeus's epyllion which would have been apparent either in the Greek original or in the translations.

With "Leander and Heroes love . . . in every mans mouth," the last thing one would expect from Marlowe is a conventional, straightforward rendering of the story. And in fact Marlowe's approach transforms Musaeus's poem—or at any rate a large part of it. The Greek text is 343 lines long, not counting a one- or two-line lacuna at line 331. Structurally the poem divides into a rising, triumphant movement narrating and celebrating the love of Hero and Leander (ll. 1–282) and a much shorter, falling, tragic movement which tells of the drowning of Leander and of Hero's suicide (ll. 282–343). Marlowe's poem, or "fragment" as it is sometimes called, does not end at just any point in the story as Musaeus tells it, but at the crucial point where triumphant love turns into tragedy, with a marked shift in pace and tone. This is the most important point established by C. S. Lewis in his well-known discussion of Marlowe's "fragment" and of Chapman's "continuation." Where Lewis goes wrong, I would argue, is in his claim that we can read Marlowe and Chapman together to obtain uniquely effective renderings of the two movements of Musaeus. Chapman expands only an eighth of Musaeus's poem, 61 lines, into 1544 lines; nothing could differ more from the swift, plummeting ending of Musaeus than the extraordinarily intricate moral and philosophical transformations of Chapman's "continuation." More important for our immediate purposes, however, is Marlowe's transformation of Musaeus's first movement. Despite his deep and generally underestimated indebtedness to Musaeus, Marlowe does not give us the "unclouded celebration of youthful passion" which Bush and many other readers have found in the poem. He gives us a poetic experience much more disturbing and ambivalent than that presented by Musaeus or by any other previous writer, including Ovid in epistles XVIII and XIX of the *Heroides*.

It is clear from the first line of his epyllion—"On Hellespont, guilty of true love's blood"—that Marlowe wanted to make his readers aware of the tragic ending of the story which they all knew so well. Critics like Clifford Leech and Brian Morris, who have argued, in opposition to the prevailing "romantic" readings of the poem, that *Hero and Leander* dramatizes the comedy and absurdity of young love, have disregarded the way in which Marlowe preserves in muted form an awareness of the final tragedy. At the same time, however, it is clear that Marlowe's interest in the story is not focused on, does not emphasize, its familiar tragic dimension. He is much more concerned with the living relationship of Hero and Leander than with their eventual tragic fate. What he depicts in this relationship includes both the comedy and the pathos of youthful romance—and it also includes more. Marlowe's recasting of the story includes a remarkably perceptive sense of the risks, limitations, and disappointments of romantic love. If Marlowe shows his young lovers, once stripped of their amusing postures and poses, to be admirable in their uncompromising passion, he also shows them to be vulnerable and unstable when confronted with the reality of actual sexual experience.

The key to Marlowe's approach to Musaeus lies partly in his heightening of the Ovidian aspects of the Greek poem. Musaeus himself may have known Ovid's Hero and Leander epistles in the *Heroides,* and in one or two passages he adopts strategies which remind us of Ovid's other elegiac amatory poems. But on the whole his more distanced and elevated narrative manner is quite unlike the intensely dramatic *ethopoeia* of the *Heroides* or the self-conscious wit of the *Ars Amatoria* and *Amores*. Marlowe's own use of the *Heroides* is, with one exception, restricted to a few descriptive details, primarily because Ovid imagines his exchange of letters taking place after Hero and Leander have consummated their love, just before the final attempted meeting. The *Heroides* epistles could offer Marlowe little direct guidance for presenting the phase of the relationship he was most interested in. But the *Ars Amatoria* and the *Amores* are a different matter altogether. Marlowe draws extensively on these poems: directly, as commentators have noted, in Leander's arguments against virginity; indirectly, and even more importantly, in establishing his narrative persona.

Marlowe's narrator is not exactly the urbane, witty *praeceptor* of the *Ars Amatoria,* nor is he the clever, tormented speaker of the *Amores*. But he partakes at times of both these voices. He sounds most like the speaker of the *Ars Amatoria* when he comments knowingly on the effect of Leander's *Amores* arguments:

> These arguments he us'd, and many more,
> Wherewith she yielded, that was won before.
> Hero's looks yielded, but her words made war;
> Women are won when they begin to jar.
> (I. 329–332)

He sounds most like the speaker of the *Amores* when he describes, with obvious delight, Hero's efforts to escape from Leander's embrace:

> But as her naked feet were whipping out,
> He on the sudden cling'd her so about
> That mermaid-like unto the floor she slid;
> One half appear'd, the other half was hid.
> (II. 313–316)

The narrator of *Hero and Leander* is as distanced from Marlowe as the speaker of the *Amores* is from Ovid; he is usually as distanced from the story he tells as the speaker of the *Ars Amatoria* is from his subject. He shares with both Ovidian voices a sophisticated, often cynical erotic expertise. Above all, he calls attention to his own presence in a way which constantly reminds us that a cunningly created and projected persona is guiding our experience of the narrative. It is this conspicuous, intrusive, self-dramatizing persona, as I have already suggested, which most clearly differentiates Marlowe's epyllionic technique from Shakespeare's.

The skill with which Marlowe uses his narrator to control the reader's experience of the narrative is nowhere more apparent than in the two opening portraits. Structurally the Hero portrait (II. 5–50) parallels the Leander portrait (II. 51–90) quite closely: both intertwine descriptions of Hero's and Leander's beauty with mythological conceits, often in the form of etiologies, telling of the effect their beauty has upon all who see them, including the gods. In verbal detail and tone, however, the two portraits are strikingly different.

The attitude of Marlowe's narrator towards Hero evolves throughout the poem into a subtle ambivalence as profoundly Ovidian as anything in the Elizabethan epyllion. Yet Marlowe's handling of Hero is also more deeply indebted to Musaeus than is generally recognized. It is from Musaeus that Marlowe derives that curious, apparently paradoxical epithet which, coming as it does in the extravagant cosmic hyperbole at the end of the opening portrait, sums up the irony of the portrait and provides the basis for much of Hero's subsequent development:

> So lovely fair was Hero, *Venus' nun*,
> As Nature wept, thinking she was undone;
> (ll. 45–46; my italics)

The phrase "Venus' nun" derives from Musaeus's reference to Hero as the priestess of the Cyprian goddess (Aphrodite). Cedric Whitman's modern English translation shows how close the relevant passage in Musaeus is to Marlowe's line:

> Hero the beautiful, heiress of Zeus-engendered blood
> Was priestess of Aphrodite. . . .
> (ll. 30–31)

The juxtaposition here of praise for Hero's beauty with the description of her relationship to Venus is significant—Musaeus goes on to develop this juxtaposition ironically, and Marlowe follows him. But the most important and most puzzling aspect of Hero's role as "Venus' nun" is that she has chosen to serve Aphrodite by dedicating herself to a life of chaste solitude (II. 31–32). Musaeus is more specific than Marlowe in explaining why Hero has made a vow of chastity to, of all goddesses, Aphrodite:

> Yet ever as she appeased Aphrodite the Cytherean
> Often she would assuage Love too with sacrifices
> Together with his Heavenly mother, fearing his quiver of flame.
> (ll. 38–40)

Musaeus's Hero has pledged herself to the service of Aphrodite in order to avoid the dangers and risks of love. This is a motive which Marlowe implies but never makes explicit. He leaves the motives for Hero's seemingly contradictory commitments to Venus vague, and we are never entirely sure why she has vowed chastity to Venus. . . .

Before examining further the way in which Marlowe builds towards the irony of "Venus' nun" in the Hero portrait, we ought to remind ourselves that classical deities, and especially Venus, had a way of transforming themselves in the Renaissance until they stood for qualities or virtues quite opposed to their original pagan significance. There was, for example, a tradition in Renaissance emblem books of using a classical figure of the celestial Venus—veiled, gowned, and surrounded by symbols of purity and chastity—as an image of *pudicitia,* or chastity. And there was the Neoplatonic tradition of the "Venus-Virgo," of Venus disguised as Diana, goddess of chastity, and regarded as a synthesis of the two apparently contradictory forces of sexual passion and chastity.

A number of interesting questions might be asked about the relevance of these allegorical traditions to Marlowe's presentation of Hero. Was he exploiting the potential ambiguity in the dual tradition of the celestial and the earthly Venus? Are we perhaps meant to see Hero as dedicating herself in Christian chastity to the celestial Venus only to be conquered by the power of the pagan earthly Venus? Or is Hero conceived as a "Venus-Virgo" who somehow combines sexual voluptuousness and chastity?

It is impossible to answer any of these questions affirmatively from the point of view of Hero's conscious motives, since Marlowe tells us nothing directly about her own conception of the goddess she serves. From the point of view of Hero's actual behavior, one can only say that if Marlowe was drawing upon Renaissance allegories of Venus, he was doing so ironically. He makes it perfectly clear from the beginning that the Venus in his poem is neither the celestial Venus nor the Venus-Virgo. And if Hero herself is seen in the image of the Venus-Virgo, it is because her vaunted chastity turns out to be a weapon of Venus that arouses the very passions it purports to discourage.

Marlowe begins preparing for the irony of "Venus' nun" by alluding early in Hero's portrait to the story of Venus and Adonis, a scene from which is embroidered on Hero's sleeve:

> Her wide sleeves green, and border'd with a grove,
> Where Venus in her naked glory strove
> To please the careless and disdainful eyes
> Of proud Adonis that before her lies.
>
> (I. 11–14)

Venus's appearance in this passage suggests that Leech is right when he comments, "Shakespeare's Venus is Hero's tyrannical goddess. . . ." Venus's nakedness stands in direct contrast to Hero's elaborately contrived costume; her behavior stands in direct contradiction to Hero's vows of chastity. At the same time the passage anticipates, even to the extent of verbal repetition, the narrator's account at the end of the poem of how Hero "trembling strove" in Leander's arms (II. 291) and of how Leander lay in bed looking at the naked Hero much as Adonis looks at Venus in this passage.

Marlowe's narrator takes advantage of every device used in Musaeus to point up the irony of "Venus' nun." He gives us a wittier and more indirect version of Musaeus's identification of Hero and Aphrodite:

> Some say, for her the fairest Cupid pin'd,
> And looking in her face, was strooken blind.
> But this is true, so like was one the other,
> As he imagin'd Hero was his mother.
>
> (I. 37–40)

Marlowe goes far beyond Musaeus, however, in describing Hero's extraordinary costume, the primary function of which is not, as has been suggested, to ridicule feminine fashions and vanity, but to point up the superficiality and falseness of her pose as a chaste nun of Venus. The ridiculously ornate costume suggests alienation from the body and from immediate sensual experience. Yet the costume includes "a myrtle wreath" (I. 17) and "sparrows" (I. 33), attributes of Venus specifically associated with her erotic power. Hero has surrounded herself with all the outward vestiges and symbols of sexual love while remaining oblivious to, or at any rate unresponsible for (again, Marlowe leaves this point ambiguous) their consequences. Her worship of Venus will be shown to be an illusion, a way of avoiding genuine participation in and understanding of what Venus represents.

While the narrator's ironic portrait of Hero is extravagantly and hyperbolically artificial and gives us only a vague, generalized sense of her physical beauty, his account of Leander is concretely sensual and erotic, full of an almost unqualified sexual admiration. The narrator's own comment later in the First Sestiad on the inevitability of human favoritism and partiality applies more tellingly to him than to Hero and Leander:

> When two are stripp'd long ere the course begin,
> We wish that one should lose, the other win;
> And one especially do we affect
> Of two gold ingots like in each respect.
> The reason no man knows: let it suffice,
> What we behold is censur'd by our eyes.
>
> (I. 169–174)

Leander's portrait makes it quite clear that, from a sexual point of view, he is the favored gold ingot in the narrator's eye, much as Hero is in Leander's eye at the end of the poem (II. 325–326). Harry Levin has pointed out that whereas in Hero's portrait the dominant visual details are filled in by an appeal to smell ("the sweet smell as she pass'd") and sound (the chirruping sparrows), in Leander's portrait the appeal is to touch and taste:

> Even as delicious meat is to the taste,
> So was his neck in touching, and surpass'd
> The white of Pelops' shoulder.
>
> (I. 63–65)

The way in which Marlowe shifts in mid-sentence here from the imagery of tasting and eating meat to the imagery of touching and seeing ivory has the effect of mitigating (without entirely dispelling) the morbidly visceral associations of the Pelops' myth (Pelops' shoulder was literally eaten by the goddess Demeter) while preserving a sense of the powerful sensual appeal Leander holds for the narrator. The narrator continues his description of Leander's body with an extremely clever, self-confessing *occupatio*:

> I could tell ye
> How smooth his breast was, and how white his belly,
> And whose immortal fingers did imprint
> That heavenly path with many a curious dint,
> That runs along his back, but my rude pen
> Can hardly blazon forth the loves of men,
> Much less of powerful gods: . . .
>
> (I. 65–71)

The fact that Leander elicits Marlowe's best erotic writing is not in itself as important as the way in which Marlowe projects a homoerotic fascination with Leander as part of the narrator's persona. The narrator is as aware as we are that Leander draws from him a different kind of response than Hero does.

Virtually all the mythological conceits in Leander's portrait dramatize his homoerotic appeal. But they are all put in the conditional mode, a strategy which enables Marlowe to acknowledge the freedom with which he is handling traditional mythological material and, at the same time, to distance Leander from actual homoerotic experience:

> His dangling tresses that were never shorn,
> *Had they been cut*, and unto Colchos borne,
> *Would have allur'd* the vent'rous youth of Greece
> To hazard more than for the Golden Fleece.
>
> (I. 55–58; my italics)

> *Had wild Hippolytus Leander seen*,
> Enamour'd of his beauty *had he been*,
>
> (I. 77–78; my italics)

This latter point is overlooked by Morris, one of the few critics who has addressed himself directly to the homoerotic aspect of *Hero and Leander*. Morris sums up his remarks on Leander's homoerotic appeal by commenting: "Leander's sexuality is, to say the least, peculiar." It is not Leander's sexuality that is "peculiar," however, but that of the various masculine figures who are attracted to him.

There are one or two details about Leander's appearance, such as his "dangling tresses" (I. 55), which might suggest that he is conceived in the tradition of the soft effeminate youth to which Narcissus, Hermaphroditus, and Adonis belong. But Leander's behavior is never effeminate in the way Adonis's behavior is. In the one passage where Leander's beauty is compared to a maiden's, the reference is to his countenance rather than to

his body, and the emphasis is on what the narrator says "some" other men
see in him:

> Some swore he was a maid in man's attire,
> For in his looks were all that men desire.
>   (I. 83–84)

These lines, like the allusion to Ganymede in line 26, look forward to the
Neptune episode, where Leander is forced to respond to Neptune's wooing
by declaring " 'You are deceiv'd, I am no woman, I' " (II. 192). Leander is
wooed by men as if he were a woman, but he is not himself womanish or
effeminate. Bush has charged Marlowe with being inconsistent in giving
effeminate traits to a young man who is supposed to be able to swim the
Hellespont, but it is apparent from the narrator's praise of Leander's back
that there is nothing weak or unmasculine about his musculature. The
narrator makes all this quite clear at the end of the portrait:

> And such as knew he was a man would say,
> Leander, thou art made for amorous play.
>   (I. 87–88)

The full significance of the homoerotic motif in the Leander
portrait does not become apparent until the Neptune episode in the
Second Sestiad. But in anticipation of a detailed examination of that
episode, let us observe that its meaning is prepared for by another striking
line in the Leander portrait:

> His body was as straight as Circe's wand.
>   (I. 61)

Morris quotes Sandys' commentary on the *Metamorphoses* in arguing that
"Circe's wand" would have suggested "sinister pleasure to any alert Renaissance reader." A more important implication of the line is that for all
its captivating charm, Leander's beauty, like Circe's wand, has the power
to turn men (and gods) into beasts. One is taken back momentarily to the
Pelops allusion, with its hint of savage aggression. The narrator's attitude
towards Leander is already becoming more ambivalent than is at first
apparent in this opening portrait.

　　Let us move on now to the first scene following the introductory
portraits and see how Marlowe extends his conceptions of Hero as "Venus'
nun" and of Leander as "made for amorous play." The citizens of Sestos
are celebrating the Feast of Adonis, and Hero goes to perform rites in the
Temple of Venus, where she will meet and fall in love with Leander.
Venus' temple is decorated with images of "the gods in sundry shapes /

Committing heady riots, incest, rapes" (I. 143–144). The goddess to whom
Hero has pledged herself in virginity stands, it seems, for riotous sexual
license. Yet Hero's ritual sacrifice in the Temple of Venus extends the
religious connotations of "Venus' nun" in a grotesque parody of what real
sacrifice to Venus will come to mean. In the midst of the lusts of the gods
depicted on the walls (I. 145–156) "a silver altar stood," and before this
altar we see "Hero sacrificing turtles' blood . . ." (I. 157–158). It is here
that we discover the cause of those curious stains on Hero's "kirtle blue"
described in the opening portrait as having been "Made with the blood of
wretched lovers slain" (I. 15–16). The difficulties commentators have had
with this earlier passage are understandable. I think Marlowe wants us to
find both passages disturbing—the initial impression of human sacrifice,
followed by the discovery of what the bloodstains are, makes us uncom-
fortably aware of the rather silly way in which Hero worships her goddess.
The muted tragic overtones mentioned previously are certainly present in
these lines—one cannot but recall the "true love's blood" of the first line
in the poem. But these tragic overtones only make more apparent the
silliness of what Hero is actually doing. In her present role as "Venus'
nun" she is sacrificing the blood of turtle doves, but true allegiance to
Venus will lead to sacrifice of a far different kind—the loss of virginity,
and ultimately the loss of her and Leander's lives. As Nigel Alexander
observes, "the rites of the goddess Venus may be rather different from the
ones that Hero appears to be practising."

It is immediately upon rising from this sacrifice on Venus' altar
that Hero looks at Leander and both are struck by "Love's arrow with the
golden head" (I. 161). Leander's response to this exchange of looks picks
up and extends the religious imagery:

> He kneel'd, but unto her devoutly pray'd;
> Chaste Hero to herself thus softly said:
> 'Were I the saint he worships, I would hear him,'
> And as she spake those words, came somewhat near him.
> (I. 177–180)

Marlowe's couplets often deliver their ironies so quickly that the reader
barely has time to savor one line, or even one phrase, before discovering
that it has become the basis for another irony, made possible by the
nimblest shift in perspective. First, Hero's line is itself ambiguous: she *is*
the "saint" Leander worships, although she does not yet realize that she
will enter into Venus' rites with him. Or does she?—her initial words,
"Were I the saint he worships," may at first seem like a confession that she
is not the chaste priestess she pretends to be. In any case, her action in

coming nearer Leander undercuts the reluctance apparently expressed in the line as a whole. Marlowe achieves the irony here through ordinary sequential syntax, but at the same time he makes one sense the simultaneity of conflicting thoughts and more deeply expressive gestures.

Marlowe is indebted to Musaeus for a number of details in his presentation of Hero's conflicting motivations. In his own way Musaeus dramatizes the simultaneous fear and desire, uncertainty and curiosity, naiveté and sophistication, of an intelligent young woman entering into her first love affair. His Hero, like Marlowe's, only gradually becomes conscious of her seductive power and of the strategy of playing the coquette. At first she is unintentionally coy:

> But she, when she recognized Leander's ensnaring desire,
> Rejoiced in his splendid charms; and quietly she also
> Once and again bent on him her own love-quickening gaze,
> With furtive gestures sending her message to Leander,
> And turned away again.
>
> (ll. 103–107)

Yet Marlowe develops Hero's fluctuating emotions far beyond Musaeus. Hero's initial response to Leander's questioning of her vows of chastity suggests that she is shocked at having been forced to realize the falseness of her previous devotion to Venus:

> 'Tell me, to whom mad'st thou that heedless oath?'
>   'To Venus,' answer'd she, and as she spake,
> Forth from those two tralucent cisterns brake
> A stream of liquid pearl, . . .
>
> (I. 294–297)

Hero quickly recovers, however, and her subsequent reaction to Leander's argument that true worship of Venus demands the very opposite of chastity indicates a remarkable coolness and poise:

> Thereat she smil'd, and did deny him so,
> As put thereby, yet might he hope for mo.
>   (I. 311–312)

Hero now appears to be in full control of the "Venus-Virgo" strategy—she is using her chastity to encourage the desire she pretends to oppose. But as Leander continues his arguments, under Hero's own subtle encouragement, Hero is made an all but helpless victim:

> Thus having swallow'd Cupid's golden hook,
> The more she striv'd, the deeper was she strook.
>   (I. 333–334)

Despite the narrator's almost callous detachment, the reader becomes involved in Hero's struggle. Dominated by love and yet capable of exerting a certain degree of control over the situation, she "strives" (Marlowe repeats the word) to retain her security and at the same time to insure the continued ardor of her suitor.

The skill with which Marlowe presents Hero's tenuous success in determining the course of the affair and, at the same time, exposes her vulnerability is perhaps best seen in her indirect invitation to Leander to visit her tower. Hero is telling of her guardian, the "dwarfish beldam,"

> That hops about the chamber where I lie,
> And spends the night (that might be better spent)
> In vain discourse and apish merriment.
> Come thither.' As she spake this, her tongue tripp'd,
> For unawares 'Come thither' from her slipp'd,
> And suddenly her former colour chang'd,
>
> (I. 354–359)

The two asides here are psychologically contrasted. The first, "that might be better spent," is a deliberately flirtatious remark, indirect enough to be safe. The second, "Come thither," is an unintentional slip of the tongue which embarrassingly exposes Hero's curiosity and desire. These lines dramatize in miniature Hero's fundamental emotional conflict.

The narrator's attitude towards Hero during this first meeting is a natural extension of the satire of the opening portrait: he clearly delights in seeing her superficial pose as "Venus' nun" exposed and used against her and in showing how her newly discovered strategies of flirtation elude her full control. As for Leander, the narrator observes him fulfilling the counsel offered in the final line of the opening portrait: "Though thou be fair, yet be not thine own thrall" (I. 90). Leander in this first meeting is the "bold sharp Sophister" who marshals argument after argument from Ovid's *Amores* in attacking every defense Hero presents—and some that she does not. But already there are hints that Leander himself is not going to be spared the narrator's satiric irony. A "sophister," Leech tells us, was a special Cambridge term for second- or third-year undergraduates, and in addition to the Ovidian echoes, Marlowe laces Leander's speech with Aristotelian definition and dicta:

> One is no number; maids are nothing then,
> Without the sweet society of men.
>
> (I. 255–256)

The point of the Aristotelian and the Ovidian echoes is to suggest indirectly what will be comically demonstrated in the second meeting, that Leander's rhetoric of love has been learned from books and has no grounding in previous experience. It may be, as Miss Tuve has shown in great detail, that much of the interest of Leander's speech stems from our simultaneous admiration for Leander's "display" of "Love's holy fire, with words" (I. 192–193) and our ability to see the speciousness of his arguments. But the fact that the arguments are specious is ultimately less important than the fact that they mask a raw and unsophisticated erotic imagination, and that they have little effect on Hero compared to Leander's sheer physical energy and attractiveness.

Miss Tuve describes Leander's arguments as "curt, acute, denuded of sensuous appeal." But in fact Leander's language is often sexually suggestive in a way which will be turned ironically against him:

> My words shall be as spotless as my youth,
> Full of simplicity and naked truth.
> (I. 207–208)

The irony here works more against Leander than against Hero, since we discover later on that Leander's youth has indeed been "spotless"—so spotless that he falters when presented with the sexual opportunity he seems to desire. Scattered throughout the rest of his speech are words which would have carried strong sexual connotations for Elizabethan readers:

> Dutiful *service* may thy love *procure*.
> (I. 220; my italics)

> Honour is purchas'd by the *deeds* we do.
> Believe me, Hero, honour is not won,
> Until some honourable *deed* be done.
> (I. 280–282; my italics)

On first reading we may think Leander a confident master of sexual pun and innuendo. But all this verbal craftiness merely sets the stage for the exposure of Leander's sexual inexperience.

Critics have been needlessly puzzled by what they have seen as a contradiction between Leander's sophisticated persuasion to love and his actual naiveté and inexperience. Marlowe gives us a quite believable portrait of a young man thoroughly versed in the rhetoric of love but as unacquainted with love's reality as Hero herself. Hero and Leander are in fact contrasted in terms of innocence and experience: Hero's pose as a chaste nun of Venus disguises her awakening sexual curiosity and sophistication; Leander's pose as an experienced rhetorician of love disguises his "spotless youth." Both will be forced out of their poses by the pressures of immediate erotic desire and made to confront the problematic realities of sexual love.

Marlowe ends the first meeting between Hero and Leander with the first of two major digressions. The episode of Mercury and the country maid may have been very freely adapted from Ovid's story of Mercury and Herse in Book II of the *Metamorphoses,* a story of which Marlowe might have been reminded by Leander's reference to Mercury's amorous adventures in Musaeus's poem (ll. 150–153). But Marlowe's digression is more interestingly Ovidian in manner than in subject. Marlowe deliberately cultivates, as Ovid so often does in his digressions, a simultaneous sense of relevance and irrelevance, of parallelism and nonparallelism, to the main story. We must read right through the Sestiad break (inserted by Chapman in the 1598 edition, we should remember, and not a feature of Marlowe's original narrative) to see how the episode is playfully woven into the primary narrative. Hero, embarrassed and shaken at having made a direct invitation to Leander to visit her in her tower, prays to Venus and renews her vows of chastity. But "Cupid beats down her prayers with his wings" (I. 369) and shoots Hero with another burning shaft of love. We do not learn of the effect of Cupid's arrow until the beginning of the Second Sestiad:

> By this, sad Hero, with love unacquainted,
> Viewing Leander's face, fell down and fainted.
> (II. 1–2)

While Cupid's arrow is taking effect, Marlowe tells how Cupid took pity on the stricken Hero and flew off to the palace of the Destinies. His request is not that Hero's prayer and vow of chastity to Venus be granted (how could Cupid support such a prayer!), but that Hero and Leander "might enjoy each other, and be blest" (I. 380). The digression which follows is an elaborate etiology explaining why the Destinies hate Love and why they therefore refuse to assent to Cupid's wish.

The digression itself seems at first glance to offer a series of entertaining parallels to the Hero and Leander affair and to give Marlowe an opportunity to comment with self-conscious irony on the present state of poetry and poets. Mercury's initial verbal wooing of the country maid is obviously meant to recall Leander's display of "Love's holy fire, with words, with sighs and tears, / Which like sweet music enter'd Hero's ears" (I. 193–194):

> And sweetly on his pipe began to play,
> And with smooth speech her fancy to assay.
> (I. 401–402)

Mercury follows up his "smooth speech" too quickly with aggressive physical gestures (I. 403–410) and is forced to retreat and resort again to verbal wooing; similarly Leander, after his long discourse, was repulsed when he tried to embrace Hero and was forced to draw out his suit and prove himself further (I. 341 ff.). But Mercury's embrace is much more sexually aggressive than Leander's; it is the embrace of "an insolent commanding lover" who "often stray'd / Beyond the bounds of shame, in being bold / To eye those parts, which no eye should behold." Mercury's behavior thus sets up the irony of Leander's fumbling naiveté in his next encounter with Hero.

As for the country maid, she is like Hero in her pretended innocence, but her freshness and naturalness serve as critical foils to Hero's artificiality:

> . . . a country maid,
> Whose careless hair, instead of pearl t' adorn it,
> Glister'd with dew, as one that seem'd to scorn it.
> Her breath as fragrant as the morning rose,
> (I. 388–391)

The parallels with Hero's hair which so charmed Apollo (I. 6) and with Hero's breath (I. 21–22) are precise. In terms of behavior, the country maid dramatizes many of the motives at work in Hero, but without the apparent idealism and insecurity which complicate Hero's attitudes. Like Hero she values her virginity, but for more overtly practical reasons—her "only dower was her chastity" (I. 412). The country maid's coyness in putting Mercury through his rhetorical paces matches Hero's, but she is more straightforwardly ambitious and self-centered in her demands. Her behavior both clarifies and brings out the subtle emotional gradations and complications in Hero's behavior.

The country maid decides to take advantage of being courted by a god and, "thirsting after immortality," requests from Mercury "A draught of flowing nectar" (I. 426–431). Mercury has to steal the nectar from Hebe, and his theft leads both to the etiological resolution of the digression and to Marlowe's comment on poets and poetry. Mercury is cast out of heaven by Jove for his theft. In revenge, Mercury persuades Cupid to make the Destinies fall in love with him so he can bring about the fall of Jove and the reign of Saturn. But because Mercury spurns the love of the Destinies, they come to hate both him and Cupid. Thus Cupid's intercession on behalf of Hero and Leander is denied (the etiology is finally completed), Jove is reinstated along with the "Murder, rape, war, lust and treachery" which characterize his reign (I. 457), and Mercury is eternally linked to poverty, with the result that the clever, learned scholar-poets associated with Mercury (and with the Elizabethan epyllion, one might add) are condemned to be poor and unknown, while fame and wealth go to "Midas' brood."

The Mercury episode is a witty *tour de force* in Ovidian digression: we are led wilfully and playfully astray by the narrator, who begins by asking us to "Harken awhile" if we want to hear why Love and Fate are enemies; at the same time, we are given just enough parallelism and relevance to the main narrative to satisfy our expectations of unity. Marlowe deliberately mutes the somber import of the episode, just as he has muted the foreshadowings of eventual tragedy all along. The enmity of Love and Fate means that Cupid's desire that the relationship of the two lovers "be bless'd" will not be fulfilled, both in the sense that their love will be tragically terminated and in the sense that under the "Stygian empery" of Jove love is inevitably and inherently troubled and tormented, much as it is in *Venus and Adonis* both before and after Venus' curse on love. The central irony of the episode is that the Destinies hate Love and oppose its fulfillment because they themselves have been wounded and frustrated by Cupid. Fate and Love are mutually frustrating in Marlowe's poem. And for Marlowe, as for Shakespeare, Love is responsible for its own lack of fulfillment and completion.

The first meeting ends with Hero coyly delaying her departure and yet afraid "In offering parley, to be counted light" (II. 5–9). But she has overestimated Leander's sophistication; the transition to the second meeting (II. 17–102) begins with a line which forecasts the exposure of Leander's lack of experience and indicates how this exposure will be related to the development of Hero's status as "Venus' nun." Hero drops her fan to give Leander a concrete excuse to visit her, but "He being a *novice,* knew not what she meant" (II. 13; my italics). This sets the stage for the comedy to follow. Hero receives Leader warmly and openly, though she is more torn than ever by her conflicting desires to yield to Leander and to protect "her name and honour" (II. 35). She begins to fear that her own misgivings will make her less appealing, however, and finally, "like light Salmacis," she throws herself upon him. In so doing she reverses her previous ritualistic offering to Venus and "offers up herself a sacrifice" (II. 44–48). But as a "novice" Leander fails to understand this kind of sacrifice—one can sense the narrator's delight in drawing out the comic irony of Leander's response:

> Like Aesop's cock, this jewel he enjoyed,
> And as a brother with his sister toyed,
> Supposing nothing else was to be done,
> Now he her favour and good will had won.
> (II. 51–54)

But finally Leander begins to suspect that "Some amorous rites or other were neglected" (II. 64) and embraces Hero passionately.

Having encouraged Leander's aggressiveness, Hero must now go on the defensive again. But her resistance only excites Leander more. She finds herself in the ironic position of unwittingly instructing Leander in the real rites of Venus, of teaching "him all that elder lovers know":

> . . . in plain terms (yet cunningly) he crav'd it;
> Love always makes those eloquent that have it.
> She, with a kind of granting, put him by it,
> And ever as he thought himself most nigh it,
> Like to the tree of Tantalus she fled,
>   (II. 71–75)

Hero's strategy during this second encounter is, from her point of view, eventually successful: she has aroused Leander's passionate love and yet "sav'd her maidenhead" (I!. 76). The narrator's comment on her struggle to save her virginity combines cynical sophistication with an element of genuine sympathy and understanding for the first time in the poem:

> No marvel, then, though Hero would not yield
> So soon to part from that she dearly held.
> Jewels being lost are found again, this never,
> 'Tis lost but once, and once lost, lost for ever.
>   (II. 83–86)

As the narrator has dealt more satirically with Leander in this encounter than in the first, he has begun to deal somewhat more sympathetically with Hero. He shows himself to be sensitive to the emotional tensions and conflicts he so knowingly exposes.

Marlowe separates the second and third meetings of Hero and Leander with a brief account of Leander's return to Abydos (II. 99–154) and with the episode of Neptune's wooing of Leander. In narrative technique the Neptune episode is less like Ovid's digressions than is the episode of Mercury and the country maid—there is less of the carefully cultivated aura of a "shaggy dog story" about it. Yet Neptune's behavior in this episode provides one of the most remarkable instances in the Elizabethan epyllion of Ovidian comic anthropomorphism. The idea for the episode may very well have come from the second of the two Hero and Leander epistles in the *Heroides*. In epistle XIX Hero petitions Neptune to calm the raging waters of the Hellespont and recalls his own amorous exploits with Anymone, Tyro, Alcyone, Calyce, and others: "Yet, Neptune, wert thou mindful of thine own heart's flames, thou oughtst let no love be hindered by the winds . . ." (XIX. 129–130). But Neptune refuses to calm the stormy sea which separates the lovers now and which will eventually cause their deaths. Marlowe's episode may therefore be read as an etiology implying, if not actually explaining, the cause of Neptune's cruelty. While the Destinies in Marlowe's first digression refuse to bless Hero and Leander because of their frustrated love for Mercury, Neptune will refuse to assist the lovers because of his frustrated love for Leander himself.

The narrator has prepared us for the Neptune episode with his account of Leander's homoerotic appeal and with his descriptions of the lechery of the gods, particularly of Jove's dallying with Ganymede (I. 148) and of Sylvanus's love for Cyparissus (I. 154–155). As Leander dives naked into the Hellespont, Neptune grows "proud" and at first imagines that Ganymede has abandoned Jove and fallen into his own realm. I have already commented on the verbal skill with which Marlowe evokes Neptune's wooing, on what Leech describes as "the double sense of the movement of the water and of the god's amorous pranks."

> He clapp'd his plump cheeks, with his tresses play'd,
> And smiling wantonly, his love bewray'd.
> He watch'd his arms, and as they open'd wide,
> At every stroke, betwixt them would he slide,
> And steal a kiss, and then run out and dance.
> (II. 181–185)

What I want to emphasize here, however, is the way in which the comedy and eroticism of Neptune's love-making constantly verge on, and occasionally become, grotesque and threatening.

J. B. Steane sees in the Neptune episode "a presentation in mythological terms and pantomime style of the nightmare intrusion of the homosexual into a normal man's life." There is indeed something dream-like, if not actually "nightmarish," in the account of Leander being pulled down to the bottom of the sea by the "saphire visag'd god" and shown the "low coral groves" where mermaids "sported with their loves / On heaps of heavy gold . . ." (II. 160–163). And dream does threaten to turn into nightmarish sick-joke when we are told that Leander "was almost dead" before Neptune realized that he was not after all the immortal Ganymede. There is also something nightmarish and grotesque in the "cartoon-like comedy" of Neptune's angry behavior later in the episode when he hears Leander cry out for the light reflected from Hero's tower:

> He flung at him his mace, but as it went,
> He call'd it in, for love made him repent.
> The mace returning back, his own hand hit,

As meaning to be veng'd for darting it.
When this fresh bleeding wound Leander view'd,
His colour went and came, . . .

(II. 209–214)

This mixing of comedy, eroticism, and sentiment with violence and grotesqueness may remind one of Ovid's technique in the *Metamorphoses* in episodes such as Jove's wooing of Europa in the form of a bull. But Marlowe's playfully detailed account exaggerates even Ovid's contrasting mixture of tones.

Brian Morris is far too optimistically single-minded, I think, in seeing in the Neptune episode a positive alternative to the "hard, jewelled, and cold" heterosexual love of Hero and Leander, in characterizing the episode as a "physical and overtly erotic description" which "enforces the peculiar power of homosexual love. . . ." Morris draws a number of apt parallels with *Edward II*, but he fails to bring out the degree of ambivalence in Marlowe's presentation of homoerotic love in both works. He notes, with insufficient emphasis, that the situation in *Edward II*, where a crafty and ambitious young man plots his appeal to a man he knows to be homosexual, is in many respects the reverse of the situation in *Hero and Leander*, where an old pederast tries to persuade a naive young man to submit to his lechery. In the former situation Marlowe shows us the exploitation and hopeless fantasy that can spring from homoerotic love; in the latter, he shows us the comic and grotesque consequences of an older lover's deluded passion for an attractive but uninterested youth.

Despite his obvious sexual interest in Leander, Marlowe's narrator is as aware of the ambivalence of homosexual as of heterosexual love. Steane gets closer to the truth about the episode when he says that it "implies . . . a sympathy with the homosexual's frustrated, hopeful, importunate, and often ludicrous state. . . ." The narrator is as aware of Neptune's ludicrousness and grotesqueness as he is sympathetic to Neptune's passion for the masculine beauty which he himself had praised so passionately in the opening portrait. It is only by seeing the homoeroticism of the Neptune episode as part of the entire vision of erotic experience which Marlowe articulates through his narrator that one becomes fully aware of its internal meaning and of its place in the poem.

As an expression of the grotesquely comic, disturbing, potentially destructive aspects of homoerotic lust, Neptune's wooing serves as a complement to the narrator's exuberant but self-ironic praise of Leander in the opening portrait. And what of Leander's role in all this? "His body was as straight as Circe's wand" (I. 61), the narrator has told us, and its effect on Neptune is in some respects like the bestializing effect of Circe's charm. Leander himself may be innocent of any Circean evil—his sympathy for Neptune's self-inflicted wound does suggest, as Steane says, the kindness a decent man will show towards non-mutual sexual solicitation. But at the same time Leander's beauty arouses a degrading, destructive lust beyond his control. This destructive aspect is played down at the very end of the episode: Neptune mistakes sympathy for love and swims off to search the ocean for gifts with which to renew his suit (II. 219–224). But what will Neptune do when he returns and finds that Leander has swum on to consummate his love with Hero? The answer, at least in Ovid's *Heroides*, comes when Hero's prayer that Neptune calm the deadly storm on the Hellespont goes unanswered.

Once again Marlowe has simultaneously and unobtrusively suggested a violent, threatening force inherent in love itself and planted the seeds for future tragedy. It is only by attending with extreme care to the mythological details of Marlowe's epyllion that one becomes conscious of the threat which often seems so remote from Marlowe's poetic concerns. Take, for instance, the one gift which Neptune has already given Leander. Helle's bracelet may at first appear to be the very opposite to a premonition of tragedy, just the thing Leander needs to insure his safety:

> The god put Helle's bracelet on his arm,
> And swore the sea should never do him harm.
> (II. 179–180)

Helle was the maiden who escaped with her brother Phrixus from their evil parents on the back of a golden ram, only to fall into a part of the sea thereafter called the "Hellespont." Neptune has thus given Leander a token of the maiden who lost her life in the Hellespont, where Leander will lose his. The very fact that Neptune presents Helle's bracelet as a guarantee of safety from the sea ironically prophesies the form Neptune's jealous revenge will take when he sees his love for Leander frustrated.

Marlowe devotes just over a hundred lines to the final meeting of Hero and Leander, a rather extraordinary feat of poetic efficiency when one considers the way in which he is able here both to sum up and to continue to develop the complexities generated in the previous seven hundred lines. The meeting begins comically, as Hero receives Leander for the first time without the contrived, artificial costume in which she was first presented:

> She stay'd not for her robes, but straight arose,
> And drunk with gladness to the door she goes.
> Where seeing a naked man, she screech'd for fear,
> Such sights as this to tender maids are are rare,
> (II. 235–238)

With this newly discovered openness and naturalness Hero may appear more admirable and attractive in the eyes of the narrator and reader, but she also appears more vulnerable. Every move she makes now will encourage Leander's sexual aggressiveness and increase her own vulnerability:

> The nearer that he came, the more she fled,
> And seeking refuge, slipp'd into her bed.
> (II. 243–244)

Hero clearly wants Leander to make love to her, but at the same time she is anxious and frightened. She has finally been drawn by Leander and by her own awakening sexual awareness out of her illusory role as a chaste nun of Venus, where she had taken on all the external manifestations of feminine sexuality but none of its actual experience, with its risks and responsibilities, into a situation where she is torn between fear of sex and sexual curiosity, between the desire to use her attractiveness to keep the upper hand and the desire to yield to an attractive and passionate lover.

Leander uses words, as before, to win Hero's consent, but it is only when words break down and his own physical exhaustion and vulnerability mingle with his passion that Hero finally surrenders:

> . . . Leander on her quivering breast,
> Breathless spoke something, and sigh'd out the rest;
> Which so prevail'd, as he with small ado,
> Enclos'd her in his arms and kiss'd her too.
> And every kiss to her was as a charm,
> And to Leander as a fresh alarm,
> So that the truce was broke, and she alas
> (Poor silly maiden) at his mercy was.
> (II. 279–285)

With Hero at Leander's mercy, the narrator begins to shift his emphasis more and more to the violence and turbulence of physical love:

> Love is not full of pity (as men say)
> But deaf and cruel, where he means to prey.
> (II. 287–288)

This is the key to Marlowe's approach to the consummation, and we can best understand his treatment by contrasting it with Musaeus's elegantly sensuous yet mystical account:

> [She] purified all his skin, and anointed his body with oil
> Sweetly scented with rose, and quenched the smell of the sea.
> And while he still breathed hard on the bed of deep coverlets
> Closely embracing her bridegroom she cried these loving words:

> "Bridegroom, heavy toiler, as no other bridegroom has ever suffered,
> Bridegroom, heavy toiler, enough now of briny water
> And the smell of fish from the sea with its heavy thunderings,
> Here on my breasts repose the sweat of your labouring."
> Thus she spoke these words, and forthwith he loosed her girdle,
> And they entered into the rites of most wise Cythereia.
>
> (II. 264–273)

Musaeus's Hero is calmly assured as she finally performs the rites which are properly due the Cyprian goddess; there is not a hint of uneasiness, fear, or guilt. Marlowe's Hero is, by contrast, victimized:

> Even as a bird, which in our hands we wring,
> Forth plungeth, and oft flutters with her wing,
> She trembling strove; . . .
>
> (II. 289–291)

Hero is far from being passively vulnerable, however—as this passage continues, the reader cannot be entirely sure that Hero's trembling is due to fear alone:

> . . . this strife of hers (like that
> Which made the world) another world begat
> Of unknown joy. Treason was in her thought,
> And cunningly to yield herself she sought.
>
> (II. 291–294)

The "unknown joy" of sexual passion finally converts Hero's fears into a desire to be an adept and cunning lover. But her moment of joy has been attained only after an internal emotional struggle more turbulent than the external physical struggle with Leander.

After the consummation insecurity and shame severely qualify Hero's sense of joy and fulfillment. She dreads the coming of day, at first because it will mean an end to their night of love (II. 301–302), then because the sun's light will shamefully display them "like Mars and Ericine" (II. 305) and will mean that she must confront Leander:

> Again she knew not how to frame her look,
> Or speak to him who in a moment took
> That which so long, so charily she kept,
> And fain by stealth away she would have crept,
> And to some corner secretly have gone,
> Leaving Leander in the bed alone.
>
> (II. 307–312)

But Leander will not allow Hero the security of privacy. He grabs her as she leaves the bed, causing her to slide to the floor and exposing her nakedness. At the end of the poem Hero is thus left standing beside the bed, naked and blushing, as Leander looks on her with the admiration of Dis contemplating a heap of gold (II. 317–326). In a sense Hero herself has finally come to realize what was ironically suggested in the phrase "Venus' nun." The allusion to Venus' shameful exposure in the arms of Mars in line 305 anticipates Hero's final predicament. To become a true "nun" of Venus she must experience the turbulence and insecurity of love as well as the joyful erotic rapture promised by Leander. And she must run the risk of becoming a sexual object—a heap of sexual gold, as it were—treated with little more sensitivity than Elizabethan playgoers would have shown towards Gosson's "Venus nunnes." The fate of the prostitute exists for Hero as only an implied and momentary threat, but it is present, along with the recollection of ecstasy, as part of the experience of love which Hero has finally come to know.

Once again Marlowe's handling of Hero may be seen as a specifically Ovidian transformation of Musaeus's narrative. Notice the parallels between Hero's behavior and that of Corinna in Marlowe's own rendering of *Amores* I.v:

> Then came Corinna in a long loose gown,
> Her white neck hid with tresses hanging down,
> Resembling fair Semiramis going to bed,
> Or Lais of a thousand wooers sped.
> I snatch'd her gown; being thin, the harm was small,
> Yet striv'd she to be cover'd therewithal,
> And striving thus as one that would be cast,
> Betray'd herself, and yielded at the last.
> Stark naked as she stood before mine eye,
> Not one wen in her body could I spy.
>
> (ll. 9–18)

> I cling'd her naked body, down she fell.
> Judge you the rest: . . .
>
> (ll. 24–25)

In looking at Musaeus through this Ovidian perspective, Marlowe has transformed Ovid as well. Corinna is an experienced courtesan, so she feels none of the threatening vulnerability and shame which beset Hero. Corinna's coy pretensions of reluctance have a very different meaning for her than they do for Hero when "cunningly to yield herself she sought" (II. 293–294). And the exposure of Corinna's beauty is described by her own lover, the "I" of the *Amores*, not by a detached narrator. The separation between actual participating observer (Leander) and fictional non-participating observer (narrator) allows Marlowe a flexibility unavailable to Ovid in this particular instance.

I have referred to the narrator as "detached" and "non-participating" to distinguish him from Leander and from Ovid's speaker. But I do not mean that he is insensitive to the emotional dynamics of the situation he describes. The sympathy which the narrator began to show for Hero at the end of the second meeting is much more openly displayed in this final meeting. He is clearly more interested in Hero's internal emotional state than in Leander's. In a sense the narrator's capacity for projecting himself into the feminine psyche balances and complements his capacity for responding to masculine sexual beauty. Yet there is not a trace of softness in the narrator's attitude towards Hero. In fact his ability to understand her emotional turmoil allows him to expose her vulnerability all the more thoroughly.

At the moment of consummation the narrator presents Leander as the conquering sexual hero now able to back up those clever arguments culled from the *Amores* with actual experience:

> Leander now, like Theban Hercules
> Enter'd the orchard of th'Hesperides,
> Whose fruit none rightly can describe but he
> That pulls or shakes it from the golden tree:
> (II. 297–300)

His final view of Leander, however, is less admiring. The comparison with "Dis, on heaps of gold fixing his look" makes clear how inferior Leander's consciousness of Hero is to the narrator's own. Sexual passion and conquest have in effect blinded Leander to Hero's internal experience. Yet there is no indication that the narrator blames Leander for his insensitivity. This, perhaps, is the ultimate expression of the narrator's cynicism, that he expects nothing more from someone "made for amorous play."

The unity of Marlowe's epyllion derives primarily from the complex but coherent evolution of the narrator's attitude towards the story he tells. He began with a cleverly critical exposure of the artificiality and superficiality of Hero's pose as "Venus' nun" and with almost unqualified praise of Leander's "spotless" masculine beauty. In working out the ironic implications of these initial attitudes, the narrator has become increasingly sympathetic to Hero's dilemma and increasingly aware of Leander's limitations. The disturbingly perceptive ambivalence with which he views the two lovers at the end represents a fully coherent extension of his view of erotic experience as it has been revealed to us in the course of the narrative.

EDWARD A. SNOW

"Doctor Faustus" and the Ends of Desire

Perhaps the most difficult thing about writing on Marlowe is finding some way of formulating and discussing his themes that will not betray the radically questioning nature of his work. For instance, if we were forced to venture a statement about the central topic of *Doctor Faustus*, it would probably not be untrue to suggest that the play, like all of Marlowe's work, is about the fulfillment of will. Yet this would scarcely suggest the extent to which the play puzzles about what the will is, and what fulfillment consists of, and how words like "will," "want," and "have" can victimize the speaker who tries to make them serve his purposes. Every time the drama raises the issue of what Faustus wants, it does so in a way that subtly deflects attention away from the ostensible objects of his desire toward the ontological ambiguities at its origin. All of his specific desires, the more randomly and recklessly they accumulate, and the more compulsively he *speaks* of them, begin to seem mere epiphenomena, attempts to rationalize an alien, anxiously prior inward restlessness by creating around it the appearance of a self that wills it and has it as "its" desire. (The problem about the subject of this sentence is the problem at the heart of the play itself.) Willing itself eventually begins to seem less a natural habitus than, as Faustus himself at one point unwittingly calls it, a "desperate enterprise." The Faustian project, we might say, becomes a matter of stabilizing the "I" by converting "wanting" in the sense of "lacking" into "wanting" in the sense of "desiring": the

From *Two Renaissance Mythmakers: Christopher Marlowe and Ben Jonson.* Copyright © 1977 by The English Institute. The Johns Hopkins University Press.

formula by which he characteristically aspires is not even "I will" or "I want" but "I'll have . . . I'll have . . . I'll have," so anxious is he to feel himself a containing self rather than merely the voice of a nameless emptiness or an impersonal rush to the void. It is not so much that there are things that he wants as it is that he needs to ensure himself that there will always be some object out there, marking extension in space and time, toward which he will be able to project "his" desire, in terms of which he can experience himself as an interior distance alive in the present and stretching continuous and intact into the future. All his negotiations with Mephastophilis leave the question of wishes to be granted pointedly unspecified and open-ended:

> I charge thee wait upon me whilst I live,
> To do whatever Faustus shall commaund, . . .
>
> (281–82)

> To give me whatsoever I shal aske,
> To tel me whatsoever I demaund . . .
>
> (339–40)

> Thirdly, that Mephastophilis shall do for him,
> and bring him whatsoever.
>
> (544–45)

And Mephastophilis is in turn reassuring Faustus at the level of his deepest anxieties when he promises that "I wil be thy slave, and waite on thee, / And give thee more than thou hast wit to aske" (486–87). Mephastophilis (besides insinuating that Faustus will get more than he bargained for) is not so much promising him "the unimaginable" as telling him not to worry about not really knowing what he wants, nor about running out of things to ask for, coming to the end of desire. Ultimate fulfillment or satiety can be the most fearful prospect of all for a self that suspects it has created itself out of nothing (in order to protect itself from nothingness), and can thus only sustain itself in the "conceited" space between desire and possession:

> CORNELIUS: The spirits tell me they can drie the sea,
> And fetch the treasure of all forraine wrackes,
> I, all the wealth that our forefathers hid
> Within the massie entrailes of the earth.
> Then tell me Faustus, what shal we three want?
> FAUSTUS: Nothing Cornelius, O this cheares my soule,
> Come shew me some demonstrations magicall . . .
>
> (177–83)

It is only with difficulty that an actor's voice, in attempting to express Faustus's enthusiasm, can overcome the resistance of the laconic, inward-turning, brooding tendencies of "Nothing, Cornelius," and block out the ominous effect of the pause that follows it. The prospect of wanting (lacking) nothing evokes just for a moment the subliminal dread of wanting (desiring) *nothing*, and perhaps lacking it—as if by a demon in language itself, *that* were what were on the other side (and at the heart) of all imagined desires. Longing and dread are an extremely unstable antithesis in this play. Like the Good and Evil Angels, they are always co-present, inseparable poles of a single impulse (and at times it seems that this impulse as a whole is what is called "the will"). It is hoped that this essay will, among other things, provide a validating frame for Empson's perception of the way in which the difficulty of giving rhetorical emphasis to the negatives in Faustus's penultimate "Ugly hell gape not, come not *Lucifer*" (1507) tends to make the voice that speaks it impatiently, even desperately invoke that which it is attempting to keep at arm's length. Whatever it is that strains against those negatives is also what resists the earlier, impatient *invocations* that the line so pointedly recalls: "come Mephastophilus, / And bring glad tidings from great *Lucifer*: / Ist not midnight? Come *Mephastophilus*, / *Veni veni Mephastophile*" (466–69). The same erotic energy charges both utterances, and the later one is the genuine consummation of the earlier one as well as its ironical inversion.

The focus of the play, then, is not so much on a theme as on the field of "terministic" ambiguities in which all its central issues are mutually implicated. An approach needs to be found that can indicate how it is that the play, being about desire, is also, necessarily, about damnation, guilt, self-transcendence, and fear of death; about the body, about self-reference, about cause, motion, place, and duration; about, ultimately, "the whole philosophical mythology concealed in language." Even more than themes and images, we need to look at the *terms* by which the play is organized—and in the process shift the focus of our attention from character-analysis and its attendant ethical judgments to the phenomenological contours of the world of the play and their relationship to those of the consciousness at the center of it. Following the language of inside-outside, or here-there, or now-then, or fast-slow, or motion-rest, through the complications of the text would, I think, put us in closer touch with the intentionality of the play than do the restrictive, morally-biased generalizations to which an approach such as "the theme of damnation" seems inevitably to condemn us.

I propose to start with the term "end" and its cognates, and follow it, especially through its interweavings with terms for body, will, and time, into whatever corners of the text it happens to lead. Of all the words in the play, it is probably the one that opens most directly upon central complexities. The language of achieving ends, making an end, coming to an end, etc., is a continual refrain of the opening soliloquy, and it recurs throughout the course of the play ("Now will I make an ende immediately" [513], "*Consummatum est*, this Bill is ended" [515], "Thy fatall time doth drawe to finall ende" [1170]), climaxing in the vacillations of the last soliloquy (" 'Twill all be past anone" [1482], "O no end is limited to damned soules" [1488]), and not culminating until the final "authorial" inscription: "*Terminat hora diem, Terminat Author opus.*" And in virtually every instance there is a tension between the speaker's attempt to say one thing, and mean it, and the tendency of the words themselves to generate ambiguity, irony, and paradox. Consider, for instance, "O no end is limited to damned soules." It is possible to take "limited" as an adjective qualifying "end," rather than as an active verb, in which case the focus of the sentence shifts from the doctrinal to the psychological, and we find ourselves on the verge of a purely phenomenological definition of the state of damnation. Even when we do hear "limited to" as a verb, there is a certain resistance to understanding it as "granted" or "allotted" (we normally think of "to limit" as the opposite of "to bestow"); and in the time it takes us to adjust to this meaning, we may hear the grammatically easier and utterly subversive "no particular end is peculiar to damned souls (all men suffer the same fate)." Finally, the awkward, apparently tautological predication of "end" by "limited" can suggest two phenomenologically opposed senses of an ending struggling within Faustus's confrontation with finality—end as extension or as circumference, as an abyss or as the boundary that keeps one from falling into it. In "Now will I make an ende immediately," to take another example, there is a rich paradox potentially involved in the notion of *making* an *end*; a possible equivocation between the volitional and temporal senses of "will"; and a transition from one experience of the time of the present to its opposite effected by the extension of "now" into the five anxious syllables of "immediately" (not unlike the transition from "dying" to dying an "everlasting death"). Or, as a last example, consider " 'Twill all be past anone." The phenomenological ambiguities of "past" tend to focus the line on the imaginative process by which the mind experiences time and death, and on the various ways in which it unconsciously preserves, gives substance to what no longer exists: "It will all have finished passing by" (on the model of "til I am past this faire and pleasant greene, / ile walke on foote"), or "It will all be the past, or in the past" (with Homer, Alexander, the Trojan War, the old philosophers, and Faustus's student days in Wittenberg). And there is an irony about transposing into the context of death itself the rather common (but still curious) act of imagining a future in which the present will be past; we are encouraged to contemplate the difficulty the mind has in including itself in the "all" or the "it," and the process by which it contrives to survive its death in the very act of projecting into it. In every instance, the more we attend to implicit ambiguities, the more we find a sceptical, nonjudgmental exploration of human consciousness tending to take the place of either an heroic, dramatistic identification with Faustus or a theological, homiletic disapproval of him.

It is in the opening soliloquy, with its careful delineation of not so much the characteristics as the *symptoms* of a Faustian personality, that the play on "end" and its cognates is most elaborately developed; it seems as a consequence the natural place for this analysis to begin. But before encountering specific instances of the term, something needs to be said about certain peculiarities of the overall texture of the soliloquy. It is virtually a patchwork of different languages: Greek, Latin, bastardized, proverbial Italian, and the "Lines, circles, sceanes, letters, and characters" of magic; or, on another axis, the specialized idioms of metaphysics, logic, ethics, medicine, law, and Christian theology. Every one of these languages implies, to a certain degree, its own world and world view: the word "end" will have slightly different connotations depending upon whether you are a Platonist or an Aristotelian, a pagan or a Christian, a Catholic or a Protestant, a metaphysician or a moralist, or a physician or a theologian. But this "Faustian" discourse, which seems capable of translating and absorbing all other languages into itself, seems correlatively to have no point of view of its own, no commitment to any particular world view or governing set of values. And it seems likewise incapable of recognizing difference or distance, or of understanding any other discourse on its own terms. The act of translation (and, less obviously, the resistances of a text) is itself a central motif of the soliloquy, and it is invariably attended by ironies of misattribution or reductive misreading. "*On cai me on*" (A's "*Oncaymaeon*") is, according to one editor, not from Aristotle, but from Gorgias, as cited by Sextus Empiricus; and if it seems implausible that Marlowe's intentions should extend to such minutiae (however appropriate it would be to the ironical tenor of the whole to discover the subversive presence of Sextus's radical scepticism lurking within Faustus's absolutist, transcendental presumptions), it surely is an aspect of the ironical design of the speech that "being and not being" connotes for Faustus not the metaphysical and ontological issues that were the heart of ancient Greek philosophy, but merely the formal, scholastic paradigms by which logical disputation is taught and mastered. *Bene disserere est finis logices* is not even from the *Analytics* to which Faustus has reduced Aristotle's works, but from the *Animadversiones Aristotelicae* of Pietrus Ramus, who "reformed" Aristotle by breaking down the division between logic and rhetoric and devising other shortcuts for mastering him—in both respects symptomatic of the character to whom this soliloquy introduces us. (In *The Massacre at Paris*, Ramus is denounced as a "flat dichotamest," and accused, in words that *Doctor Faustus* pointedly recalls, of "having a smack in all, / Yet didst never [sic] sound anything to the depth." If Faustus would seem to be antithetical in his resolve to "sound the deapth" of all that he professes [32], the condemnation of Ramus nevertheless describes perfectly the shallowness he betrays in the process.) His inability to attend to the full contexts of the Biblical passages has become a critical commonplace; it may also be of ironical significance that he quotes (with slight mistakes) from *Jerome's* Bible, thus emphasizing that it is already a translation with which he is involved (and scarcely the translation one would expect a precocious student at Wittenberg to be reading, given Marlowe's anachro-nistically contemporary dramatization of Faustus), intrigued even here by the presumptuousness of human authorship (underscored by the rhythmic stress on "*Jeromes*"), and haunted as well by its derivative, interpolated nature.

It is interesting to compare, as a means of grasping at least one aspect of Marlowe's elusive critical perspective, the way in which this opening soliloquy reduces every "foreign" language that enters it with the manner in which "*O lente lente curite noctis equi*" (1459) intrudes into the final soliloquy. Here, too, technically, is misquotation: the original is "lente currite, noctis equi." Here too, if you wish, is a flagrant violation of the original context: what in Ovid is a wish to extend a night of erotic pleasure serves for Faustus as an expression of apocalyptic dread. Once again a pagan (or epicurean) sensibility is distorted when it is appropriated by a Christian (or Faustian) one. Yet the difference in effect is complete. The line from Ovid wells up spontaneously from the depths of Faustus's being: it *originates* in him (no time or need for translation here!). Burning his books will not get it out of his system. Beneath its apparent inappro-priateness, it is profoundly expressive of the obscure erotic energy in-volved in his religious passion. And against the feeling that Ovid's guilt-free, flesh-and-blood eroticism is betrayed in this Faustian setting, there is an equal sense that the setting deepens the Ovidian sense by creating a cosmic and spiritual background against which the erotic embrace it celebrates can take on its full, intrinsic value. (Jump comments that the transposition "adds immeasurably to [the words'] power and poignancy.") Faustus's misquotation here seems literally an improvement of the original, in its own language—as if he were further inside the poetry, feeling it more deeply, than Ovid himself. And the haunting, paradoxical inwardness of the line can become even more complex if it happens to remind us that Marlowe himself began his literary career and first achieved notoriety with a translation of the *Elegies*. The contrast between the line's perfunctory Englishing there—"Stay night, and run not thus"—and its spontaneous, originative upwelling (and remembering) at the end of *Faustus* then takes its place as a facet of a complex meditation by Marlowe, implicit throughout the play, on authorship and its consequences—specifically, on his relationship to his protagonist, and on the distance that bringing him into being places between him and his more superficial, complacent Ovidian origins. Certainly no less crucial to the final, lingering effect of the play than Faustus's own passionate breakdown is the accompanying collapse of the authorial perspective, from the ironical, mocking detachment established by the opening soliloquy into the experience of immediacy and emotional identification that the closing soliloquy thrusts upon us. Whatever the actual chronology of Marlowe's plays, no work of art—not even *The Tempest*—communicates more powerfully the *sense* of a "last work" than does *Doctor Faustus*.

When we turn specifically to the motif of "end" and "ending" in the opening soliloquy, what seems crucial about the method of reiteration is a discrepancy between the pointed awareness in the text of the different words that can be translated as "end"—and the correspondingly different senses of "end-ness" that language can suggest—and the speaker's incapacity to respond to the concept in any other than an eschatological, self-alienating sense of "end-point" or "termination." For instance: "disputing well" (already a symptomatically Faustian translation of the potentially less disputatious *bene disserere*) is the "end" (*finis*) of logic in the sense of final cause, abiding concern, reason for being: one is always in the midst of logic, once one *has* achieved its end. Yet Faustus seems instinctively to assume that having "attained" this end means that he has arrived at the end of it, used it up, finished with it—and that as a result there is nothing to do but move on to something new. It is much the same with *ibi desinit philosophus, ibi incipit medicus*. This is what amounts to an ethical statement about the limits of the *field* of philosophy, a reminder that the health of the body and the knowledge of its functions and its orders lie outside the scope of philosophy, yet that philosophical wisdom should involve a respect for the body and the knowledge by which physical well-being is maintained. (And in the context of Marlowe's own "post-Christian" vision, the aphorism acquires a gnomic significance beyond anything Aristotle would have intended: that to go all the way in the realm of philosophy is to arrive at the all-important starting-point of the body, to discover it as the unanalyzable phenomenon toward which every thread of philosophical speculation, no matter what its ostensible subject, ultimately leads us. As if *only* a philosopher could know the true significance of medicine.) But Faustus seems to take it to mean simply that when you are finished with philosophy, then it is time to take up medicine. His experience as a physician has no bearing on his experience as a philosopher, nor vice versa. One art follows directly upon another, each beginning precisely where the last left off, each neatly condensed, predigested, and encapsulated within the covers of its own book.

If Faustus were more at home within the metaphor of "sounding the depths," then the "end" of an art might be a moment of creative fulfillment, an opening upon immanent horizons. But "levelling at the end," which seems so much more obviously expressive of the acquisitive impatience and narrow, projective vision that characterize him throughout the soliloquy, condemns him to traverse only surfaces, and to arrive only at terminations. It seems paradoxically the very nature of his will to go forward, his eyes aiming at a goal posited beyond him, that fates him to find himself always back where he started, empty-handed. As the soliloquy unfolds, the impression of an heroic capacity to originate and conclude ("Settle thy studies *Faustus*, and beginne") gradually yields to that of a more passive, compulsive insertion into the ambiguities of "having commencde." The spectacle of a virtuostic progress through the human sciences is displaced by a growing awareness of static self-imprisonment; the gestures of an insatiable thirst for the profound gradually betray the existence of a grasp that turns everything it touches into "external trash."

Against the emphasis in the first soliloquy on the order of books—on compartmentalization and inventory, on hierarchical ordering, on the programmatic acquisition of knowledge—and against the goal-oriented obsession with horizon and transcendence that it reinforces, the shape and texture of the play itself poses an altogether more complicated picture of the structures within which a human life unfolds:

> As are the elements, such are the spheares,
> Mutually folded in each others orbe,
> And *Faustus* all jointly move upon one axletree,
> Whose terminine is tearmd the worlds wide pole . . .
> (667–70)

On the one hand, of course, this is simply Mephastophilis's devilishly laconic recapitulation of the Ptolemaic commonplace: against Faustus's desire for privileged awareness, he reasserts the truth of what has always been and what every schoolboy already knows; against Faustus's submerged longing for a pluralistic universe ("Tel me, are there many heavens above the Moone?" [664]), he insists upon the closed world of classical and medieval order. But the words themselves, excerpted from their immediate context, are descriptive less of a classical world picture than of a field of Pyrrhonist or Montaignian "experience" (or of what a modern sensibility might term a "problematic"): the various spheres of what we experience as the world are not discrete and hierarchically ordered but "mutually folded in each others orbe"; the same is true even of the elements themselves. The very notion of distinct, separable professions, or of explanatory and evaluative sets of finite, static irreducibles (whether it be the four elements, the seven deadly sins, the faculties of psychology, or the entities with which the language of religion populates and fragments the inner life) is an arbitrary imposition upon an "ever moving" field of circulation where everything is made up of and interanimated by everything else. All revolves upon a single axis, while the concept of end-point and polarity (Good and Evil Angels as well as East and West, North and South) is just a "terministic" reduction of what is really spherical extent. Although any attempt to prove that the play endorses, as well as evokes, this vision of things would ultimately become problematical, one can feel a cherished atmosphere of human kindness and well-being, a sense of grace itself, suddenly descend over the play when Faustus describes to the Duke and his pregnant Duchess a circular movement within which the mind's and language's divisive oppositions and linear sequences are imperturbably accepted and contained:

> DUKE: Beleeve me master Doctor, this makes me wonder above the rest, that being in the dead time of winter, and in the month of January, how you shuld come by these grapes.
> FAUSTUS: If it like your grace, the yeere is divided into twoo circles over the whole worlde, that when it is heere winter with us, in the contrary circle it is summer with them, as in *India*, *Saba*, and farther countries in the East, and by means of a swift spirit that I have, I had them brought hither, as ye see, how do you like them Madame, be they good?
> DUCHESS: Beleeve me Maister doctor, they be the best grapes that ere I tasted in my life before.
> FAUSTUS: I am glad they content you so Madam.

> (1245–57)

If one looks at the form of Faustus's fortunes rather than at the frames in terms of which he consciously experiences himself, one can also discover a "whole worlde" in which all disciplines, all approaches to knowledge, are simultaneously implicated in one another, lead to one another not sequentially but dialectically. The Biblical texts at which Faustus balks confront him with what would seem strictly a matter of divinity; yet it is with an ethical sensibility (however impure) that he instinctively responds to it, while both ethical and theological crisis unfold within the framework of an exercise in elementary syllogistic reasoning. The language of magic, which seems so opaque and autonomous in the opening soliloquy, borrows heavily from the language of Christianity, and its invocations turn out to be efficacious (or so at least the devil claims) only because of the negative significance that theology attributes to them. Blasphemy, too, turns out not to be self-consummating, but must be accomplished through a legal contract. The congealing of blood is a resistance to pacts with the supernatural that can be understood either medically or theologically, as a confirmation of either Augustinian or Epicurean wisdom—ultimately at stake are two antithetical visions of the nature of Faustus's damnation. When Lucifer responds to Faustus's desperate cry for salvation with "Christ cannot save thy soule, for he is just" (714), part of our difficulty in coming to terms with the reply has to do with the convergence of theological, ethical, and contractual perplexities on the single word "just."

Nothing that Faustus dismisses in the opening soliloquy really goes away; whatever he banishes returns as a theme woven into the very fabric of the play. The result is a curious disjunction between the gestures that he makes and the fortunes that befall him, between what he undertakes at the level of conscious, rhetorical selfhood and what he undergoes at the level of flesh and blood, "textual" experience. He is strangely out of place in this play that seems at first glance but the logical extension of his personality: if he is the prototype of the "forward wit" condemned by the final chorus, he seems conceived and framed by the "patient judgment" to whom the opening chorus appeals. In the moments when the issue of what is happening to him most concerns Faustus himself, there is always an exasperating feeling of the inability of the mind to make contact with the sphere where its life is taking place, in spite of what would seem the stable locus of the body. This obscure sensation crystallizes in moments such as Faustus's attempt, as he watches his blood congeal, to interpret what it means, and only succeeding when he can manage to *read* it as a text; it is present most obscurely but intensely throughout the final soliloquy.

This disjunction between the organization of Faustus's mind and the shape and rhythm of the experience to which the play submits him (along with the growing conviction that, *contra* Mephastophilis, no amount of the latter will ever "change" the former) is what is at the bottom of the feeling that he is fated, in spite of all his compulsive gestures of bidding farewell and making final ends immediately, to experience it all over and over again ad infinitum—beyond even the twenty-four years of the contract, into the fatal round of the play itself. As the play takes its course, one can sense evolving, through the dialectic between Faustus's forward progress and the depths of the work that Marlowe is shaping around it, a meditation on what is really involved in "settling" and taking stock of a life, and on what is really required in order to "get over and done with, conclude, come to a form, achieve resolution in the self and of the self's works." Against all of Faustus's conclusions and resolutions, Marlowe allows himself only that final, laconic "*Terminat hora diem, Terminat Author opus*"—an ending that, in spite of all *its* ambiguities, rings true with the force of an epitaph.

LAWRENCE DANSON

The Questioner

In our better moments we welcome controversy about Shakespeare because in our better moments we trust Shakespeare: we trust that our controversies testify to Shakespeare's ability to embrace multitudes. With Marlowe the case is different. Marlowe has from the start failed to inspire trust. He "was intemperate & of cruel hart," according to his roommate, Kyd; and in various ways the idea persists that his defects of character or quirks of psychology account for the difficulties we have with him. Marlowe is blamed for our critical perplexity; our difficulties are laid to the charge of his supposedly uncertain control over or self-divided perception of his material. Especially in the matter of Marlowe's relation to the "opinions" of his time—the notorious Elizabethan World-Picture—Marlowe's "damnable" inaccessibility to interrogation, by Privy Council or critic, may seem positively scandalous.

Without quite assuming that Marlowe never made an artistic miscalculation, I want here to suppose that basically Marlowe did know what he was doing, and that the problems we encounter are often part of his artistic method. I want to suppose that Marlowe did understand his own ideas and feelings—as much as that is ever possible—and that the major plays are not the gropings of a neurotic rebel. These suppositions should not lead to any diminution of Marlowe's stature as an explorer of the tensions, heterodoxies, and tragic possibilities in the *ethos* he dramatized. For clear-sighted is not simple-minded: it was not Marlowe but his damned Faustus who asked for a devil to "resolue [him] of all ambiguities."

From *English Literary Renaissance* (1982). Copyright © 1982 by University of Massachusetts Press.

The fact that Faustus *asks* is significant: it is something Marlowe's heroes often do. (In this essay I will be concerned only with Barabas, Tamburlaine, and Faustus.) The questions they ask, and the ways they ask them, are worth attending to for a variety of reasons. We should attend because, oddly, Marlowe's questioners themselves tend *not* to; frequently they will not pause for an answer. And this peculiarity may lead us to consider the problematic relationships—dramatic, philosophical, emotional—between Marlowe and his characters, and between those characters and us. Also it is worth attending to the Marlovian questions because they are too easily drowned out by another characteristic rhetorical device, the hyperboles so well analyzed by Harry Levin.

The interrogative mood would not, perhaps, seem to sort well with the assertive declarations of the Overreacher. But Puttenham (among others) distinguishes a variety of rhetorical questions whose effects are potentially various and surprising. There is, for instance, *erotema* or "The Questioner": "a kinde of figurative speach when we aske many questions and looke for none answere, speaking indeed by interrogation, which we might as well say by affirmation." *Erotema* is as tricky a figure as hyperbole. With the latter, which Puttenham also calls "the loud lyer," there is the risk of over-taxing the audience's credulity. So, too, with *erotema*: the questioner who wants to affirm had better be sure that his question will get the intended response. Puttenham gives as an example of *erotema*, "Medea excusing her great crueltie vsed in the murder of her owne children which she had by Iason . . . . : "*Was I able to make them I praie you tell, / And am I not able to marre them all aswell?*" For an uncomfortable instant the question admits answers beyond the scope of the obviously intended one. And to the extent that it does, it makes the audience active rather than passive: Medea's question forces us to realize, as though we were discovering it ourselves, the horror in this ostensible propriety of the maker marring her creatures. In Marlowe's characters' mouths, too, "the questioner" may allow an audience to hear something quite different, in dramatic effect, than what would be said "by affirmation."

Barabas' first rhetorical question, for instance (after several non-rhetorical questions about weather and shipping) is a notable *erotema*:

> What more may Heaven doe for earthly man
> Then thus to powre out plenty in their laps,
> Ripping the bowels of the earth for them,
> Making the Sea their seruant, and the winds
> To driue their substance with successefull blasts?
>
> (145–47)

I begin with *The Jew of Malta* because the relationships it establishes between author and character and between character and audience are typically Marlovian but more easily discerned than in the other plays, partly because of its more overtly satirical stance. In Barabas' question the antithesis *heaven-earthly* is explicit (in *Tamburlaine* it is strikingly implicit); and the antithesis makes it possible to find other plausible answers to complement Barabas' intended one. The questioner invites us to take a wicked delight in his reduction of all values to the "earthly" measure—a pleasure it would be hard to refuse. But one would have to redefine radically the conventional meanings of "heaven" and "earthly" in order to give full assent to Barabas' affirmative. Marlowe's rhetorical and philosophical control is evident in his manipulation of this semantic fact. He pulls us shockingly toward a reductive redefinition of his terms, at the same time that he makes ironic profit out of the impossibility of immediately effecting that redefinition. Our attitude toward Barabas is complex: we are with him in knowing more about the ways of the world than the "haplesse man" of conscience who "for his conscience liues in beggery" (158); but we are also with the author who knows that the inescapable traditional values of "heaven" will leave Barabas' "earthly man" absurdly self-defeated.

Marlowe has been establishing an uneasily conflicting relationship between the audience and Barabas from the start, where his long soliloquy gives ample opportunity for both complicity and distance. It begins in wish-fulfillment, with Barabas literally mounding up his very disposable assets: "So that of thus much that returne was made: / And of the third part of the *Persian* ships, / There was the venture summ'd and satisfied" (36–38). But the pleasure of playing with money is short-lived; Barabas pauses, tired and disgusted with his labors: "Fye; what a trouble tis to count this trash" (42). The belief that worldly wealth is heaven's trash is part of the pious baggage the Elizabethan theatergoer inevitably brings with him to this odd Malta. But Marlowe allows the orthodox reminder to obtrude only an instant, as Barabas goes on to protest against the intolerable coarseness of his own proceedings—not, however, by the "heavenly" but precisely by the "earthly" measure. First we are abashed, then again delighted as Barabas introduces us to the less vulgar ways of being earthly rich. But then, again, we're caught: in what follows, the vision of this finer way begins by disarming us, then again alarming us, as we hear, ironically undercutting Barabas, the tones of that value-system which will be made explicit in the "heaven-earthly" antithesis:

> Giue me the Merchants of the *Indian* Mynes,
> That trade in mettall of the purest mould;
> The wealthy *Moore*, that in the *Easterne* rockes

> Without controule can picke his riches vp,
> And in his house heape pearle like pibble-stones;
> Receiue them free, and sell them by the weight,
> Bags of fiery *Opals, Saphires, Amatists,*
> *Iacints,* hard *Topas,* grasse-greene *Emeraulds,*
> Beauteous *Rubyes,* sparkling *Diamonds,*
> And seildsene costly stones of so great price,
> As one of them indifferently rated,
> And of a Carrect of this quantity,
> May serue in perill of calamity
> To ransome great Kings from captiuity.
> This is the ware wherein consists my wealth.
>
> (54–67)

Will not some in the audience remember, in this talk of "costly stones of so great price," a merchant who sold all he had to purchase one pearl of great price? What really, "in perill of calamity," has served "To ransome great Kings from captiuity"? Barabas' speech is ingeniously hyperbolic as it searches for ever-smaller ways of enclosing wealth. And it shows the affinity between hyperbole and *erotema*: overreaching himself, Barabas stumbles into the language of transcendence; and once we hear that language it is difficult not to feel some distance between ourselves and the speaker. That distance is the sort we feel when a rhetorical question provokes an unexpected response.

This first soliloquy, then, begins to establish the play's ironic attitude toward Barabas and his wealth, and to place us in our interestingly active position between enjoyment of Barabas' wit and the recognition of a range of spiritual meanings beyond his conceiving. Now he is interrupted by his merchants bringing news. The pace (84–140) is brisk; there is no opportunity for reflection; we are caught up in the excitement of getting and spending until, alone again, Barabas resumes the work of his first speech:

> Thus trowles our fortune in by land and Sea,
> And thus are wee on euery side inrich'd:
> These are the Blessings promis'd to the Iewes,
> And herein was old *Abrams* happinesse:
> What more may Heaven doe for earthly man
> Then thus to powre out plenty in their laps?
>
> (141–46)

The identification of the Jews' promised blessings and earthly riches is the kind of iconoclastic wit with which Marlowe shocked Richard Baines. Here, it is functional in establishing the ironic limits of the Maltese universe, in which "Euery ones price is written on his backe" (764). But Barabas has introduced a leaky allusion which, like the open-ended *erotema*, allows the audience to take an active part, hearing both what the character intends and something more. Marlowe allows his audience to go outside Malta's slavish perspective: it would have taken no special exegetical skill to know that, in the contemporary understanding, the family treasure of "old *Abrams* happinesse" was Christ and that the promised blessing was a spiritual one. Barabas is comically outrageous in his richly carnal mistaking of the Bible's promise.

The game is not simply that of one-upping Barabas with our privileged knowledge. The two rhetorical questions that immediately follow Barabas' first slippery one—"Who hateth me but for my happinesse? / Or who is honour'd now but for his wealth?" (150–51)—show Barabas in his dual role, as much the satirist as the object of satire. The lesson Barabas takes from these questions is, within the Maltese scheme of things, amply justified by the Christian characters:

> Rather had I a Iew be hated thus,
> Then pittied in a Christian pouerty:
> For I can see no fruits in all their faith
> But malice, falshood, and excessiue pride,
> Which me thinkes fits not their profession.
> (152–56)

The concluding line is deliciously understated. What less fits a Christian profession than the rotten fruits Barabas sees? And who can doubt that the Christians of Malta are reaping a rich crop of them?

(In fact, to take up my own rhetorical question, I suspect that many in Marlowe's audience might fail to hear this satire against Christian hypocrisy—which is why it would have been supererogatory for a savagely indignant Marlowe to have written, in Elizabethan England, a satire against Jews.)

"We doo aske oftentymes, because we would know: we do aske also, because we woulde chide, and sette furthe our grief with more vehemencie, the one is called *Interrogatio*, the other is called *Percontatio*." Thus, in a *percontatio*, Barabas asks the Christian governor, Ferneze: "Are strangers with your tribute to be tax'd?" (290). And thus a Christian knight in reply: "Haue strangers leaue with vs to get their wealth?" (291). Thomas Wilson's nickname for *percontatio* is "snappishe askying"; in this exchange between Barabas and the governor's man we see the snappish asker out-snapped. It is a model for the relationship between Barabas and Ferneze throughout the play.

Marlowe's relationship with Barabas is oblique, as is Barabas' with us. Ferneze's relationships—with author, audience, and the entire cast of characters—are more nearly opaque. With Barabas we must be on guard both because he takes us into his confidence, thus making us complicit in his Machiavellian game, and also because he reserves the right to trick us, his accomplices. Ferneze is another confidence man, but unlike Barabas he never acknowledges the con. Macheuil warns us in his Prologue:

> Admir'd I am of those that hate me most.
> Though some speake openly against my bookes,
> Yet will they reade me, and thereby attaine
> To *Peters* Chayre.
>
> (9–12)

Only a covert Macheuil is a consistent Macheuil. Ferneze, who keeps his counsel, by the end keeps all: Barabas' wealth, the Turkish tribute, the slave trade, Malta. The obliquity of Marlowe's presentation of Ferneze makes him worth a moment's study, before we go on to more Marlovian questioners.

This Christian champion enters on a question: "Now Bassoes, what demand you at our hands?" Again: "What's *Cyprus*, *Candy*, and those other Iles / To vs, or Malta?" (230, 234–35). Is this asking or chiding, *interrogatio* or *percontatio*? In fact Ferneze knows perfectly well what the Turk wants, but his moment of deceptive rhetoric helps us, by putting us on our guard. We should know now how to react to Ferneze in the game of question-and-answer he plays with Barabas. For instance Barabas snappishly asks if the Jews must be taxed "equally" with the Christians, and Ferneze replies:

> No, Iew, like infidels.
> For through our sufferance of your hatefull liues,
> Who stand accursed in the sight of heauen,
> These taxes and afflictions are befal'ne,
> And therefore thus we are determined.
>
> (294–98)

Does Ferneze believe that his "sufferance" of the Jews has caused the Turkish affliction? Does Marlowe expect us to believe that Ferneze believes it? Marlowe's satire, like Ferneze's gamesmanship, is consummate.

Again Barabas tries a snappish question: "Will you then steale my goods? / Is theft the ground of your Religion?" (327–28); and again Ferneze has the reply pious:

> No, Iew, we take particularly thine
> To saue the ruine of a multitude:

> And better one want for a common good,
> Then many perish for a priuate man.
> (329–32)

This is (as Boas points out in his edition) essentially "the plea of Caiaphas" (John 11.50). The overly-revealing allusion, perfectly controlled and slyly understated, is as typically Marlovian as any splendid hyperbole.

Barabas' struggle to keep from being preached out of his possessions continues in the interrogative mood and theological vein:

> Some Iewes are wicked, as all Christians are:
> But say the Tribe that I descended of
> Were all in generall cast away for sinne,
> Shall I be tryed by their transgression?
> The man that dealeth righteously shall liue:
> And which of you can charge me otherwise?
> (345–50)

A question not to be asked, that last. Ferneze's reply begins in righteous indignation and ends in transparent twaddle:

> Out, wretched *Barabas*,
> Sham'st thou not thus to iustifie thy selfe
> As if we knew not thy profession?
> If thou rely vpon thy righteousness,
> Be patient and thy riches will increase.
> Excesse of wealth is cause of covetousnesse:
> And covetousnesse, oh 'tis a monstrous sinne.
> (351–57)

Ferneze's last line, with its portentous polysyllables surrounding the vacuous ejaculation, is as close as he comes to showing any pleasure in his own Machiavellianism.

"Policy," Barabas concludes, playing on some Maltese key-words, "that's their profession" (393). As the play turns more broadly comic after the initial scenes its satire against misprofessing Christians becomes unmistakable. We are in no doubt, for instance, about Marlowe's attitude toward the "religious caterpillars" who lament that Abigail, dying a Christian, dies "a Virgin too, that grieues me most" (1497), and whose attempts to bring Barabas to repentance end in a fratricidal struggle for his fortune. But what does the play say about the "profession" itself, apart from its woefully inadequate professors?

The Jew of Malta is more concerned with moral values than with specifically theological; the question of Marlowe's attitude toward Christianity in it can therefore be answered only in part. We can know that

Barabas is wicked and, more significantly, that Ferneze is too because we tacitly recognize the play's coherent moral view. We can answer its sly rhetorical questions and understand the range of its ironic allusions because we know not only what the characters know, but also what Marlowe knows. That moral view and that knowledge are no less consistent with a Christian profession than is satire against nominally Christian hypocrites. Never has *Te deum* rung more hollowly than in Ferneze's concluding couplet, "So march away, and let due praise be giuen / Neither to Fate nor Fortune, but to Heauen" (2409–10). If we cannot be sure in this play that Marlowe himself gives praise to heaven, we can be sure of his ironic distance from the obdurate Machiavellian who mouths the praise.

II

The situation is more complicated in *Tamburlaine*. And surely we will mistake it if we assume that the Scythian shepherd is really only the Cantabrigian Marlowe in fancy-dress. Yet such an identification is frequently made, with the result that either Marlowe or his play is impugned. In his own day, Greene implied that Marlowe would dare "God out of heaven with that atheist Tamburlaine"; more recently, J. B. Steane continues the tradition of *ad hominem* criticism: "It is clear that, whether in pleasure or repulsion, Marlowe was attracted to cruelty; and here in *Tamburlaine*, although the mind is divided, the division is unequal and the larger part seems to rate violence and cruelty as among the enviable excitements of life." Examining "The Strange Case of Christopher Marlowe," L. C. Knights takes Tamburlaine's "regressive craving for effortless and unlimited power" as a symptom of Marlowe's own parlous state; and Wilbur Sanders detects in the play "a bad breath of psychic decay." Steane condemns the play's "Fascist spirit"; before him, Willard Farnham, less outraged but similarly identifying author with character, had written that Marlowe "gave himself completely to a drama of untrammeled worldly success." That these opinions do not fit all the evidence is noticed by the critics, who therefore either posit an extraordinarily sudden change of heart—"Needless to say, Marlowe outgrew this young man's worship of pomp, or he could not afterward have written the tragedies that he did write"—or a divided mind. Wilbur Sanders goes further, assuming not a divided but an absent mind: "moral ambiguity" accounts for "the rival interpretations of *Tamburlaine*," in which we have "the problem of deciding where precisely Marlowe stands"—and Sanders wonders if "perhaps he stands precisely nowhere."

But there is a coherent moral vision in *Tamburlaine*, however indirectly it is made to emerge; it is neither reductively moralistic nor foolishly Promethean. And it is coherent throughout both parts of the drama. The distinction Harry Levin draws obscures this continuity: "By the end of the First Part [Tamburlaine] is a candidate for apotheosis. But the Second reveals the self-proclaimed god as a mortal, a human being whose strength is his inhumanity and whose weakness is his mortality." Did we need Part Two to tell us that? Were we ever to believe that Tamburlaine held "the Fates bound fast in yron chaines" or with his hand turned "Fortunes wheel about" (369–70)? Tamburlaine's "working words" need not work on an audience exactly as they do on his impressionable antagonists. Certainly the plays' vision does not depend on any last-second retribution. Tamburlaine's death by spontaneous combustion may indeed carry, as Roy Battenhouse tells us, the traditional idea that "God is casting His Scourge into the fire" of his own rage. But we might as well take its inclusion as a sop to the softer-minded Christians in Marlowe's audience or a joke at their piously expectant expense, for it neither alters nor even necessarily confirms what has come before. The Prologue has bid us "View but his picture in this tragicke glasse / And than applaud his fortunes as you please." The astonishing thing is not only that Tamburlaine is allowed to make good so many of his threats, but that we really are expected to use our judgment in interpreting the dramatic image—and to applaud that image only as we please.

A person who believes himself to be immortal is probably not to be trusted with strenuous philosophizing. From the colorful, if childish, question early in his career,

> Is it not braue to be a King, *Techelles*,
> *Vsumcasane* and *Theridamas?*
> Is it not passing braue to be a King,
> And ride in triumph through *Persepolis?*
> (756–59)

—from that *erotema*, which shows as much a delight in pretty sounds as it does anything else, Tamburlaine passes on to consider man's place in "The wondrous Architecture of the world" (873). The speech, which is in two parts, divided by a significant rhetorical question, has occasioned much critical debate. It begins as a kind of *apologia* addressed to the defeated, weak King Cosroe:

> The thirst of raigne and sweetnes of a crown,
> That causde the eldest sonne of heauenly *Ops*,
> To thrust his doting father from his chaire,

> And place himselfe in the Emperiall heauen,
> Moou'd me to manage armes against thy state.
> What better president [precedent] than mightie Ioue?
> (863–68)

Tamburlaine takes a somewhat squalid family quarrel—the picture of Jove throwing his "heavenly" father out of his chair is neither heroic nor pretty—as the model for his project of world conquest. The ironic iteration of the words "heaven" and "heavenly" would make it especially difficult for an alert member of the audience not to compare this example of filial revolt with the Christ-story of love, obedience, and reconciliation. Tillyard's famous terse dictum is worth repeating: "The orthodox scheme of salvation was pervasive in the Elizabethan age. You could revolt against it but you could not ignore it." The success of Marlowe's rhetorical and dramaturgical indirectness depends on the impossibility of ignoring it, even when an Oriental despot invokes a Roman deity.

The part of Tamburlaine's speech following his question has attracted the most critical commentary. What kind of worldview is this? What are we to make of its disturbing conclusion?

> Nature that fram'd vs of foure Elements,
> Warring within our breasts for regiment,
> Doth teach vs all to haue aspyring minds:
> Our soules, whose faculties can comprehend
> The wondrous Architecture of the world:
> And measure euery wandring plannets course,
> Still climing after knowledge infinite,
> And alwaies moouing as the restles Spheares,
> Wils vs to weare our selues and neuer rest,
> Vntill we reach the ripest fruit of all,
> That perfect blisse and sole felicitie,
> The sweet fruition of an earthly crowne.
> (869–80)

Scholars have sought without much success a provenance for this surprising notion that nature, whose essence is supposed to be strife, teaches us to imitate its incessant internecine warfare. In all the putative models, nature's strife actually suggests an ideal of eventual or subsistent harmony: the absence of such an ideal from Tamburlaine's speech has been taken, therefore, either as evidence of Marlowe's prescient modernity or of his confusion. But the assiduity with which we cull the history of ideas may obscure the simple fact that we have here Tamburlaine's ideas, not Plato's, Aristotle's, Empedocles', DuBartas', Tennyson's or Darwin's—not even, dramatically speaking, Marlowe's. What is at issue is neither Mar-

lowe's modernity nor his confusion, but his ironic distance from his character. The precedent Tamburlaine takes from his notion of a "warring,"
self-divided nature is grander sounding but no more convincing than the
precedent he draws from the unquiet homelife of the gods. He sees nature
disturbed and sets about imitating it, as though one were to draw from the
observation of cancer the lesson that men should behave in their moral
lives like metastasising cells.

The conclusion of the speech most decidedly demands that we
distinguish Marlowe from his speaker. The brilliant periodic sentence
swells, carrying us literally towards "Heaven"—by way of the loaded
phrases "ripest fruit," "perfect bliss," "sole felicity"—only to drop us
rudely on "The sweet fruition of an *earthly* crown." The techniques are
similar to those Marlowe was to use, in a comic vein, in *The Jew of Malta*.
Tamburlaine's earthly bliss is intended to make no more sense than
Barabas' "Oh girle, oh gold, oh beauty, oh my blisse" (695). The attempt
to press words indelibly associated with a transcendental ideal into the
service of worldly aspiration is indeed challenging, and perhaps disturbing,
but it cannot be wholly successful. Denying us the satisfaction of the word
"heavenly," which syntax and semantics lead us powerfully to expect,
makes the substituted "earthly" inescapably ironic. You can deny heaven,
as Tamburlaine does, but without a willful act of cultural, linguistic
amnesia you cannot ignore it.

Harry Levin denies that there is anticlimax in the vision of "an
earthly crown":

> Tamburlaine's conception of bliss is not less climactic because it is
> heresy. . . . [W]hereas a heavenly crown was the pious hope of every
> Christian, an earthly crown is the notorious emblem of worldliness,
> heterodoxy, and pride of life. In short, it is not bathos but blasphemy.

It sounds better, of course, to be grandly defiant rather than merely
stupid, or blasphemous rather than bathetic. But Marlowe makes the
distinction hard to maintain: they are different perspectives on the same
thing. Part of the play's great originality is its admitting the aggrandizing
perspective. This is indeed a different dramatic world from the one in
which, for instance, the rebelling Lucifer in the Corpus Christi plays is by
necessity a fearful, farting grotesque. But Marlowe's play is also dramatur-
gically notable for the various indirect ways, including the rhetorical, that
it keeps us aware of the possibility of a *heavenly* crown: and where there is
that possibility the striving for an earthly crown must be seen as the perverse
choice of a lesser good. Levin calls the Marlovian hero an "overreacher";
it would suggest the complementary truth if we called him an underachiever.

"Is it not passing braue to be a King?"—and the play, in the manner of a cleverly wry *erotema*, makes us wonder, all the more because Marlowe does not take away the wonder by pointing the moral. As with Barabas, our relationship to Tamburlaine is dynamic: at times we feel the seductive power of his "working words," at times recoil from them, at times feel torn between the conflicting possibilities Marlowe carefully contrives. Grand sin or foolish mistake? Both possibilities are there, but finally they are not equal. Tamburlaine, taught by his warring nature to aspire, climbs and climbs. It is by turns an impressive and a repulsive spectacle. But at the end he has gotten no further than the earth from which he began. And that is either frightening or funny.

Out of the death of his "divine Zenocrate" Tamburlaine creates the most astonishing image of himself as a self-baffled earthly possessor. His hyperbolic rage is what we have come to expect:

> What, is she dead? *Techelles*, draw thy sword,
> And wound the earth, that it may cleaue in twaine,
> And we descend into th'infernall vaults,
> To haile the fatall Sisters by the haire,
> And throw them in the triple mote of Hell,
> For taking hence my faire *Zenocrate*.
>
> (3064–69)

The problem with this is not only that we have heard its like before. Here in Part Two we see explicitly what has been implicit throughout, that the real object of Tamburlaine's revolt is mortality itself. Because he cannot be immortal or make others so he has perversely made himself the agent of death, bursting "The rusty beames of *Ianus* Temple doores, / Letting out death and tyrannising war: / To match with me vnder this bloody flag" (3082–84)—none of which, however, will make the shepherd's love "Come downe from heauen and liue with me againe" (3086). But if he cannot have Zenocrate's body and soul he can, extraordinarily, have her body:

> Where ere her soule be, thou shalt stay with me
> Embalm'd with Cassia, Amber Greece and Myrre,
> Not lapt in lead but in a sheet of gold,
> And till I die thou shalt not be interr'd.
>
> (3097–100)

Zenocrate's embalmed presence onstage here in Act Two and again at the play's conclusion can hardly be for the audience the triumphant or consolatory image it is for Tamburlaine. It is merely the most gruesome confirmation of his ordinary mortality.

In what he takes to be love Tamburlaine is, on his own terms, doomed to defeat, even as he is doomed in war. His great speech on Zenocrate's beauty—"What is beauty saith my sufferings then?"—is an example of Puttenham's *antipophora* or "Figure of responce," "when we will seeme to aske a question to th' intent we will answere it ourselues." *Antipophora* "is a figure of argument and also of amplification"—the latter, says Puttenham, because in answering our own question we "spend much language." Tamburlaine spends much language in this set-speech only to purchase an ironic emptiness. For what he amplifies is absence: beauty is what, when all the poems are written, still will not be expressed; its "argument" is its own negation. The mode is startlingly lyrical, but in other ways the speech is typical: there is something stirring in the idea of the unattainable ideal, but something disturbing too in the inevitable defeat it promises.

Even in his more customary role as warrior Tamburlaine dooms himself by the nature of his perverse ideal: "Giue me a Map, then let me see how much / Is left for me to conquer all the world" (4516–17). In an interesting variation on the sorrows of Alexander, Tamburlaine weeps because there will always be more to conquer: "And shall I die, and this vnconquered?" (4543, 4551). For once, the rhetorical question admits no alternatives. Death itself is what Tamburlaine would need to conquer to satisfy his imperial ideal.

There is not much place in Tamburlaine, the play or the character, for introspection. But at times there are intimations of an emotion, call it melancholy or despair, which Marlowe will explore in *Doctor Faustus*. Tamburlaine sorrows for Zenocrate and at his own partial recognition that death will conquer him. In Part One, when he is about to slaughter the virgins of Damascus, he appears "all in blacke, and verie melancholy"—and asking some of his most alarming questions:

> What, are the Turtles fraide out of their neastes?
> Alas poore fooles, must you be first shal feele
> The sworne destruction of *Damascus*[?]
> They know my custome: could they not as well
> Haue sent ye out, when first my milkwhite flags
> Through which sweet mercie threw her gentle beams
> Reflexing them on your disdainful eies:
> As now when furie and incensed hate
> Flings slaughtering terrour from my coleblack tents,
> And tels for trueth, submissions comes too late.
>
> (1845–54)

Tamburlaine's "melancholy" is as noteworthy as his insane rigidity. Erwin Panofsky's analysis of Dürer's engraving *Melencolia I* is apposite to Tamburlaine's condition as it will also be to Faustus': "Melancholia belongs in fact to those who 'cannot extend their thoughts beyond the limit of space.' Hers is the inertia of a being which renounces what it could reach because it cannot reach for what it longs." *Tamburlaine* is neither a homily against presumption nor an exhortation to dream the impossible dream. It presents an emotionally complex vision of how man may lose the full potential of his humanity in pursuit of an inhuman goal.

III

For all the differences in dramatic mode, Doctor Faustus is caught in Tamburlaine's dilemma and he more fully is a Marlovian version of *Melencolia I*: "Winged, yet cowering on the ground—wreathed, yet beclouded by shadows—equipped with the tools of art and science, yet brooding in idleness, [he] gives the impression of a creative being reduced to despair by an awareness of insurmountable barriers which separate [him] from a higher realm of thought." But it is not immediately plain what the nature of those "barriers" are or why Faustus remains shut out from "a higher realm" even in the excruciating finale where desperately he tries to "leape vp to my God" (1462). Who pulls Faustus down is indeed a question; and it is interesting that the play, for all its theological explicitness, should occasion the most controversy about the nature of Marlowe's theology. Obviously it is not an atheist's play in any sense beyond what an Elizabethan Privy Council might construe. Marlowe told Baines that the Roman liturgy would be most attractive to him were he inclined to be attracted to any religion. Recent critics have explored possible connections between Faustus' despair and Calvinist or Lutheran doctrine. I want to return to these questions by way of Faustus' own questions.

Faustus' opening soliloquy is, in Levin's phrase, "an inventory of the Renaissance mind"—or, at least, of the departments of study open to it. For I do not think it true that "Whatever the contemplative life can teach . . . Dr. Faustus has learned." Scholars who have achieved a reputation like Faustus' are in danger of being trusted: but from Faustus' first rhetorical question Marlowe does his best to assure that we listen warily, with an almost undergraduate skepticism, to the rest of Faustus' vaunting speech:

> Settle thy studies *Faustus*, and beginne
> To sound the deapth of that thou wilt professe:
> Hauing commencde, be a Diuine in shew,

Yet leuell at the end of euery Art,
And liue and die in *Aristotles* workes:
Sweet *Anulatikes* tis thou hast rauisht me,
Bene disserere est finis logicis,
Is, to dispute well, Logickes chiefest end[?]
Affords this Art no greater myracle[?]
Then reade no more, thou hast attaind the end.
(A-text, 3–40; question marks only in B)

Marlowe's creative detachment from his speaker is evident even in such apparently innocuous phrases as "sound the depth" or "live and die," to which a terrible burden of tragic irony will accrue by the end of the play. Faustus scornfully seeks a "miracle" in Aristotle: as C. L. Barber has written of "the irony which attends Faustus' use of religious language to describe magic"—and as we have seen in Barabas' and Tamburlaine's use of religious language—"the rebels seem to stumble uncannily upon words which condemn them by the logic of a situation larger than they are." The rhetorical questions also open out to that larger situation.

"Is, to dispute well, Logickes chiefest end[?]" Faustus cites Aristotle but he quotes the anti-Aristotelian Peter Ramus. A modern scholar who noticed the apparent confusion declares that "everyone of [Marlowe's] educated hearers . . . every Cambridge undergraduate" would have recognized Ramus in *Bene disserere est finis logicis.* Surely this grants too much to the efficacy of even the best Elizabethan education; but Marlowe does call attention to the substitution both by having Faustus translate the phrase and by the effect of the *erotema* itself. For some, at least, in his audience Marlowe has given two allusions for the price of one, and warranted our looking briefly at how both the Aristotelians and the Cambridge Ramists were answering the question of "logic's chiefest end."

Thomas Wilson's *The Rule of Reason* (1551) was the first text-book of logic written in English. It was widely known, although old-fashioned by the time Marlowe was doing logic at Cambridge, and it is firmly Aristotelian. Wilson asks, "Whereof, or to what ende Logique is," and answers:

Manne, by nature hath a sparke of knowledge, and by the secrete workying of God, iudgeth after a sort, and discerneth good from euil. Before the fall of Adam, this knowledge was perfect, but through offence, darknesse folowed, and the bright light was taken awaie. Wise men therefore, consideryng the weakenesse of mannes witte, and the blyndnesse also, wherein we are all drounded: inuented this arte, to helpe us the rather, by a naturall order, to finde out the truthe. For though before Adams fall, knowledge was naturall, and came without labor, yet no man can now of hymself, attain the truth in al thynges, without help and diligent learnyng.

The end of logic, then, is "to finde out the truthe" in discerning good from evil. Even with logic's aid truth will not, in our fallen state, be easily achieved: the diligence and "naturall order" Wilson commends is in striking contrast to Faustus' recourse to the desperate infantilism of magic, with its "Lines, circles, [signs,] letters and characters: / I, these are those that *Faustus* most desires" (81–82). The truth that is the end of Wilson's logic goes far beyond that "world of profit and delight" at which Faustus draws up short (83). Although Faustus declares that magic's dominion "Stretcheth as farre as doth the minde of man" (91), Wilson's logic "extendeth, not onely to knowe worldly affaires: but also to knowe God, & all his heauenly workes, so farre as nature may comprehend." That knowledge of God is the "chiefest end" of *all* learning was not a new idea with the traditionalist Wilson, but neither was it outmoded. The great Renaissance ideal was still to be powerfully stated by Milton: "The end then of Learning is to repair the ruines of our first parents by regaining to know God aright, and out of that knowledge to love him."

Abraham Fraunce's *The Lawier's Logike* (1588) is aggressively Ramistic. (Fraunce had been at Cambridge from 1575, and was a fellow of St. John's when Marlowe matriculated at Corpus Christi in 1581.) According to Fraunce, "to reason well and artificially is the duetie and ende of Logike." The art is proposed quite frankly as a way for lawyers to get ahead: the difference in tone between this pragmatic new man and the pious Wilson is striking. But so is the difference, although it appears at first merely technical, between Fraunce's interpretation of Ramus and Faustus'. The latter renders *bene disserere* as "to dispute well"; but Fraunce worries the proper translation: "This our English word, Reasoning, is more proper and fit to express the nature of Logike, than either that other word, of disputing, derived from *disputare*, or the like, as *disserere*, and *docere*." Fraunce acknowledges that Ramus and his translators use both *disserere* and *disputare* (Faustus' two choices); therefore "I do not reiect, but by their leaue leaue their Latin words behind our English," the humanistically resonant *to reason*:

> As farre then as mans reason can reach, so farre extendeth it selfe the use and virtue of this art of reasoning [i.e., logic], whose most ample and almost infinite use and power, hath never had in any tong a more generall and yet proper name, than this of reasoning, as we use it now adaies.

Thus from neither the traditional Aristotelian nor the new Ramist would Faustus find support for his conclusion that "to dispute well [is] Logickes chiefest end." In either system, "this art" does afford a greater miracle, whether it be the sort that belongs to "God, & all his heauenly workes," or the more narrowly humanistic one implied in Fraunce's choice of "reasoning." The Ramist declares that logic can reach as far as man's reason can reach: it is not, in its "end," only a set of debating points; and the traditionalist makes explicit that its reach extends to the divine realm from which, with all his devilish aids, Faustus will find himself excluded. Faustus dismisses logic: "A greater subject fitteth *Faustus* wit" (41); and he thereby confirms himself the merest technician of knowledge, familiar with the number of celestial spheres, their revolutions and axial wobbles, but incapable of considering "who made the world" (694). Faustus mistakes the end of logic because he neglects its full context; he sees the art's letter but not its spirit. It is a mistake to which he is prone not because he is a scholar but because he is human. It is a mistake he will make repeatedly, in the rest of the speech and the play.

Hardly a word of this questioning first soliloquy is not charged with tragic ironies that accrue through allusiveness and dramatic context. Marlowe's demands upon us to listen—and to hear both what is said and what is significantly left unsaid—make it worth a moment's further consideration. Faustus goes on to question the ends of the various arts, and repeatedly in his answers he draws up short. And increasingly, I think, the speech's intellectual subtext appears more plainly, that the letter kills but the spirit gives life.

With a parting glance at Aristotle, Faustus curtly dismisses the philosophical problem of being and not-being (42). And from the apparent inconsequence and abstraction of philosophy he turns where students seem always to turn: "Be a physition *Faustus*, heape vp golde, / And be eternizde for som wondrous cure" (44–45). But what cure is so wondrous that we could be "eternizde" by it? The image of the good physician Christ thus enters the speech. The image is crucial for us, although to the very end the sight of his cure, "Christs blood stream[ing] in the firmament" (1463), will be less compelling to Faustus than that of God's "irefull browes" (1469).

Faustus bids Galen come but quotes Aristotle: "*Summum bonum medicinae sanitas*, / The end of physicke is our bodies health" (46–47). The dismissive rhetorical questions he now asks are predicated on a limited notion of "the end of physicke":

> Why *Faustus*, hast thou not attaind that end?
> Is not thy common talke sound Aphorismes?
> Are not thy billes hung vp as monuments,
> whereby whole Citties haue escapt the plague,
> And thousand desprate maladies beene easde[?]
> Yet art thou still but *Faustus*, and a man.
>   (48–53)

Context and allusion make it hard for us to exclude our knowledge of what, in another scale of values, "our bodies health" itself is for: "Know ye not, that your bodie is the temple of the holie Gost, which is in you, whome ye haue of God? and ye are not your own" (1 Cor.6.19, Geneva Bible). According to values the play acknowledges in its rhetorical structures, "the end of physicke" is *not* the body's health: or, the end of the body's health is not the *body's* health. Faustus' own desperate malady, like Tamburlaine's, is his dependent humanity: "Yet art thou still but *Faustus*, and a man."

Contemptuously dismissing medicine for what he thinks it cannot do, Faustus' questions direct us still more explicitly to a realm where man's sickness is already cured: "wouldst thou make man to liue eternally? / Or being dead, raise them to life againe? / Then this profession were to be esteemd" (54–56). Only in his panicky last half hour will Faustus realize that life *is* eternal, and his is eternally damned (1481–95). Here at the start the injunction Christ ironically let be applied to himself silently informs Faustus' insufficient examination of the end of physic: "Physician, heal thyself" (Luke 4.23).

From medicine Faustus turns to law:

> where is *Iustinian?*
> *Si vna eademque res legatus duobus,*
> *Alter rem, alter valorem rei, &c.*
> A petty case of paltry Legacies,
> *Exhereditari filium non potest pater, nisi—*
> Such is the subiect of the institute,
> And vniuersall body of the law.
> (B-text, 54–60)

The case of one object willed to two parties will, of course, be Faustus' case, shortly to be argued by a Good and a Bad Angel. But under the universal body of the law it is everyman's case. According to the spiritual lawyer St. Paul, all men are condemned to death under the law but saved by Christ who fulfills the law. The conclusion to the seventh chapter of Romans passionately fights out a version of what Faustus describes as "A petty case of paltry Legacies":

> I delite in the Law of God, concerning the inner man: But I se another law in my membres, rebelling against the law of my minde, & leading me captiue vnto the law of unne, which is in my membres. O wretched man that I am, who shal deliver me from the bodie of this death! I thanke God through Iesus Christ our Lord. Then I my self in my minde serue the Law of God, but in my flesh the law of sinne.
> (Rom. 7.22–25, Geneva)

Faustus reads that a father cannot disinherit his son unless—and he breaks off at precisely the question that will most plague him: at what point, for what cause, is *this* son disinherited by the father? But because Faustus is the kind of legalist he himself contemptuously describes, "a mercenary drudge, / who aimes at nothing but externall trash" (64–65), the magnitude of the question will not obtrude on him until, in the desperate plea-bargaining of his last soliloquy, he finds that his case is lost.

"When all is done, Diuinitie is best" (67): Faustus' error is not in coming too late to divinity or even in dismissing it. For the point, surely, is that any of the previous branches of learning, properly understood, could have done as well. The repeated error has been in failing to grasp the "chiefest end" of *any* human endeavor. That, at any rate, is one way of understanding the situation, a way that was available to Marlowe's audience and which Marlowe's allusive technique, his dramatic ironies, and his rhetorical questions seem to me to make inescapable. That pillar of English orthodoxy Richard Hooker provides a good gloss on Faustus' intellectual and spiritual tragedy:

> Now that which man doth desire with reference to a further end, the same he desireth in such measure as is unto that end convenient; but what he coveteth as good in itself, toward that his desire is ever infinite. So that unless the last good of all, which is desired altogether for itself, be also infinite, we do evil in making it our end. . . . Nothing may be infinitely desired but that good which indeed is infinite. . . . No good is infinite but only God.

Hooker's syllogism leads to God as "the chiefest end"; in a moment Faustus will construct out of half-sentences from scripture a syllogism that leads to damnation. Marlowe and Hooker do make, as it were, strange bedfellows. But the fact is that Hooker's ideas, by virtue of their very traditionalism, were available ideas, the sort you could not ignore.

Faustus turns to Jerome's Bible, bidding himself "view it well" (68). Why his view extends only to the first part of the passages he finds—to the syllogistic conclusion that we must sin and "consequently die . . . an euerlasting death" (75–76), while leaving it for us to hear the merciful conclusion of the unspoken parts—raises the play's thorniest set of questions. They are questions that involve inextricably theological and dramaturgical issues. In the B-text Mephostophilis seems to provide an answer:

> 'Twas I, that when thou wer't i'the way to heauen,
> Damb'd vp thy passage, when thou took'st the booke,
> To view the Scriptures, then I turn'd the leaues
> And led thine eye.
>
> (1989–92)

But this answer only makes explicit the question of Faustus' free-will or lack of it: is Faustus damned or does he damn himself? And this in turn raises the question of the dramatic status of Marlowe's palpable devils, angels, and the gaping hell-mouth Henslowe was at cost to provide for this play about the spiritual state of evil.

Wilbur Sanders thinks Marlowe is inconsistent or trying to have things both ways. At times in the play "damnation has . . . a sharp physical actuality," which seems to Sanders a "medieval" way of looking at it; at other times there is a "modern . . . insight into the depths of the damned mind." Mephostophilis, for whom "Hell hath no limits, nor is circumscrib'd / In one selfe place" (567–68), presumably takes an informed modern view, whereas Marlowe himself too often subscribes to "an older mechanistic demonology." Either hell is real or it is a symbol: that it seems to be both in *Doctor Faustus* is for Sanders a symptom of Marlowe's confusion. The really "modern" thing here, however, is the unwillingness to entertain an actuality which *is* fully symbolic. Symbolically, it is perfectly appropriate that the literal-minded Faustus should be carried to hell by Henslowe's hired men dressed as "realistic" devils.

The dramaturgic problem will trouble us only if we see things with Faustian literalism. Even the B-text's explicitness, with Mephostophilis claiming credit for Faustus' predicament, is not inconsistent, although I think it is artistically unfortunate. While Mephostophilis is the cause, he is the cause (as he might say) *per accidens*; essentially, the cause will always lie "Within the bowels of these elements," ourselves. The problem of conceptualizing the spiritual is inevitable: "The inadequacies of language and man's constant inclination to anthropomorphism led sixteenth century daemonologists—especially the occult—to speak sometimes of spirits with a circumstantiality not consonant with their knowledge. . . . Though daemons possessed personal form and existence, the minds of men had no images of them any more than of abstract good and evil." When Mephostophilis first appears to Faustus as a dragon, he is told by the magician to "Goe and returne an old Franciscan Frier, / That holy shape becomes a diuell best" (269–70)—but no better or worse than another: "Was this the face that lancht a thousand shippes? / And burnt the toplesse Towres of *Ilium?*" (1357–58).

The apparent dramaturgical problem reveals a real theological one. When Faustus tries to leap up to his God, who does pull him down? Is Faustus unwilling still to repent?—for repent he does not, however much he may in his panic regret his fate or plead for leniency. Or is Faustus unable to repent because it is God's will that he be damned? Concerning his syllogism of damnation, Faustus asks "What doctrine call you this, *Che sera, sera,* / What wil be, shall be?" (77–78). Recently, Charles Masinton has answered the rhetorical question by calling the doctrine "Luther's deterministic theology":

> Faith in God saves the sinner, but the man who does not already possess it as a gift from God cannot simply decide to have it, since his mind and will are in the devil's control. And without faith, the fallen man— unable to believe that the salvation he fervently desires is possible for him—lapses into despair. This is exactly the case with Faustus.

Certainly it is part of Faustus' case; the movement toward repentance and the lapsing into despair is the frenetic piston that drives the lurching central portion of the play. But that Marlowe shares Faustus' desperate theology cannot be proven. In the midst of one especially imbecilic prank, his cozening the horse-courser, Faustus pauses, killing time till the punch-line:

> what art thou Faustus but a man condemnd to die?
> Thy fatall time doth drawe to finall ende,
> Dispaire doth driue distrust vnto thy thoughts,
> Confound these passions with a quiet sleepe:
> Tush, Christ did call the thiefe vpon the Crosse,
> Then rest thee Faustus quiet in conceit.
>
> (1169–74)

For Faustus the recollection of the saved thief is merely a soporific; for others it may be another reminder of the unspoken, merciful half of Faustus' syllogism. The play has its Evil Angel to say "Too late," but its Good Angel too: "Neuer too late, if Faustus can repent" (707–08; in the B-text "will" replaces "can"). Despair does conquer: Faustus' spiritual death-in-life is caught in the frightening oxymoron, "I do repent, and yet I do dispaire" (1330). But just who killed John Faustus is one Marlovian question that remains eternally open.

Faustus despairs and does not repent—or vice-versa. His end is fully implied in his dramatic beginning, when we hear him questioning the ends of learning and stopping in every case at the killing letter. The questions he asks and the answers he seeks are throughout the play those of the literal-minded man whose finding the knowledge of the world entails the losing of his soul. Panofsky, in his analysis of Dürer's *Melencolia I*, summarizes Henry of Ghent in a way that is strikingly relevant to *Faustus*. (The word "imagination," as it is used in the passage, is associated literally with images as opposed to ideas):

> There exist . . . two kinds of thinkers. On the one hand, there are the philosophical minds which find no difficulty in understanding such purely

metaphysical notions as the ideas of an angel or of extramundane nothingness. On the other hand, there are those "in whom the imaginative
power predominates over the cognitive one." They "will accept a dem-
onstration only to that extent as their imagination can keep step with
it. . . . Their intellect cannot transcend the limits of imagination . . .
and can only get hold of space [*magnitudo*] or of that which has a
location or position in space. . . . Therefore such men are melancholy,
and become excellent mathematicians but very bad metaphysicians,
for they cannot extend their thoughts beyond location and space which
are the foundations of mathematics."

Faustus is a dramatic adumbration of those sad thinkers who "cannot
extend their thoughts beyond location and space." The questions he asks
can be poignant or ludicrous; in either case they reveal an aspiration
stunted by the narrow scope of a mind that will not climb after knowledge
infinite.

IV

Marlowe's own questions are less naive than those of his heroes. Often
they are angry questions. They account for some of the basic difficulties
we have in establishing the plays' tone and genre. For a rhetorical
question can work in two radically different directions: it can call attention to
the obviousness of the correct response or to the distance between the
expected response and the correct one. That the question is asked at all
implies that something is amiss. It is unsettling because it implies a gap
between the standard used in responding and the situation which gives
rise to the question, between the affirmation and the interrogation.
Marlowe's plays often inhabit that space between affirmation and interrogation, that satirical space where *interrogatio* (when "we do aske . . .
because we would know") must be heard as *percontatio* (when "we do aske
. . . because we woulde . . . sette furthe our grief with more vehemencie").

The depressing obviousness of the correct response, for instance,
strikes us in the question posed by Orcanes, the King of Natolia, in
Tamburlaine: "Can there be such deceit in Christians, / Or treason in the
fleshly heart of man, / Whose shape is figure of the highest God?"
(2893–95). The play's action, in which we witness that Christian deceit,
directly answers the first part of the question, turning it from *interrogatio* to
its more bitter rhetorical neighbor. We cannot so directly witness the
disparity between "the highest God" and man's fleshly heart, but the

question itself pushes us toward the discovery of it. Neither a statement of the fact ("There is deceit in Christians") nor a simple question ("Is there deceit in Christians?") would carry the force of the rhetorical question, "Can there be such deceit?"—for it makes us freshly aware both that there is such deceit and that there ought not to be. Although it is spoken by Orcanes, its artful "vehemencie" as a question identifies it as Marlowe's own.

Barabas asks a different kind of rhetorical question:

> why, is not this
> A kingly kinde of trade to purchase Townes
> By treachery, and sell 'em by deceit?
> Now tell me, worldlings, vnderneath the sunne,
> If greater falshood euer has bin done.
> (2329–33)

If Orcanes' question about deceit was sad because the answer was too obvious, Barabas' question about deceit is outrageous because there is no obvious answer. The difficulty of responding is the point. Apparently it *is* "kingly" to use treachery and deceit, for kings (we see) use them; but even as we give that response we are doing violence to our standard notion of how kings ought to behave—not merely as an ethical commonplace but as a matter of language: "kingly" means *not* treacherous, *not* deceitful. The question divides one kind of knowledge from another, the knowledge of what *is* from the knowledge of what ought, by an absolute standard, to be. Marlowe's play exists in the space created by that division, where the language appropriate to one kind of knowledge is forced to speak for the other kind of knowledge. The rhetorical question therefore has the subversive effect of changing any value-laden word into a pun: "kingly" and "deceit" have each come to mean at least two different things simultaneously, as in *Doctor Faustus* "heavenly" came to mean both itself and its opposite.

This is, in small rhetorical compass, the kind of subversiveness Marlowe practices in larger dramatic strategies as well. To write in the vein of *erotema* is to assume on the one hand an absolute standard which can supply the question's answer and on the other a disparity between the absolute standard and the questioner's situation. It is inevitably, therefore, to write in the vein of satire. In Marlowe the satire can be harsh or rueful, broad or delicate; it can tend toward farce or toward tragedy. These plays have the trappings of a tragic conclusion, but the sense of tragic completion is subverted by the sense of disquieting incompleteness attendant on the questioning mode.

KIMBERLY BENSTON

Beauty's Just Applause:
Dramatic Form and the
Tamburlanian Sublime

The language of poetry naturally falls in with the language of power. . . .
The principle of poetry is a very anti-levelling principle. It aims of no
medium. It is everything by excess. It rises above the ordinary standard
of sufferings and crimes. It presents a dazzling appearance. It shows its
head turretted, crowned, and crested. Its front is gilt and bloodstained.
Before it 'it carries noise, and behind it leaves tears.' It has its altars and
its victims, sacrifices, human sacrifices. . . . It puts the individual for the
species, the one above the infinite many, might before right.

T hus wrote Hazlitt of Coriolanus; but,
as A.D. Hope suggests in his essay on Tamburlaine in *The Cave and the
Spring*, Hazlitt's evaluation of the poetry of power would be an even more
apt critique of Marlowe's triumphant, bloody *magus*. In his observation
that Tamburlaine's Argument of Armes is like an Argument of Poetry,
Hope verges on but stops short of the central truth that Tamburlaine is a
transcendentally solipsistic *poet* of the Sublime. His pitiless conquests are
the poems of a powerful, antithetical quest for power, his *sword* the
creative principle of agonistic eloquence, an unnaming weapon that cuts
foreign territory into metonymic signs of his own will:

First published in this volume. From *The Shaping of the Marlovian Sublime*. Copyright © 1985
by Kimberly Benston.

> I will confute those blind Geographers
> That make a triple region in the world,
> Excluding Tudor Regions which I meane to trace,
> And with this pen reduce them to a Map,
> Calling the Provinces, Cities and townes
> After my name . . .
>
> (1715–20)

Marlowe's hero, then, is a consummate yet unconditioned tyrant, unambiguously cruel yet absolutely triumphant, a transcendentally rebellious force with which other princes should be loath to "*presume* to manage *armes*" (my emphases). But if Marlowe thereby dissipates the *Vita Tamerlanis*'s Humanist tension between violence and nobility, its consistent endorsement of *de caribus* convention, he more radically amends his sources in order to press the identification of Scourge and orator, of arms and presumption, denied by his historian contemporaries. For *Tamburlaine, Part One* (hereafter simply "*Tamburlaine*") as is clear from literally every line and scene, conflates verbal and physical power in the structure of rhetorical conflict which theorists from Longinus to Thomas Weiskel have termed the sublime. From his first appearance, Tamburlaine puts the ideological premises of rhetorical humanism to the dramatic test, literally making words into "woorking" instruments of desire while appropriately throwing off the limits of convention with the trappings of his "Parentage":

> Lie here ye weedes that I disdaine to weare,
> This compleat armor, and this curtle-axe
> Are adjuncts more beseeming *Tamburlaine*.
> (237–39)

This, then, is the crucial import of Marlowe's revisionary insight into the immediate and secondary sources of Tamburlaine's character: in them Marlowe saw the fundamental lineaments of the antithetical temperament, however obscured by a contradictory metaphysical bias; and, concomitantly, he so shaped, intensified, and augmented them as to isolate the sublime crisis of violence and language for a dramatic examination of unprecedented vigor and complexity in English literature. In his resolute depiction of Tamburlaine as *tyrant-rhetor*, Marlowe evokes not the Ciceronian ideal of Tudor Humanists' ethical Orator King, but the sophistic wielder of violent *peitho*, the abrogator of law so feared by Plato for his realization of rhetoric as *tyrannikon ti*—a "soveraigne" mode of will.

From its inceptive invocation of Tamburlaine's engendering "high astounding tearms," the play emphasizes the conflictual aspect of rhetorical encounter from which the self emerges. The aura of excess and extremity suffusing such interchanges imbues Tamburlaine's claims upon divinity with significance beyond anything implied by liberal notions of "Renaissance individualism." At its most intense, the hero's linguistic assertion is also a defense against death and the primacy of Creation evoking the sublime's defining effort to appropriate the authority of origins. In the literature of the sublime, the *locus classicus* of this daring assertion is the thirty-fifth chapter of *Peri Hypsous*:

> Nature appointed us, mankind, to be no
> mean nor ignoble creature, but led us
> into life and the whole universe as if
> into some great assemblage, to be, as
> it were, spectators (*theatas*) of all her
> creation and most zealous competitors
> therein, and breathed at once into our
> souls an unconquerable love of what is
> forever great and, in comparison to us,
> more devine. . . . Therefore for the
> contemplation and thought within the
> scope of man not even the whole cosmos
> suffices, but his conceptions often pass
> beyond the limits which confine him; and
> if one should scan life about in a circle
> [and] see how much in everything the
> extraordinary, the great, and the noble
> have the larger part, he will soon know
> for what we have been born.

The revisionist evolution from subservience to rivalry in relation to Creation is the distinguishing trait of Marlowe's major works; the Marlovian magus, no less than the Longinian genius, is not content to remain passively attentive in his assigned (and privileged) station of audience to the "assemblage" of "the whole universe." What begins as admiration, as pure wonder, inevitably becomes, given the demiurgic expansiveness of man's mind, a dynamic struggle for priority.

We discover this sublime imagination most startlingly in the famous reproach to Cosroe early in Part One ("The thirst of raigne and sweetness of a crown," etc.—863–80), a superb poem of annunciation in which the Apollonian hero asserts a "climing after knowledge infinite" that, as is typical in later annunciation poems (vid. Keats' "Ode to Psyche" or Shelley's "Hymn of Apollo"), is truly a will toward the vast *unknown* the poet means to colonize alone. The speech, which Swinburne praised in Tamburlainian rhetoric as "perhaps the noblest in the literature of the world," must be quoted in full:

> The thirst of raigne and sweetness of a crown,
> That causde the eldest sonne of heavenly *Ops*,
> To thrust his doting father from his chaire,
> And place himselfe in the Emperiall heaven,
> Moov'd me to manage armes against thy state.
> What better president than mightie *Jove*?
> Nature that fram'd us of foure Elements,
> Warring within our breasts for regiment,
> Doth teach us all to have aspyring minds:
> Our soules, whose faculties can comprehend
> The wondrous Architecture of the world:
> And measure every wandering plannets course,
> Still climing after knowledge infinite,
> And alwaies mooving as the restless Spheares,
> Wils us to weare our selves and never rest,
> Untill we reach the ripest fruit of all,
> That perfect blisse and sole felicitie,
> The sweet fruition of an earthly crown.
>
> (863–80)

This passage proposes not only a denial of the *de casibus* pattern in every sense represented by Cosroe; it is Tamburlaine's fullest declaration of the agonistic sublime, an explanation of desire as the disruption of a prior tyranny that is truly a figural (hence enabling) myth of authority. Tamburlaine's celebration of endless striving has been long abused and misinterpreted, not least for being read out of dramatic context. It is, first of all, a triumphant defense against Cosroe's self-contradictory portrayal of Tamburlaine's ambition as "unnatural" and his own as resolved of "one wholsome aire [and] proportion of Elements" (836–37), a view cruelly ironized by his shattered "state"—

> Barbarous and bloody *Tamburlaine*,
> Thus to deprive me of my crowne and life.
> Treacherous and false *Theridamas*,
> Even at the morning of my happy state,
> Scarce being seated in my royall throne,
> To worke my downfall and untimely end.
> An uncouth paine torments my grieved soule,
> And death arrests the organe of my voice.
>
> (853–60)

Belatedly sensing the essential relations among power, being, and voice, Cosroe reveals the fault of his quest to be the end implicit in its means, the need for a secure, final, thus finite position (the very "sitting" on "my royall throne" *is* the quest's "untimely *end*").

Tamburlaine's response employs similar terminology ("thirst," "crown," "state," "Nature," "chaire," "Elements," as well as the allusion to Jove's unseating of Saturn, all form an explicit re-inscription of Cosroe's language) but expresses a contrary ethos of "restless" movement through techniques of *energeia*. He answers Cosroe's contradictory claim for harmonious ambition by enunciating the more profound (and heretical) paradox of natural discord, a striking catachresis of the Renaissance theory of *discordia concors* in its assertion that the elements' permanent instability, their insistent and incessant rivalry, is the very *telos* of nature.

This is the sublime tyrant-rhetor's necessary vision of 'human nature': dynamism, restlessness, voracity, and contention are his proper "state" as a *speculum* for the desire of "us all." Tamburlaine's glorification of "insatiate" strife and disorder as the *final* cause of *natura naturans* is, in turn, aptly framed by the dying Cosroe's explication of conventional theories of physiologic and cosmic order (viz. 835–50 and 891–901), thereby lending its 'shocking' thesis dramatic intensity and authority. The speech's unresolved crux, however, has always been the presumed *internal* contradiction between the sublime project of endless "climing after knowledge infinite" and the bathetic goal of "an earthly crown." The solution to the dilemma thus posed by the last line's discordant effect resides partly in a reinterpretation of Tamburlaine's rhetorical strategy, partly in a realization of contextual significance, but also in the recognition that "knowledge infinite" is not a literal objective but a trope for the goalless intentions of the will. To "know" merely and particularly—as learned Cosroe does—is to be "doting": fixed, old, and "ripe" for displacement. Tamburlaine's rhetoric thus defends the aspiring soul against meaningless or simply accumulated confirmations, against mere repetition of an epistemologically plethoric but imaginatively poverty-stricken 'comprehension.' The soul does not seek a given cognitive moment, but rather the force to proceed past the astonishment (or 'wonder') of discovery—to undergo, that is, like Longinus's *theates*, the transformation from what Weiskel labels a reader's to an agonistic sublime. Tamburlaine seeks "knowledge" in the sophistic not the Humanist sense: to know is to make; and in Marlowe's Creation Myth—as in Longinus's—to create is to begin over and over as a perpetually dis-covering usurper (that is, dissolver or represser) of original knowledge. In this formula, the world is conquered by thinking it into being, an aggrandizement that makes human will tyrannical or totalizing as it imagines the world as the reified form of its own desire (thus the soul "measures" or competes with an image—Spheare—that is also its metaphorical substitute). Tamburlaine claims a desire for final knowledge, but he has in fact been 'taught' to desire or soar ("aspire"—cf. 1881–84)—the (pre)condition of conquest over the vast expanse of the *un*mapped world.

When the recognition of the numinous becomes particularized, however, the figure of boundless "mooving" is pressed into a visualizable form, the world's limitless Architecture now become the envisioned height of a ripened fruit awaiting appropriation by the "thirsting" soul. Rather than suffering a breakdown of discourse as in the awe-fullness of the eighteenth-century sublime, Tamburlaine's vision seems to seek a hasty protection in the signified correlative of "knowledge," which apparently rescues the possibility of articulating meaning from the terror of unknowing exploration—but at genuine risk. The movement from aim to object seems too radical, the control or definition of will too strict, suggesting an uneasiness with the disequilibrium so boldly proclaimed. The common charges of disjunctive "bathos" made against the speech's conclusion, whatever their absolute merit, do therefore point suggestively to the submerged (albeit integral and ultimately liberating) challenge to the sublime's essential need for perpetual persuasion, a crisis Tamburlaine will "suffer" more seriously and transcend more triumphantly again in the famous soliloquy of V.ii. Here the sublime mentality of the Marlovian hero, in its anxiety about the very fury of its own imagined powers, begins to reveal its inherently *dramatic* structure, the necessity of *internal* tension (however sublimated, as it is just barely here) erupting into expressive, externalized conflict. Instructed by a transcendent force to challenge even its primacy, the hero can assert the priority of his own voice only by first transferring that power to a tractable object, a metonym of elevating greatness (hence the turn to the "earthly crown"). Sublime desire is a perspective on, a metaphor of bathos; its object must seem intrinsically inadequate and, if attained, sordid, puny, and shameful (what Faustus will disdainfully term "external trash"). Explication or definition of the goal of the striving will thus betrays a *desire for expression per se*; seeking to soar beyond the aporia between self-transcendence and self-fulfillment, Tamburlaine's oration frames its rhetoric of demand (accompanied by imagery of extension and wholeness) with the rhetoric of presence (marked by imagery of height and fullness). Thus representation of the self's intention as "the sweet fruition of an earthly crowne" reinforces the hero's capability of articulating desire's demands and so strengthens his will-to-persuasion.

However hyperbolic an image of the will's pursuit, the "earthly crowne" is still a metonymy of the mind's aspiration and so calls for further explication with respect to both rhetorical and dramatic contexts. That Tamburlaine's heroic fury and vertical defiance of limit should conclude with a pronouncement of the primacy of *human* interests on *earth* is, first of all, a signal not of disappointment but of defiance. The evident

Neo-Platonic overtones suggestive of spiritual energy should lead to a reconciliation of pleasure and virtue in a "wholly non-material, ensphered form of world-soul." Again, we must come to see *bathos* as a key not an embarrassment to the nascent aesthetic of the sublime. Indeed, as Weiskel has observed, only irony distinguishes *bathos* and the sublime, yet Tamburlaine's exemption from *de casibus* convention (a structure which from the *fallen* Prince's view is indeed an ironic semiotic) emancipates him from such mocking perspective.

The scene of Tamburlaine's assumption, completing its utter reversal of previous coronations, culminates with the choric shout of "Long live *Tamburlaine*" (915), a parodic revision of Cosroe's followers' "God save the King" (196). Tamburlaine has supplanted not simply a king but every traditional idea of kingship: "I know not how to take their tyrannies" laments Cosroe (892), and neither could have the political theorists of Marlowe's age. Tamburlaine's heretical rebellion is not, finally, against any particular kingship but against canonical investiture itself; thus he faces a series of increasingly powerful monarchs, each representing a different type of sovereignty, each eliciting from Tamburlaine a different transgression of law. Before even entering, Tamburlaine is spoken of as "that sturdie Scythian thiefe" (44), and, indeed, once present, Tamburlaine declares himself beyond the conventions of both arms and more peaceful forms of interchange:

> But now you see these letters & commandes
> Are countermanded by a greater man:
> And through my provinces you must expect
> Letters of conduct from my mightinesse.
> (217–20)

Like the rival stars of external influence, all authority is "countermanded" by an act of appropriation seen as more verbal than physical, its codes expressly suspended only to be reasserted by a newly established authority ("these *letters . . . letters* from *my* mightinesse"). From the beginning, Tamburlaine grasps language's function as a technique of personal and political mastery, understanding as no one else does its ability to enslave the other through imaginative violence or seduction. And, as one of Cosroe's supporters, Ceneus, observes, the menace of the crisis thus engendered—the crisis of tyranny—is that its form is inevitably one of irreconcilable discontinuity between privileged individual and the polis composed, in every sense, of his "subjects":

> [Tamburlaine] durst in disdaine of wrong and tyrannie,
> Defend his freedome gainst a Monarchie.
> (509–10)

II

Tamburlaine's abrogation of external authority, like all efforts to oppose the self to any idea of otherness, is a defense against time and space, and hence is *apparently* anti-dramatic. Some of Marlowe's most sympathetic critics, perceiving the danger of draining from the stage the reality of conflict which the dynamic subjectivity of the play's style necessarily incurred, have gone further in pronouncing *Tamburlaine* finally *un*dramatic, at best a seminal but not itself a fully realized formal structure. Must we, as U.M. Ellis-Fermor suggests, "separate the play from the great central figure that dominates it," regarding Marlowe's injury or inattention to form as the price of his exploration of the verbal and philosophical resources of a distinctively English drama, an innovation which it took a Shakespeare to forge into a truly theatrical art?

Tamburlaine, in fact, possesses a brilliant if subtle dramatic design. Nevertheless, criticism of the play has either ignored questions of form altogether or judged it inappropriately or artlessly shaped, monotonously episodic, or intrinsically atheatrical. Ellis-Fermor sets the terms of this opinion:

> Tamburlaine, so far from interpreting life by indicating its form, appears as formless and incoherent as life itself. The final triumph and marriage of Tamburlaine is perhaps a climax, but it is too long deferred to have a direct connection with the original impulse. . . . Tamburlaine's rise to power cannot fill five acts of a play without complications, and a complication would be a denial of the very nature of Tamburlaine's genius, which triumphs, not after a struggle, but without it. Thus, before his play was begun, Marlowe had committed himself to a theme that was in its essence undramatic. It is a foregone conclusion, then, that there will be no dramatic form.

As William J. Brown has observed, Ellis-Fermor's pronouncement has set the tone for all subsequent commentary, whether pejorative or celebratory (formlessness seen alternately as a residium of Tamburlanian hysteria or as a desideratum of Tamburlanian bravura). One major *leit-motif* of these critiques is that the theme of voracious ambition leads Marlowe to eschew principles of composition in favor of a paratactic, almost random series of episodes. But the antithesis of desire and form is, I will suggest, operative only for the hero; to the dramatist, it is necessarily a thematic concern to be rendered with formal rigor. More interesting (and more often argued) is the notion that formal considerations beyond "episodes . . . of more or less arbitrary sequence," as Steane puts it, are deliberately subordinated to the "basic function of manipulating sympathies for or against the hero" in relation to Christian-Humanist ideals. Thus, it is argued, the play's opening injunction to

> View but his picture in this tragicke glasse,
> And then applaud his fortunes as you please
> (7–8)

proposes that audience response, not dramatic structure, determines the essential nature of the play. Whether Tamburlaine's extremities of language and action invite us to indulge his aspirations or call emphatically for his ultimate rejection, Marlowe *is* clearly interested in the problem which a figure such as Tamburlaine poses to interpretation as such. He therefore structures *into* his play a composite audience: the "passionately" impressed Theridamas of I.ii, the confounded Cosroe of II.vi, the awed and the resigned Agydas of III.ii, the mentally as well as physically overwhelmed Bajazeth of V.ii, and the alternately shocked and literally admiring Zenocrate are only the most prominent members of a dramatic community that is nothing so much as a collective exegete of the overpowering text that is "Tamburlaine," a hermeneutic body less choric than confuted. Audience "sympathy" is not centrally an issue—indeed, the Prologue, in contrast to the ploddingly normative Tudor interlude's Presenter whom Marlowe clearly evokes, provokes the spectator to question rather than simply implement received notions of authority, morality, and heroism. Marlowe then proceeds in the play itself to put the major premises of contemporary "high" drama into doubt by courting pious formal assumptions—that the *de casibus* concept of providential intervention and moral retribution will foreshorten the hero's rise to power; that the Virgilian progression from pastoral to epic will place the hero in a romantic context of fulfilled national mission; that the evident *psychomachia* of an assured, ambitious, and thus presumably damned protagonist will, as in Morality structure, ultimately stabilize his dangerous relation to the audience through formulaic dogmatic display—only for the extraordinary and self-contained nature of the hero to suspend them continually. The play's evolving pattern of action and reaction undermines *a priori* notions of dramatic shapeliness and hence is fundamentally concerned to subvert, not enroll, theatrical orthodoxy; by forcing us relentlessly to confront the phenomenon of "Tamburlaine" without the benefit of stable models and theories, Marlowe craftily demands attention to new, disturbing, and immensely consequential propositions about the art of tragic drama. Indeed, Marlowe's exploitation of convention reflects an effort to shift emphasis from story to meaning, which is not, of course, to say from form to content. Critics, quick to assume Marlowe's intention to be primarily that of securing our enthusiasm or antipathy for the hero, fault the playwright for apparently "arbitrary" construction; looking at plot, they ignore design. Yet Marlowe was daringly original, his mastery of composition just as superb as his mastery of language, and his conception of form opened a new era of theatrical experimentation.

We must begin, certainly, with the play's episodic organization, but in order to recognize it as a key not an impediment to Marlowe's presentation of thematic detail. It is helpful to isolate the basic, interrelated critical conclusions drawn from recognition of *Tamburlaine*'s scenic copiousness: Tamburlaine (it is commonly said) does not develop psychologically or essentially; the play, like the hero's rhetoric, suffers from an excess of substance, its repetitiveness characterizing the action as "bombastic" or featureless (meaningless) through mere extension; and the secular implications implied by a progressive, chronicle-like exposition clash disruptively with an "inherently moral" judgment against any purely heroic impulse. Thus Marlowe is depicted as following strictly his sources' characterization of Tamburlaine through a few exemplary "sayings and deeds" (Le Roy's phrase), juxtaposing an increasingly wondrous hero with a series of foes whose challenges merely provide Tamburlaine opportunities for fashioning self-accelerating spectacles of power. But Tamburlaine is, in fact, engaged in a perpetual project of self-begetting which necessarily entails a *developmental* presentation of his relation to authority and otherness— specifically, to Fortune, the Sun, Jove, and, concomitantly, his own self-conception. Tamburlaine evolves ceaselessly (and, to his immediate audience, incomprehensibly), but as an agonistic rather than a moral force; thus the play offers, as Harry Levin and Eugene Waith suggest, a gradual and increasingly hyperbolic revelation of heroic character, a process for which, I submit, the narrative contiguity of metonymic contests is ideally suited. *Tamburlaine*'s dramatic parataxis creates a theatrical *energeia* in keeping with the hero's rhetorical exigencies; like Diderot's *style coupe*, it is breathless and tense, moving forward by sudden bursts of freshly ritualized impulse. This is a dramaturgy of *anaphora* (the figure which Thomas Wilson termed "the marcher"), its procession of battles forming by accumulation a catalogue of triumph reinforcing the underlying linguistic pulse and causing a kind of incantatory effect. Insofar as dramatic syntax appears to dissolve principles of subordination so that each scene has an absolute value, hermetically reproductive of an underlying principle, *Tamburlaine*'s dramatic strategy is to magnify the very idea of conflict, organizing without ethical or metaphysical perspective microscosmic rivalries into a hypnotic discourse of violence. We thus are made to witness in the movement of episodic *anaphora* the expansion and incremental repetition of agonistic encounter which corresponds to the Scythian's own self-authoring mode of rhetorical display. Theatrical repetition here is, therefore, not an indication of limited material or imagination but a device of emblematic purpose which, echoing the vast geographical and dynastic enumerations of Tamburlaine's hyperbolic catalogues, constitutes a *ritual* design. Hence the action is punctuated by emblematic stage images and ritualized theatrical effects—the succession of coronations; the ceremonial robings and disrobings; the Morality-esque confrontation between Four Virgins of Mercy and Tamburlaine, God of Wrath; the progression and tableaux of triumph; the concluding preparations for funeral and wedding—the literally central instance of which is the highly symmetrical and overtly symbolic flyting of III.iii, an agon in which (as if in a late medieval mummer's play) Tamburlaine plays exalted St. George to Bajazeth's vainglorious Turkey Snipe in a wholly rhetorical fable of prowess.

Tamburlaine, in short, is structured in perfect accord with its philosophical and linguistic interests: it is a theatrical hyperbole, presenting the protagonist through an intensifying accumulation of conflicts (Tamburlaine's opponents, we recall, are increasingly formidable) which individually and collectively correlate heroism with violent, will-ful eloquence. The plot appropriately consists of a nearly unbroken chain of debates; as Donald Peet concluded, "there is scarcely a moment when one of the characters is not pursuing the primary goal of the rhetorician— persuasion." Form, like content, is here in a profound sense rhetorical. In saying this, we might seem to echo those who have found in Tudor rhetoric the embryonic model for Elizabethan drama and court with them the rejoiner that, as George Hunter has himself observed, the opposition of debate may be inherently dramatic but fine drama is more than argument. Effective theater, that is to say, must seek *movere* through dialectic and not simply dichotomy. This is precisely why it is crucial to understand Marlowe's rhetoric from a sophistic and sublime rather than a Humanist perspective: it is as a contest of *will* (*pathos*) and not of logic (*logos*) or attribute (*ethos*) that Marlovian heroism is enacted and realized. Rhetoric is thus not merely a vehicle of conflict but becomes, indeed, its essence; so that far from speaking in a uniform and monotonous manner *Tamburlaine's* characters variously seek and achieve a heroic idiom articulated perfectly only by Tamburlaine. Marlowe's restriction of the figurative texture of his characters' speech to a few basic versions of 'amplification'—comparison, division, accumulation, etc.—is not the mark of poetic youth but of profound insight into the *agonistic* nature of hyperbole, the "outdoing" trope. Tamburlaine, we are to see, is first among rivals in a constantly escalating war for what Longinus called "the foremost place" in poetic competition.

Still, the basis for a view of *Tamburlaine* as 'merely' or statically rhetorical persists in the view that no conflict could logically have complicated the protagonist's unmimetic if dynamic rise to power—such a drama "would be a denial of the very nature of Tamburlaine's genius, which triumphs, not after a struggle, but without it." The episodic structure we have praised as a mechanism of agonistic persuasion would thereby be judged a reflection of a self-absorbed or even narcissistic egoism that precludes any strictly dramatic engagement or activity. *Tamburlaine*'s dramaturgic hyperbole is "moving" in a fully theatrical sense, however, because it is not, in fact, strictly paratactic and so is not thoroughly a ritualized glorification of an inherent lack of feeling. In the spirit of the Longinian sublime, Tamburlaine's greatest *hypsos* must arise from crisis, resulting not, to be sure, from any external foe but from any enemy within: the temptation to adopt a weakening mode of vision that deflects desire from the antithetical rewards of pure self-fulfillment to the communalizing pleasure of Eros or Beauty. Thus G.I. Duthie emphasizes the "ultimate" conflict in the hero between war-making and love-making— though he, too, withdraws from close *dramatic* analysis of Eros' effect on Tamburlaine in declaring that "the aspiring mind hardly furnishes promising pyschological material for drama." The sublime, with its combative purpose and underlying anxiety for expressive power, is a potential ground for tragic conflict—as the sophistic roots of Hellenic theater suggest. Hyperbole, we must remember, encompasses the topos of "inexpressibility" (*meioxis*) as well as that of "outdoing" (*auxesis*); it can thereby represent not only competitive surpassing (a "mounting" or "augmenting" trope) but, contrarily, the "inability to cope with the subject" associated with Weiskel's reader's sublime, and so can be assimilated by ethical or metaphysical purpose to a self-effacing valorization rather than a self-elevating overcoming of external, prior 'truth.' Tamburlaine "suffers" (cf. 1. 1941) this crisis, dramatically speaking, because of Zenocrate's presence; her embodiment of sexuality, pity, and community—in short, the challenge of otherness—establishes a recondite subtext to the ritualistic movement of escalating triumph, a subtext which ultimately, if only momentarily, arrests the prevailing paratactic movement by forcing Tamburlaine to confront the problem of feeling and so test his rhetorical energies in a new way. This moment is the soliloquy of V.ii ("Ah Fair *Zenocrate*," etc.—1916 ff.)—possibly the most important passage in pre-Shakespearean drama—a speech which constitutes the climax to a complication woven subtly into a construct of otherwise purely symbolic syntax.

The interaction in *Tamburlaine* between ritual and psychological interests is the cornerstone of Marlowe's innovation in tragic form. The literary historical dimension of this contribution must await later study; for the present it suffices to provide a model of Tamburlaine's remarkable structural precision which, following Doran's discussion of Shakespearean plotting in terms of visual arts, we might term an achievement of "multiple unity." Such an approach allows for simultaneously narrative, thematic, and theatrical analyses, and, moreover, reveals a highly purposeful scenic organization. Borrowing Mark Rose's methodology of "applied rhetorical analysis" we would map this design as follows:

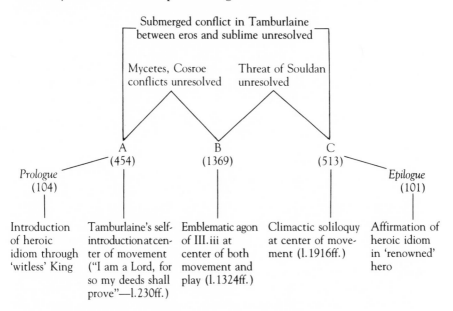

Key: A: *Nature of Hero*: Emergence and Definition (Prologue–Act I: 1–454)
  B: *Exposition of Hero*: Incremental Agons vs. Mycetes, Cosroe, Bajazeth, Souldan (Acts II–IV:455–1781)
  C: *Nature of Hero, II*: Complication and Resolution/Reaffirmation (Act V: 1782–2215)

N.B.: Numbers in parentheses under A, B, and C indicate numbers of lines, not line numbers

This model suggests that Marlowe, contra even his friendliest critics' assessments, sought a unity far beyond that offered by his sources or customarily found in *psychomachia* drama. His design incorporates both a continuous emphasis on agonistic encounter as the play's basic thematic principle (with the ritualized flyting of III.iii coming at the play's center) and a developing movement of potentially tragic significance (with the crescendo of Tamburlaine's inner conflict between Eros and the sublime— introduced covertly as early as I.ii—reaching a climactic resolution in the play's only soliloquy). In this way, inward elements of Marlowe's thought are aptly rendered in outward aspects of his formal technique, so that structure and meaning become inextricably interwoven in an imaginative mode of revolutionary implications. It is to the climactic moment of these developing patterns—the crucial soliloquy of the last act—and its relation to Tamburlaine's heroism which we finally must turn.

III

The theatrical *anaphora* of Tamburlaine's triumphs reaches a peak of intensity with the conquest of Bajazeth; with the formally balanced 'flyting' between Zenocrate and Zabina, the thematic ideal of the equivalence of speech and action is rendered in succinct dramatic form. Other battles await Tamburlaine, but no military foe will enlist the hero's Argument of Armes so elaborately or so pointedly. Yet Tamburlaine's most exacting trial *follows* the conquest of Bajazeth, and its importance and severity result from the very difference between its source and the external threat of rival potentates. I refer, of course, to the *inner* struggle with the appeal of Beauty or otherness which erupts in the soliloquy of V.ii.

The scene preceding Tamburlaine's confrontation with the Damascan Virgins brings to a climax the pattern of failed persuasion initiated by Mycetes and highlighted by Cosroe and Bajazeth while at the same time crystallizing Tamburlaine's monopolization of language as tyrant-rhetor. For Tamburlaine asserts here the prestige of his voice as transcendental master signifier, the mystified source of all authority, law, and power. Like the *theates* overwhelmed by the awesome power of sublime force—a crisis engendered by a compelled aphasia—Tamburlaine's victims are trapped by the "antifestival" of the hero's tyrannical reign over expression. Tamburlaine's claim in this scene to be utterly beyond emotion is shrewdly rendered in terms relevant to the threat posed by the "lovely Virgins" (1815)—the hero would not change his "mind"

> For all the wealth of Gehons golden waves,
> Or for the love of *Venus*, would she leave
> The angrie God of Armes, and lie with me.
> (1904–06)

Thus Tamburlaine's easy assurance of superiority over the gods in the relation of self to the urgings of Eros is suddenly challenged by the intrusion of emotions so far denied or suppressed—a challenge waged on an interior battlefield and so dramatized in the play's crucial soliloquy.

The soliloquy proceeds from the famous apostrophe to Zenocrate (1916–31), whose sorrows for her people and fears for her father, the Souldan, are disturbing yet related to Beauty; through a discourse on Beauty's challenge to Tamburlaine's own sensibility and on the incomprehensible nature of Beauty itself, something ever remaining "which into words no vertue can digest" (1934–54); to a culminating effort to 'resolve' the threat to heroic self-conception by "conceiving and subduing" Beauty (1955–71).

To Tamburlaine, the crisis posed by Beauty is inevitably a threat to those very rhetorical powers that establish his presence, political and dramatic. It is the possibility of silencing wonder, an arrest of self-potentiating linguistic power by a force outside the mind, that most "moves" the hero:

> If all the pens that ever poets held,
> Had fed the feeling of their maisters thoughts,
> And every sweetnes that inspir'd their harts,
> Their minds, and muses on admyred theames;
> If all the heavenly Quintessesence they still
> From their immortall flowers of Poesy,
> Wherein as in a myrrour we perceive
> The highest reaches of a humaine wit.
> If these had made one Poems period
> And all combin'd in Beauties worthinesse,
> Yet should ther hover in their restlesse heads,
> One thought, one grace, one woonder at the least,
> Which into words no vertue can digest.
>
> (1942–54)

The remarkable order and control of this verse almost belies its own subject and is, therefore, exactly suited to the expression of an ascesis leading to inexpressibility. Kocher has demonstrated that this passage constitutes, in fact, a perfectly autonomous sonnet; further, the gradual development of assonantal rhyme climaxed by the concluding couplet lends the verse an impression of climax and closure in "one Poems period." Such formal precision and aesthetic finality in a conventional mode is a subtly apt vehicle for presentation of this Kantian or "reader's" sublime. For Zenocrate's face is imaged precisely as a natural "woonder" that Tamburlaine sees essentially as a text, a text which creates for the interpreter the powerful but potentially traumatic challenge of "apt" spectatorship. Zenocrate's face, in fact, poses the double challenge of the rhetorically and naturally incomprehensible, an object beyond the grasp of both reason and sensation, evoking at once semiological indeterminacy and visual vastness. As with the cosmographical expanses Tamburlaine would reduce to the sensible and tractable order of cartographical inscription, Zenocrate's natural Beauty must be formulated as a linguistic phenomenon, albeit one initially outside textual circumscription. Thus the hero, the maker of self-elevating spectacles of awful terror, is here put into a negative or 'subdued' relation to an exalted, distant, and inexpressible Other, an overdeterminedly 'meaningful' signifier which renders the subject mute. In the figure of Zenocrate's hyperbolic Beauty—the prosopopeia that yet escapes representation—the tyrant-rhetor is himself potentially dis-figured, suffering language as a kind of privation rather than celebrating its seductive violence. As with Weiskel's version of the Kantian negative sublime, the subject (here Tamburlaine, specifically portrayed in terms of verbal capacity), in its inability to comprehend wholly the object (here Zenocrate, depicted as the natural text of the Beautiful) intuits its relation to a freshly imagined numinous domain (the singular "heavenly Quintessence" beyond the alchemy of "humaine wit"). Indeed, to pursue the Kantian formulation, the opposition between the object which cannot be compressed within limits and the subject whose faculties of knowledge seem baffled or checked, suggests it is the former rather than the latter that is properly "sublime."

The text of Zenocrate's beauty asserts—particularly in the internal sonnet—that the mind's intuition of magnitude, power, or wonder can be the intimation of its own finitude. Genius loses its aura of Longinian *hypsos* and glimpses the possibility of its basis in a general "humaine" inadequacy. This humanizing effect of Beauty presupposes a recognition of what Kant calls a "ground external to ourselves," a sense of the Other amounting to a reverence that checks the outflow of vital and all-excluding forces. It is therefore the link between pity and beauty that threatens Tamburlaine's discourse (and which, rhetorically, accounts for the otherwise curious oscillation between consideration of the Souldan's fate and worship of Zenocrate in the soliloquy's first section); and it is against their communalizing and anti-heroic authority that the final section of the soliloquy is addressed.

This final passage is nothing less than a grand act of sublime revision and restitution. What it revises—by recasting the soliloquy's essential terms of Beauty and virtue—is the relation between Eros and imagination; what it restitutes is the primacy of agonistic eloquence. The underlying anxiety of the lyricism in the first three sections is now made overt.

> But how unseemly is it for my Sex
> My discipline of armes and Chivalrie,
> My nature and the terrour of my name,
> To harbour thoughts effeminate and faint?
> Save onely that in Beauties just applause,
> With whose instinct the soule of man is toucht,
> And every warriour that is rapt with love,
> Of fame, of valour, and of victory
> Must needs have beauty beat on his conceites.
> (1955–63)

Here we confront in the passage an important syntactical ambiguity: is Tamburlaine giving Beauty, as object of the soldier's regard, the recognition due its "worthinesse," or is Beauty the active, applauding subject? Beauty's essential antagonism to both heroic self-conception and its expression (1963) is, in any case, the point to which Tamburlaine's complex utterance moves. The transition from regard to subjugation of Beauty is suggested by the striking notion that the heroic self is "rapt with love" of "fame, of valour, and of victory." Encomium has become defense, *laus* almost transformed to *vituperatio* but certainly dissolved into *correctio*. For the soliloquy proceeds to save Tamburlaine from his own desire for the Beautiful, and thus from the potentially tragic dilemma it confronts: the debilitation of heroic self-conception caught between the rival pressures of ego and community. This, and not any logical analysis or consistent, referential lyricism, is the true purpose of its final lines. The very hyperbole which figures the presence of the divine Zenocrate as threat to Tamburlaine's integrity diffuses the opposition of her claims, subtly recasting the function of "vertue" from that which cannot "digest" (consume, possess) thoughts of Beauty to that sole sum of glory which masters whatever would make Tamburlaine "effeminate and faint," and thereby raising him above the gods in resistance to the false flame of erotic dalliance:

> I thus conceiving and subduing both
> that which hath st[o]opt the tempest of the Gods,
> Even from the fiery spangled vaile of heaven,
> To feele the lovely warmth of shepheards flames,
> And martch in cottages of strowed weeds,
> Shal give the world to note for all my byrth,
> That Vertue solely is the sum of glorie,
> And fashions men with true nobility.
> (1964–71)

Whether we accept Dyce's emendation of "stopt" or "stoopt" and Deighton's change of "tempest" to "topmost" (and whether we construe "That" as a conjunction or as a demonstrative adjective) does not alter Tamburlaine's fundamental reaffirmation of the agonistic sublime, the hunger for perpetual deification by a rhythm of conception and subjugation, of fabrication and possession, which is the very impulse of the tyrant-rhetor seen heretofore. Moreover, the renewed concern with origins and the attendant conflict with transcendental authority initiated in I.ii (cf. especially Tamburlaine's transformation from shepherd to warrior and the reference to Jove's masking "in a Shepheards weed" for erotic pleasure—394 ff.) reasserts Tamburlaine's desire to be meaning's source and not its servant (the confusion of expression and creation in the metaphorical progression from 'conceit' to 'conception' is in this context telling).

Tamburlaine's speech thus undertakes a subtle revision both of Beauty's relation to imagination (the text of nature no longer subverting heroic expression but, instead, finding expression solely through the mind's articulation) and of *vertue*, which is returned to its Longinian signification of *nobilitas*, the *arete* that shines behind "the terrour of my name" (cf. 1768–69). Beauty is conquered by the very *arete* it engenders and becomes merely an element of the violent project of oratorically-based *virtù*. Concomitantly, the aphasia of the reader's sublime is cured by a Longinian celebration of *hypsos* (an elevation of *poesis* over the objects imagination 'makes' which the scribal corruptions rather more reflect than obscure); persuasion of self (soliloquy) recalls Tamburlaine to the cruel ends of verbal mastery.

The reaffirmation of Tamburlaine's hunger for power is, in fact, dramatically established after the soliloquy with characteristic Marlovian irony in Tamburlaine's jarring query, "Hath *Baiazeth* ben fed to day?" (1973). Metaphors of "digestion" thereby bind the soliloquy to its surrounding dramatic contexts (cf. 1895 f. and 1942 f). The dual appetites for power and language, that is to say, are related to one another dramatically as elements of a temperament restored to its confidence in voracious conquest.

It is not surprising, therefore, that following the soliloquy Tamburlaine does not (as so many would wish) dissolve into the harmonious, Virgilian hero of *communitas*, but instead ascends again, and with greater vigor, to the unstilled tempest with the gods:

> The God of war resignes his roume to me,
> Meaning to make me Generall of the world,
> *Jove* viewing me in armes, lookes pale and wan,
> Fearing my power should pull him from this throne.
> (2232–35)

Tamburlaine's ethos of ceaseless strife and dynastic displacement, rendered in the imagery of unassuaged thirst for rule (2236 ff.), establishes the prevailing tone of the play's conclusion. Thus the final coronation of Zenocrate, with its preparation for "truce" and "mariage" (2311, 2316), is striking not for its sense of resolution which the gesture to romance convention implies but for its very lack of closure, its characteristically anticipatory and ambitious self-presentation that accents the "Wil and Shall" of unfulfilled desire:

> As *Juno*, when the Giants were supprest,
> That darted mountaines at her brother *Jove:*
> So lookes my Love, shadowing in her browes
> Triumphes and Trophees for *my* victories:
> Or as *Latonas* daughter bent to armes,
> *Adding more* courage to my conquering mind.
> To gratify the sweet *Zenocrate,*
> Egyptians, Moores and men of Asia, . . .
> *Shall* pay a yearly tribute to thy Syre.
> And from the boundes of *Affrick* to the banks
> Of *Ganges, shall* his mighty arme extend. . . .
> Thy fist betrothed Love, *Arabia,*
> *Shall* we with honor (as beseemes) entombe, . . .
> Then *after* all these solemne Exequies,
> We *wil* our rites of marriage solemnize.
>
> (2292–99, 2301–03, 3212–13, 2315–16;
> emphases, except for proper names, are
> mine)

The elaborate arrangement for triumphal procession and display intimates the expression of yet another statement in the ritual syntax of Tamburlanian achievement, another instance but not a singular completion of the hero's "ma[r]tiall deeds" (2305). For the truce is proclaimed by a change of costume which, like the metamorphosis of I.ii it notably evokes, suggests a tendency to dramatic and contentious transformation—here signalled by the disposition to remove weapons hung at the readily accessible threshold of the warrior's temple (2310):

> Cast off your armor, put on scarlet roabes.
> Mount up your royall places of estate,
> Environed with troopes of noble men,
> And there make lawes to rule your provinces.
>
> (2309–09)

Upsetting formal and "moral" patterns, Tamburlaine returns to the soaring idiom of those visions of unqualified subjugation which motivated his career at its inception. Speaking thus in defiance of all forces of externality, Tamburlaine stands outside the "lawe" his word alone authorizes, enunciating not finally but once more the inner principle of the perpetual beginner.

IV

It is Tamburlaine's capacity as both warrior and poet (indeed to him they are one) for (re)creating himself and all extrinsic things which makes him the true compeer of the Longinian genius. And, indeed, it is this capacity that, both within and outside the play itself, makes "Tamburlaine" so difficult to interpret with finality. As he fashions and defends a self "beyond the limits" confining the *theates*, so does he elude the forms others seek to impose on him. Thus the overdetermining plethora of epithets applied to him—"the man ordain'd by heaven" (506), "divelish shepheard" (812), "monster turned to manly shape" (827), "wondrous man" (831), "Monster of five hundred thousand heades . . . the hate and Scourge of God" (1577, 1579), "this man or rather God of war" (1782), etc.—ultimately yields the impression of a figure inclusive of yet beyond all available "tytles." Defining Tamburlaine is the play's inner purpose, and the most sustained effort to image the hero within its action—Menaphon's famous description of 461–84—suggests the impossible or, more accurately, endless nature of the enterprise. Menaphon's similes and epithets oscillate among earthly, divine, and superhuman portrayals, employing conceits of aesthetic perfection (467, 480 ff.), natural power (468 ff.), worldly achievement (471 f.), divine authority (461 f., 473 ff.), and heroic prowess (477 ff.)—all of which are meant to account for the figure who is

> In every part proportioned like the man,
> Should make the world subdued to *Tamburlaine*.
> (483–84)

Menaphon's breathless hyperboles (expressive of the insuperable difficulty of grasping the sublime presence) are 'resolved' in the disjunctive realization of their futility: "Tamburlaine" and the "man" it presumably designates remain somehow differentiated, the "meaning" of the former always inadequate to the ultimately inexpressible character of the latter. What does emerge with clarity is the imperious fury to 'subdue' all to the will within the man, to effect the sublime subjugation of every opposing thought through the Longinian power of *hypsos*:

Smile Stars that raign'd at my nativity:
And dim the brightnesse of their neighbor Lamps,
Disdaine to borrow light of *Cynthia*,
For I the chiefest Lamp of all the earth,
First rising in the East with the milde aspect
But fixed now in the Meridian line,
Will send up fire to your turning Spheares,
And cause the Sun to borrowe light of you.
                                             (1477–84)

This is the last time, in Marlowe—indeed, in the English canon—that we are to hear such sublime rhetoric as more than compensation for tragic loss. For in Marlowe's rigorous self-revisions (starting with the second part of *Tamburlaine* itself) we find increasingly compelling evidence that, through Tamburlaine, he had become his own "president" and that he had begun to revalue his most audacious proclamation of imaginative freedom in terms of the innate limitations and external oppositions imagination seeks to overcome. Only the Tamburlaine of Part One, among Marlowe's splendid gallery of *pathos*-ridden heroes, could achieve a sublime continuity of self, a ceaseless, more-than-Icarian flight beyond the tragic fall and conflagration wrought by the Beautiful, mortal world.

Chronology

1564   Christopher Marlowe born in Canterbury to John Marlowe, a cobbler. Christened at the church of St. George the Martyr, Canterbury, on February 26.

1579–80 Scholar at the King's School, Canterbury.

1580–87 Attends Corpus Christi College, Cambridge. Marlowe awarded a Parker scholarship for his years at Cambridge; presumably he was expected to be preparing for holy orders. Receives his B.A. in 1584. Graduates with an M.A. after intervention of Queen's Privy Council. Goes to London.

1587   *Tamburlaine*, Parts I and II performed by Lord Admiral's Men, with Edward Alleyn in title role.

1589   Marlowe arrested in a street brawl, briefly imprisoned in Newgate.

1590   Publication of Parts I and II of *Tamburlaine*.

1592   Marlowe bound over to keep the peace. Although he must have been writing *Faustus*, *The Jew of Malta*, *Edward II* and *The Massacre at Paris* during these last few years (*Dido* may well have been written while Marlowe was at Cambridge), we have no reliable dates either for the composition or the chronological sequence of these plays.

1593   The Privy Council issues a warrant for Marlowe's arrest on May 18, six days after Marlowe's friend Thomas Kyd had been arrested on suspicion of treason and had, under torture, accused Marlowe of atheism, unclean living and possibly, treason. On May 30, Marlowe spends the day with four companions, at the tavern of Eleanor Bull, in Deptford. After supper, he quarrels with one of them, Ingram Frizer, and is mortally stabbed through the eye by him. Frizer, successfully claiming self-defense at the inquest, is pardoned on June 18. A few days after Marlowe's death, an informer, Richard Baines, accuses Marlowe of various blasphemies, treasons and atheistic opinions. Marlowe is buried at St. Nicholas Church, Deptford.

1594   *Edward II* and *Dido, Queen of Carthage* published.

1598   *Hero and Leander* published. Chapman finishes *Hero and Leander*, and this new version published. Marlowe's version of Ovid's *Elegies* published.

1599   *The Passionate Shepherd to his Love* published.

1600   *Lucans First Booke Translated Line by Line* published.

1601   Or 1602: *The Massacre at Paris* published.

1604   A-text of *Doctor Faustus* published.

1616   B-text of *Doctor Faustus* published.

1633   *The Jew of Malta* performed at the Cockpit and the Court; published.

Contributors

HAROLD BLOOM, Sterling Professor of the Humanities at Yale University, is the author of *The Anxiety of Influence, Poetry and Repression* and many other volumes of literary criticism. His forthcoming study, *Freud: Transference and Authority*, attempts a full-scale reading of all of Freud's major writings. He is the general editor of *The Chelsea House Library of Literary Criticism*.

HARRY LEVIN is Irving Babbitt Professor Emeritus of Comparative Literature at Harvard University. His numerous books include studies of Shakespeare and Joyce.

DAVID BEVINGTON is Professor of English at the University of Chicago and the author of *Tudor Drama and Politics*.

A. D. HOPE is Australia's leading poet. His works include *Collected Poems* and *The Cave and the Spring*.

WILBUR SANDERS is Professor of English at the University of Sydney, Australia. He is the author of *The Dramatist and the Received Idea*.

DAVID DAICHES is Regius Professor Emeritus of English at Edinburgh University. His many books include studies of Robert Burns and Willa Cather.

CLEANTH BROOKS, Gray Professor Emeritus of Rhetoric at Yale University, is the author of three studies of Faulkner and of *Modern Poetry and the Tradition*.

A. BARTLETT GIAMATTI is President of Yale University. His books include *The Earthly Paradise and the Renaissance Epic* and a study of Spenser.

ERICH SEGAL teaches Classics at the Universities of Yale and Oxford. His best-known novel is *Love Story*. He is also the author of *Roman Laughter*, a study of Plautus.

JACKSON I. COPE is Professor of English at the University of Southern California. His books include *Joyce's Cities* and *The Metaphoric Structure of "Paradise Lost."*

WILLIAM KEACH is Professor of English at Rutgers University. His books include *Elizabethan Erotic Narratives* and a study of Shelley.

EDWARD A. SNOW is Professor of English and of Art History at Rice University. He is the author of *A Study of Vermeer*.

LAWRENCE DANSON is Professor of English at Princeton University. He is the author of *The Harmonies of "The Merchant of Venice"* and *Max Beerbohm and the Mirror of the Past*.

KIMBERLY BENSTON is Professor of English at Haverford College. His books include studies of Imamu Baraka and of the modern drama. Forthcoming is his *The Shaping of the Marlovian Sublime*.

Bibliography

Allen, D. C. "Renaissance Remedies for Fortune: Marlowe and the *Fortunati*." *Studies in Philology*, vol. 38 (1941): 188–97.

——. "Marlowe's *Dido* and the Tradition." In *Essays on Shakespeare and Elizabethan Drama in Honor of Hardin Craig*. Edited by Richard Hosley. Columbia, Mo.: University of Missouri Press, 1962.

Babb, Howard S. "Policy in Marlowe's *The Jew of Malta*." *English Literary History*, vol. 24 (1957): 85–94.

Barber, C. L. " 'The Form of Faustus' Fortunes Good or Bad'." *The Drama Review*, vol. 8 (1964): 92–119.

——. "The Death of Zenocrate: 'Conceiving and Subduing Both' in Marlowe's *Tamburlaine*." *Literature and Psychology*, vol. 16 (1966): 15–24.

Battenhouse, Roy W. *Marlowe's Tamburlaine: A Study in Renaissance Moral Philosophy*. Nashville: Vanderbilt University Press, 1941.

——. "Protestant Apologetics and the Subplot of 2 *Tamburlaine*." *English Literary Renaissance*, vol. 2 (1973): 30–43.

——. "The Relation of *Henry V* to *Tamburlaine*." *Shakespeare Survey*, vol. 27 (1974): 71–79.

Bawcutt, N. W. "Machiavelli and Marlowe's *The Jew of Malta*." *Renaissance Drama*, vol. 3 (1970): 3–49.

Bevington, David M. *From Mankind to Marlowe: Growth of Structure in the Popular Drama of Tudor England*. Cambridge, Mass.: Harvard University Press, 1962.

Bluestone, Max. "*Libido Speculandi*: Doctrine and Dramaturgy in Contemporary Interpretations of Marlowe's *Doctor Faustus*." In *Reinterpretations of Elizabethan Drama*. Edited by Norman Rabkin. New York: Columbia University Press, 1969.

Bowers, Fredson. "The Text of Marlowe's *Faustus*." *Modern Philology*, vol. 49 (1952): 195–204.

Boyette, Purvis E. "Wanton Humour and Wanton Poets: Homosexuality in Marlowe's *Edward II*." *Tulane Studies in English* (1977): 33–50.

Brooke, C. F. Tucker. "Marlowe's Versification and Style." *Studies in Philology*, vol. 19 (1922): 186–205.

Brooke, Nicholas. "The Moral Tragedy of Doctor Faustus." *Cambridge Journal*, vol. 7 (1952): 662–87.

Bush, Douglas. *Mythology and the Renaissance Tradition*. New York: Pageant Book Co., 1937.

Cole, Douglas. *Suffering and Evil in the Plays of Christopher Marlowe*. Princeton: Princeton University Press, 1962.

Collins, S. Ann. " 'Sundrie Shapes, Committing Headie Ryots, Incest, Rapes': Functions of Myth in Determining Narrative and Tone in Marlowe's 'Hero and Leander'." *Mosaic*, vol. 4 (1970): 107–22.

Cutts, John P. *The Left Hand of God: A Critical Interpretation of the Plays of Christopher Marlowe.* Haddonfield, N.J.: Haddonfield House, 1973.

Davidson, Clifford. "Doctor Faustus of Wittenberg." *Studies in Philology*, vol. 59 (1962): 514–23.

Deats, Sara Munson. "Myth and Metamorphosis in Marlowe's *Edward II*." *Texas Studies in Literature and Language*, vol. 22 (1980): 304–21.

Duthie, G. I. "The Dramatic Structure of Marlowe's *Tamburlaine the Great* Part I." *Shakespeare's Contemporaries.* Edited by Max Bluestone and Norman Rabkin. Englewood Cliffs, N.J.: Prentice-Hall, Inc., 1961.

Egan, Robert. "A Muse of Fire: *Henry V* in the Light of *Tamburlaine*." *Modern Language Quarterly*, vol. 29 (1968): 15–28.

Eliot, T. S. *Elizabethan Essays.* London: Faber & Faber, Ltd., 1934.

Ellis-Fermor, Una M. *Christopher Marlowe.* London: Methuen & Col, Ltd., 1927.

Fraser, Russell. "On Christopher Marlowe." *Michigan Quarterly Review*, vol. 12 (1973): 136–59.

Friedenreich, Kenneth. " 'Huge Greatnesse' Overthrown: The Fall of the Empire in Marlowe's *Tamburlaine* Plays." *CLIO*, vol. 2 (1972): 32–48.

————." 'You Talks Brave and Bold': The Origins of an Elizabethan Stage Device." *Comparative Drama*, vol. 8 (1974): 239–53.

Frye, R. M. "Marlowe's *Doctor Faustus*: The Repudiation of Humanity." *South Atlantic Quarterly*, vol. 55 (1956): 322–28.

Gardner, Helen. "Milton's 'Satan' and the Theme of Damnation in Elizabethan Tragedy." *English Studies* 1 (1948): 46–66.

Glenn, John Ronald. "The Martyrdom of Ramus in Marlowe's *The Massacre at Paris*." *Papers on Language and Literature*, vol. 9 (1973): 365–79.

Godshalk, W. L. *The Marlovian World Picture.* The Hague: Mouton, 1974.

Goldberg, Jonathan. "Sodomy and Society: The Case of Christopher Marlowe." *Southwest Review* 4, vol. 69 (1984): 371–90.

Greenblatt, Stephen. *Renaissance Self-Fashioning.* Chicago: The University of Chicago Press, 1980.

Gregg, W. W. "The Damnation of Faustus." *Modern Language Review*, vol. 41 (1946): 97–107.

Hattaway, Michael. "The Theology of Marlowe's *Doctor Faustus*." *Renaissance Drama*, vol. 3 (1970): 51–78.

Hawkins, Harriet. *Poetic Form and Poetic Truth.* Oxford: At the Clarendon Press, 1976.

Homan, Sidney R. "Chapman and Marlowe: The Paradoxical Hero and the Divided Response." *Journal of English and Germanic Philology*, vol. 68 (1969): 391–406.

Honderich, Pauline. "John Calvin and Doctor Faustus." *Modern Language Review*, vol. 68 (1973): 1–13.

Hoy, Cyrus. "Shakespeare, Sidney and Marlowe: The Metamorphosis of Love." *Virginia Quarterly Review*, vol. 51 (1975): 448–58.

Hunter, G. K. "The Theology of Marlowe's *The Jew of Malta.*" *Journal of the Warburg and Courtauld Institutes*, vol. 27 (1964): 211–40.

———. "Five Act Structure in *Doctor Faustus.*" *The Drama Review*, vol. 8 (1964): 77–91.

Kernan, Alvin, ed. *Two Renaissance Mythmakers: Christopher Marlowe and Ben Jonson.* Baltimore: The Johns Hopkins University Press, 1977.

Kimbrough, Robert. "1 *Tamburlaine*: A Speaking Picture in a Tragic Glass." *Renaissance Drama*, vol. 7 (1964): 20–34.

Kirschbaum, Leo. "Marlowe's *Faustus*: A Reconsideration." *Review of English Studies*, vol. 19 (1943): 225–41.

Knights, L. C. "The Strange Case of Christopher Marlowe." In *Further Explorations.* London: Chatto & Windus, 1965.

Kocher, Paul, H. *Christopher Marlowe: A Study of His Thought, Learning and Character.* Chapel Hill: University of North Carolina Press, 1946.

Leech, Clifford. "Marlowe's *Edward II*: Power and Suffering." *Critical Quarterly* 1 (1959): 181–96.

Lever, Katherine. "The Image of Man in *Tamburlaine.*" *Philological Quarterly*, vol. 35 (1956): 421–27.

Levin, Richard. *The Multiple Plot in English Renaissance Drama.* Chicago: The University of Chicago Press, 1971.

Lewis, C. S. *English Literature in the Sixteenth Century Excluding Drama.* Oxford: At the Clarendon Press, 1954.

Mahood, M. M. "Marlowe's Heroes." In *Poetry and Humanism.* London: Jonathan Cape, 1950.

Manheim, Michael. "The Weak King History Play of the Early 1590's." *Renaissance Drama*, vol. 2 (1969): 71–80.

Manley, Frank. "The Nature of Faustus." *Modern Philology*, vol. 66 (1969): 218–31.

Masington, Charles G. *Christopher Marlowe's Tragic Vision: A Study in Damnation.* Athens, Ohio: Ohio University Press, 1972.

Matalene, H. W. "Marlowe's *Faustus* and the Comforts of Academism. *English Literary History*, vol. 39 (1972): 495–519.

McAlindon, T. "The Ironic Vision: Diction and Theme in Marlowe's *Doctor Faustus.*" *Review of English Studies*, vol. 32 (1981): 129–41.

Morris, Brian, ed. *Christopher Marlowe.* London: Mermaid Critical Commentaires, 1968.

Morris, Harry. "Marlowe's Poetry." *The Drama Review*, vol. 8 (1964): 134–54.

Neuse, Richard. "Atheism and Some Functions of Myth in Marlowe's *Hero and Leander.*" *Modern Language Quarterly*, vol. 31 (1970): 424–39.

O'Brian, Margaret Ann. "Christian Belief in *Doctor Faustus.*" *English Literary History*, vol. 37 (1970): 1–10.

Ornstein, Robert. "The Comic Synthesis in *Doctor Faustus.*" *English Literary History*, vol. 22 (1955): 165–72.

Palmer, D. J. "Magic and Poetry in *Doctor Faustus.*" *Critical Quarterly*, vol. 6, (1964): 56–67.

Peet, Donald. "The Rhetoric of *Tamburlaine*." *English Literary History*, vol. 26 (1959): 137–55.

Poirier, Michel. *Christopher Marlowe*. London: Chatto & Windus, 1951.

Powell, Jocelyn. "Marlowe's Spectacle." *The Drama Review*, vol. 8 (1964): 195–210.

Quinn, Michael. "The Freedom of *Tamburlaine*." *Modern Language Quarterly*, vol. 21 (1961): 315–20.

Ribner, Irving. "The Idea of History in Marlowe's *Tamburlaine*." *English Literary History*, vol. 20 (1953): 251–66.

———. "Marlowe and Machiavelli." *Comparative Literature*, vol. 6 (1954): 349–56.

———. "*Tamburlaine* and *The Wars of Cyrus*." *Journal of English and Germanic Philology*, vol. 53 (1954): 569–73.

Richards, Susan. "Marlowe's *Tamburlaine* II: A Drama of Death." *Modern Language Quarterly*, vol. 26 (1965): 375–87.

Riggs, David. *Shakespeare's Heroical Histories: "Henry VI" and its Literary Tradition*. Cambridge, Mass.: Harvard University Press, 1971.

Rousseau, G. S. "Marlowe's *Dido* and a Rhetoric of Love." *English Miscellany*, vol. 19 (1968): 25–49.

Sachs, Arieh. "The Religious Despair of Doctor Faustus." *Journal of English and Germanic Philology*, vol. 63 (1964): 625–47.

Sanders, Wilbur. *The Dramatist and the Received Idea: Studies in the Plays of Marlowe and Shakespeare*. Cambridge: Cambridge University Press, 1968.

Sewall, Richard B. *The Vision of Tragedy*. New Haven: Yale University Press, 1959.

Singer, Irving. "Erotic Transformations in the Legend of Dido and Aeneas." *Modern Language Notes*, vol. 90 (1975): 767–83.

Smith, James. "Marlowe's *Doctor Faustus*." *Scrutiny*, vol. 8 (1930): 36–55.

Smith, Warren D. "Substance and Meaning in *Tamburlaine*, Part I." *Studies in Philology*, vol. 67 (1970): 155–66.

Steane, J. B. *Marlowe: A Critical Study*. Cambridge: At the University Press, 1964.

Stroup, Thomas B. "*Doctor Faustus* and *Hamlet*: Contrasting Kinds of Christian Tragedy." *Comparative Drama*, vol. 5 (1972): 243–53.

———. "Ritual in Marlowe's Plays." *Comparative Drama*, vol. 7 (1973): 198–221.

Swinburne, Algernon Charles. *The Age of Shakespeare*. London: Chatto & Windus, 1909.

Thorp, Willard. "The Ethical Problem in Marlowe's *Tamburlaine*." *Journal of English and Germanic Philology*, vol. 29 (1930): 385–89.

Tomlinson, T. B. *A Study of Elizabethan and Jacobean Tragedy*. Cambridge: At the University Press, 1964.

Turner, Myron. "Pastoral and Hermaphrodite: A Study in the Naturalism of Marlowe's Hero and Leander." *Texas Studies in Literature and Languages*, vol. 17 (1975): 397–414.

Turner, Robert. "Shakespeare and the Public Confrontation Scene in Early History Plays." *Modern Philology*, vol. 62 (1964): 1–12.

Waith, Eugene M. *The Herculean Hero*. New York: Columbia University Press, 1962.

————. *Ideas of Greatness: Heroic Drama in England*. London: Routledge & Kean Paul, 1971.

Walsh, William P. "Sexual Discovery and Renaissance Morality in Marlowe's *Hero and Leander*." *Studies in English Literature, 1500–1900*, vol. 12 (1972): 33–54.

Warren, Michael J. "*Doctor Faustus*: The Old Man and the Text." *English Literary Renaissance*, vol. 11 (1981): 111–47.

West, Robert H. "The Impatient Magic of *Dr. Faustus*." *English Literary Renaissance*, vol. 4 (1974): 218–40.

Wilson, F. P. *Marlowe and the Early Shakespeare*. Oxford: At the Clarendon Press, 1953.

Acknowledgments

"*Edward II*: State Overturned" by Harry Levin from *The Overreacher: A Study of Chrisopher Marlowe* by Harry Levin, copyright © 1952 by the President and Fellows of Harvard College. Reprinted by permission.

"*The Jew of Malta*" by David Bevington from *Mankind to Marlowe: Growth of Structure in the Popular Drama of Tudor England* by David Bevington, copyright © 1962 by the President and Fellows of Harvard College. Reprinted by permission.

"*Tamburlaine*: The Argument of Arms" by A. D. Hope from *The Cave and the Spring: Essays on Poetry* by A. D. Hope, copyright © 1970 by The University of Chicago Press. Reprinted by permission.

"Dramatist as Realist: *The Jew of Malta*" by Wilbur Sanders from *The Dramatist and the Received Idea: Studies in the Plays of Marlowe and Shakespeare* by Wilbur Sanders, copyright © 1968 by Cambridge University Press. Reprinted by permission.

"Language and Action in Marlowe's *Tamburlaine*" by David Daiches from *More Literary Essays* by David Daiches, copyright © 1968 by David Daiches. Reprinted by permission.

"The Unity of Marlowe's *Doctor Faustus*" by Cleanth Brooks from *A Shaping Joy* by Cleanth Brooks, copyright © 1971 by Cleanth Brooks. Reprinted by permission.

"The Arts of Illusion" by A. Bartlett Giamatti from *The Yale Review* (1972), copyright © 1972 by Yale University. Reprinted by permission.

"Marlowe's *Schadenfreude*: Barabas as Comic Hero" by Erich Segal from *Veins of Humor* by Erich Segal, copyright © 1972 by the President and Fellows of Harvard College. Reprinted by permission.

"Marlowe's *Dido* and the Titillating Children" by Jackson I. Cope from *English Literary Renaissance* (1974), copyright © 1974 by University of Massachusetts Press. Reprinted by permission.

"*Hero and Leander*" by William Keach from *Elizabethan Erotic Narratives* by William Keach, copyright © 1977 by Rutgers University. Reprinted by permission.

"*Doctor Faustus* and the Ends of Desire" by Edward A. Snow from *Two Renaissance Mythmakers: Christopher Marlowe and Ben Jonson* edited by Alvin B. Kernan, copyright © 1977 by The English Institute. Reprinted by permission.

"The Questioner" by Lawrence Danson from *English Literary Renaissance* (1982), copyright © 1982 by University of Massachusetts Press. Reprinted by permission.

"Beauty's Just Applause: Dramatic Form and the Tamburlanian Sublime" by Kimberly Benston, copyright © 1980 by Kimberly Benston. Published for the first time in this volume. Printed by permission.

Index